VIENNA
1890-1920

VIENNA
1890-1920

Edited by Robert Waissenberger

With contributions by
Hans Bisanz, Kurt Blaukopf,
Günter Düriegl, Renata Kassal-Mikula,
Harald Leupold-Löwenthal,
Wendelin Schmidt-Dengler,
Robert Waissenberger
and Reingard Witzmann

THE WELLFLEET PRESS
WELLFLEET

Published by
WELLFLEET PRESS
110 Enterprise Avenue
Secaucus, New Jersey 07094

ISBN: 1-55521-258-1

Printed and bound in Hong Kong.

CONTENTS

FOREWORD

Robert Waissenberger

During the period spanning the turn of the century, Vienna, then one of the most important cities in the world, experienced a brilliant efflorescence. For many years, however, its achievements in the cultural and intellectual fields failed to gain adequate recognition, nor was it until quite recently that connoisseurs began to appreciate the full importance of Viennese Art Nouveau which, as a late expression of the style, was quite distinct from similar manifestations elsewhere. At a time when the School of Paris, German Expressionism and other modern movements had long since been given their due, the work of great Viennese artists such as Gustav Klimt, Egon Schiele and Josef Hoffmann was still regarded as being of little more than peripheral significance.

In music, Vienna occupied a position no less important than in the visual arts. Brahms and Bruckner were both active in the city towards the end of the nineteenth century, for many years the Court Opera prospered under the distinguished directorship of Gustav Mahler, while the composers of the Viennese School, notably Schoenberg and his pupils Alban Berg and Anton von Webern, were attracting considerable attention though as yet little if any acclaim.

Architecture and literature were also fields in which Viennese artists excelled. Otto Wagner and Adolf Loos, who made their mark with buildings of a highly individual nature, are now universally recognized as pioneers of modern architecture, while the renown of such Viennese writers as Arthur Schnitzler and Hugo von Hofmannsthal has steadily grown, nourished by a greater understanding of the context in which they worked and to which they so materially contributed. For without them *fin-de-siècle* Vienna would have been a much less interesting place.

Needless to say, the concentration of artistic creativity in Vienna was not *sui generis* – a unique and unheralded manifestation – but rather belonged within the framework of a definite tradition. Nor were its more enduring products merely the luxuriant emanations of the hot-house atmosphere then prevailing in the capital. For nowhere else was the premonition of change, of imminent collapse, so much in evidence – a premonition born, not only of the complexity of Austria-Hungary's political and national circumstances, but also of the awareness that all this hung on one frail thread – the life of the aged Emperor Francis Joseph I of Austria.

Yet the question as to why there should have been this sudden burst of artistic creativity is one that has never been satisfactorily answered. The absence of any apparent relation between contemporary social conditions and the rarefied qualitative standards set by art leads us to assume that art, subject as it often was to profound misapprehension, represented in some degree a reaction to the disquieting nature of reality. And, indeed, the role of the artist, in confrontation with the world around him, may be regarded to some extent as a prophetic one.

In brief, the products of the best artists and craftsmen – particularly those of the Secession and the Wiener Werkstätte – were accessible only to a select few, namely the liberal bourgeoisie with its more eclectic tastes and better-lined pockets. But that clientele constituted no more than a very small minority in a rapidly growing metropolis whose population was increasing by leaps and bounds. These developments inevitably went hand in hand with pauperization and a housing shortage so acute that people had to live in grossly overcrowded tenement blocks. It was a state of affairs that gave rise to considerable political and social tension, the more so since Vienna had now become a microcosm of the multinational Austro-Hungarian Monarchy.

On the one hand, then, was the problematical situation engendered by the rapid growth of the city, on the other an art all too susceptible to excessive aestheticism – the art of an upper middle-class culture. Thus the literature of the time was largely concerned with the needs and preoccupations of an over-refined society increasingly aware of its own predicament.

It cannot therefore be regarded as a coincidence that, at this particular time and in this particular place, Sigmund Freud should have evolved his theory of psychoanalysis. Whether the same could have happened anywhere else is a moot point. There is, however, an undeniable connection between social conditions in Vienna and psychoanalysis. In this book, then, it is treated as an intellectual phenomenon which bridges the gulf between those social conditions and the striving after perfection witnessed in art.

The life of a city such as Vienna, even over so short a span as thirty years, presents a panorama too vast to be comprised within the covers of a single book. We have therefore had to confine ourselves to individual examples. By according each the importance that is its due, we hope to provide the reader with a balanced as well as a convincing picture. Superb as are Vienna's artistic achievements, they cannot be discussed in isolation without conveying a false impression. But here we run the risk of failing to distinguish between the aims of art and the aims of its period, which would again be false. For only by a consideration of the contradictions that exist between the art and its period can we hope to form a tolerably accurate picture.

I PORTRAIT OF A CITY – CONFIGURATION AND CHANGE

Günter Düriegl

A guidebook, published in 1908, contains the following passage:

On the Continent, Vienna is second only to Paris in size and brilliance and, until the time of the International Exhibition of 1873, had maintained its title to the role of most distinguished German city. Yet the events of 1866 had already robbed it of its political preeminence in Germany and reduced it to being nothing more than the hub of the Monarchy, a position which, morever, since the dualist Constitution of 1867, it had also in part forfeited to Budapest. Though its development had suffered as a result of these setbacks, Vienna has remained by far the greatest city of the Empire; it is not only the permanent residence of the dynasty, but also the seat of the joint administration and the diplomatic corps; here, too, are concentrated all the larger industrial and capitalist concerns as well as the most important institutions devoted to the arts and sciences. Vienna is thus the hub, not only of the Austrian state, but also of the Monarchy as a whole. Of late it has experienced a notable revival. Since 1871, when its population was outstripped by that of Berlin, it has been the second largest German city, and the third largest on the European mainland. Among cities of over a million inhabitants in all parts of the world, Vienna ranks fifth after London, New York, Paris and Berlin, with Chicago and Tokyo already hard on its heels.[1]

Despite the restrained, not to say critical tone – in keeping with a bourgeois outlook characterized by moderation and reserve – this account is not altogether devoid of pride.

For when all is said and done, Vienna was the centre of Austria-Hungary, the heart of a great European power, and as such symbolized for some 54 million inhabitants of a mighty empire, the object of their heart's desire. Moreover, it had attained that position within the few decades following the collapse of the 1848 revolution, when the bourgeoisie actually responsible for that revolution were consolidating their position by establishing a *modus vivendi* between liberalism and the backward-looking conservatism of the legitimists. During that period, known as the *Gründerzeit*[2] – a distinctly anodyne word for a time of hectic and often unfounded exuberance, of dizzy heights and horrifying depths – Vienna became a great city and, ultimately, a brilliant metropolis.

Unity of town and suburbs

In 1857 work began on the construction of the Ringstrasse, the opulent successor to the bleak and forbidding belt of fortifications surrounding the Inner City. On completion

9

of the project, the unity of town and suburbs, which had existed on paper since 1694,[3] became a tangible, if almost immeasurable, reality. On this boulevard, planted with plane trees, ailanthi and limes, the best architects had applied their minds to the concept of a *Gesamtkunstwerk* (total work of art), a glittering *via triumphalis* symbolic of the capital. No longer was any distinction drawn between Inner City and suburbs, the

whole being now divided into nine districts, excluding, however, the outer suburbs.

The Lines, erected in 1704 as a second girdle of fortifications between the inner and outer suburbs, still survived, though they now constituted a topographical and physical barrier rather than a defense work. They also played a fiscal role, being furnished with toll gates where, since 1829, a tax had been levied on food entering the city.

Plan of the City of Vienna.

10

1 Anton Hlávaček: *Blick vom Nussberg auf den regulierten Donaustrom* ('View of the Regulated Course of the Danube from the Nussberg'). 1881, oil on canvas, 44.4 x 63 cm. Historisches Museum der Stadt Wien.
In the course of only a few decades the fortified city of Vienna had become an open city in which local changes were carried out in conformity with an overall plan. In 1875, when the part of the Danube lying within the city had finally been regulated, the left bank was accorded recognition as an integral part of the capital. It was incorporated in 1904.

2 Stephansplatz. *C.* 1900, photograph. Historisches Museum der Stadt Wien.
The changes that took place in the city impinged upon its very core. The new buildings on the north-west side of the Stephansplatz were put up between 1867 and 1895. Attempts to preserve the historic heart of the city were foiled by a new generation of town planners.

3 Court Opera House. *C.* 1900, photograph. Historisches Museum der Stadt Wien.
The Imperial and Royal Court Opera House, one of the most striking examples of architectural historicism, may be seen on the right, beside the intersection of the Ringstrasse and the Kärntner-strasse.

4 Carl Müller: *Strasse in Wien* ('Street in Vienna'). Water-colour on black chalk, 27.3 x 37.7 cm. Historisches Museum der Stadt Wien.
Carl Müller was a little-known member of the Klimt group. In his painting of an unnamed street he has included a striking poster by the Trieste artist, Giulio Angelo Liberali, advertising Schlesinger's paprika.

From the mid-nineteenth century onwards, the economic ties between Inner City and suburbs had become ever closer. However, the incorporation of the latter was hampered, not only by fear of a 'malevolent proletariat', but also by the Inner City's downright refusal to shoulder the added burden of financing the police and poor relief.[4] On the other hand, the independence of the increasingly urbanized outer suburbs repeatedly gave rise to difficulties which gravely impeded the modernization of the city as a whole. Thus, while building development in such localities was not necessarily unplanned (the submission of plans having become obligatory under a ministerial decree of 4 November 1862),[5] it was carried out with little or no regard for the requirements of neighbouring communities or of the Inner City.

A typical example of this state of affairs is the request sent by the Vienna Municipal Council to the mayors of the outer suburbs on 4 March 1879 to the effect that they should ensure the cleanliness of streets and squares and disinfect canals and cesspits.[6]

The immediate circumstances of 1848 and the fears they engendered may, perhaps, explain the short-sighted and altogether questionable attitude adopted towards the outer suburbs upon which the economic life of the city largely depended. Indeed, at the turn of the eighteenth century, similar fears, nurtured by the turbulent days of the French Revolution, had impelled the Emperor Francis II to decree that industrial production should be shifted from the city centre to the outer suburbs. As a result, those summer resorts so dear to the Viennese rapidly changed from rustic retreats for romantic sentimentalists into densely inhabited industrial centres. For mechanization enabled the metal-working industries, in particular, to experience seemingly endless growth. Not only did manufacturing capacity expand along typically capitalist lines, but the pool of labour increased in such a way as to bring about a marked change in traditional demographic patterns. The most populous community at this time was Hernals in Lower Austria, with some 70,000 inhabitants.[7]

5 The Lines. C. 1895, photograph. Historisches Museum der Stadt Wien.
The Lines had long ceased to serve any defensive purpose. In the final decades of the nineteenth century they became something of an eyesore, acting only as a boundary which divided suburbs from outer suburbs and prevented their growing into an organic whole.

Nor was there any slackening of the flow of immigrants into the capital. The wages obtainable in Vienna, modest though they may have been, attracted people from all over the Monarchy. The immigrants were largely of peasant origin, the majority being natives of the Sudetenland, a region which, by the turn of the nineteenth century, accounted for no less than 25 per cent of the Viennese population. On arrival, they settled in the dormitory areas where the housing was disposed in a grid pattern about the new centres of industry. The proximity of domicile to the place of work was wholly in accord, not only with the peasant but also with the craft tradition and, more significantly still, eliminated travelling expenses. Again, outside the Lines no duty was levied on foodstuffs and this, along with other circumstances conducive to a lower cost of living, acted as a further incentive to settlement in the outer suburbs. Thus the influx continued unabated, despite the nature of the accommodation which, poor even by the standards of the day, might have been expected to discourage such a trend. For the vast majority lived in huge blocks of minute tenements, often of no more than one room. Each dwelling normally housed ten or more occupants, and this in return for a rent which might consume up to a quarter of a man's wage.

So disparate were the aspects presented by the outer suburbs that the attitude adopted towards them could hardly be other than ambivalent. On the one hand their economic advantages and potential spoke strongly in favour of their incorporation into the city, on the other, a consideration of their social circumstances and the overwhelming pressures these involved militated against a move which demanded so large a measure of humanitarian commitment.

On 6 December 1889 the Vienna Municipal Council, with the agreement of the government, resolved that the area subject to food-tax – hitherto bounded by the Lines – should be extended to include forty-three outer suburbs. On 19 December 1890 the emperor gave his assent to a law providing for their incorporation. One day later, with the promulgation of a 'Municipal Statute for the Imperial Capital and Royal Residence of

7 Taborstrasse, 2nd District.
C. 1900, photograph. Historisches
Museum der Stadt Wien.
The Taborstrasse is one of the
oldest and most important of
Vienna's arteries and the houses
that line it are very much in the
urban tradition. But even quarters
such as this did not shun radical
change.

8 Hainburgstrasse, 3rd District.
C. 1900, photograph. Historisches
Museum der Stadt Wien.
It is evident from the old houses
on the right that this was once a
farming area. The adjoining apartment block belongs to an entirely
different tradition and is typical of
the late *Gründerzeit* style found in
the inner districts.

9 Ferdinand Weckbrodt: *Die Ge-
gend des Hernalser Friedhofs mit
Blick gegen Dornbach* ('Dornbach,
seen from the neighbourhood of
Hernals cemetery'). *C.* 1890,
water-colour, 27.8 x 43 cm.
Historisches Museum der Stadt
Wien.
Hernals (17th District) underwent
a drastic transformation from a
rural parish to an industrial district with a different social
structure and a new pattern of
building.

10 Franz Kopallik: *Der Franz-
Josephs-Bahnhof* ('The Francis
Joseph Station') *C.* 1905,
water-colour, 23.2 x 34.9 cm. Historisches Museum der Stadt
Wien.
The station, with the city beyond,
seen from the Gürtel line viaduct.
This was the terminus of the
Kaiser-Franz-Josephs-Bahn. The
line, which opened in 1870, ran
between Vienna, Prague and Eger
(now Cheb).

16

Vienna', the latter's elevation to the status of major city (officially known as Greater Vienna) was endorsed by the Legislature. These laws took effect from 1 January 1892, following a proclamation by the governor of Lower Austria in the previous month, in which he announced the incorporation of the hitherto autonomous communities. Here it should be explained that Vienna formed part of Lower Austria and as such was subject to the authority of its governor.

Thus the total area of Vienna increased from 55 to 178 square kilometres, while nineteen new districts[8] were created to achieve the decentralization necessitated by such tremendous expansion. The population rose from 801,176[9] in 1890 to 1,355,979[10] in 1891. Between then and 1918, when Vienna as an Imperial capital and royal residence ceased to exist, these demographic changes were responsible for urban modifications which, in many areas, still determine the face of the city today.[11]

Architectural achievements

The architectural achievements of the final years of the *Gründerzeit* comprise, alongside new buildings, the reconstruction of already extant ones. A steady rise in the price of land, advances in building technology and, last but not least, the growing demand for comfort provided both a stimulus and a framework for the creation of fresh architectural forms. New building was largely confined to the nine inner districts, where preservation orders did little or nothing to prevent the demolition of the existing stock. An additional incentive for the development of these areas was a regulation permitting buildings of six storeys in the 1st District, and of five storeys in the other eight, while only four were allowed in the outlying districts. However, a loophole existed in that basement, ground-floor, mezzanine, intermediate storeys and attic did not officially rate as storeys, so that taller buildings could in fact be put up. In vertical terms, then, the regulations were stretched to their limits, and similar licence reigned on the horizontal plane. In most cases a very liberal interpretation was placed on a ruling of 1893 whereby no more than 85 per cent of any one site might be built over. Again and again, we find typical solutions of this period in the form of buildings where the central court is omitted, and whose multiple ranges are a veritable warren of lights and stair-wells. Notwithstanding the obvious disadvantage inherent in a spatial organization aimed solely at a handsome financial return, it should be noted that some importance already attached to the provision of sanitary arrangements, a bath being more or less *de rigueur* in middle-class apartments of two and a half rooms upwards. Another characteristic was the similarity of the apartments, irrespective of the range or storey in which they were situated. The desirability or otherwise of an apartment's position no longer played any part in the choice of layout. Thus there evolved a type of dwelling, the basic design of which was to be retained in, notably, the Municipality's tenement blocks of the inter-war years.

In the late *Gründerzeit* the infiltration of the suburbs by numerous craft industries came to an end, not least for economic reasons, since businesses run by skilled tradesmen were being hard pressed by com-

11 The Lines office at Währing. *C.* 1890, photograph. Historisches Museum der Stadt Wien.
Since 1829 offices located on the Lines had had the task of collecting the so-called food-tax. With the incorporation of the forty-three outer suburbs on 1 January 1892 the system was abolished. Officially the city was now known as Gross-Wien or Greater Vienna.

18

12 The Danube Canal above the Ferdinand Bridge. 1895, photograph. Historisches Museum der Stadt Wien.
It was not until the turn of the century and the regulation of the Danube Canal that the transport system could be fully reorganized.

13 Platz am Hof, exemplifying the redevelopment of the Inner City. 1913, photograph. Historisches Museum der Stadt Wien. The unbounded urge to replace old houses with new ones was given free rein, more particularly in smart squares such as this one.

petition from the factories. On the other hand, the landlords' obsession with profits led, in the inner district, to a dire shortage of small workshops[12] for craftsmen who, if lucky, might find refuge in a basement, a storey lying below street level and immediately above the cellar. The migration of the craft industries to the outer suburbs scarcely affected the earlier factories which tended to adapt themselves to the growth of housing. Of particular economic interest, and hence also of relevance in the socio-spatial sphere, are the businesses in the 'outlying' districts. Here the former village streets, which led towards the city, evolved into important commercial and industrial thoroughfares, of which each district possessed at least one.

The changes that took place in Vienna's new districts were not occasioned solely by private enterprise nor, as it were, by organic growth, but might also be dictated by the needs of the public sector. For so vast had the Municipality grown, in terms of both area and population, that its proper government called for some degree of decentralization. Local councils were therefore created to carry out, on behalf of the mayor, those tasks which fell within their competence. This in turn necessitated the building of council offices whose sites were usually chosen with an eye to the future popularity of the district. That these hopes were sometimes dashed is evident from the new schools and churches which, built in areas reserved for housing development, were doomed to remain mere isolated outposts.

Railways

The railways exerted a considerable influence on the socio-spatial development of the city in the widest sense of the term. The fact that they had been built in the decades preceding the integration of the suburbs[13] shows yet again how mistaken it was to have delayed that move for so long. Almost without exception, the termini of these railways were situated near the Lines, an obstruction which could not be razed until handed over to the Municipality in 1893. That tracks did not have to traverse densely built-up areas was, of course, an advantage, but it also deprived Vienna of the amenity of a central station.

In due course the railway lines leading to the city became physical boundaries of prime importance,[14] as is clearly evident from the routes taken by the Südbahn and

Regulation of the waterways

The completion of the Gürtelstrasse and the regulation of the River Wien and of the Danube Canal brought about marked changes in the city. The course and condition of both these waterways were unsatisfactory and the problems arising from them called for a solution that was long overdue. That these difficulties were eventually tackled around the turn of the century was chiefly due to the recent completion of a grandiose plan for a public transport system, namely the Vienna *Stadtbahn* (city railway). The Danube Canal passes close by the heart of the city. Between 1870 and 1875 the Danube itself was the subject of a major operation when a new bed was dug.[15] The scheme was evidently linked with the subsequent straightening of the lower course of the Danube Canal and the installation of a ship caisson at its entrance. But this did not mean that further regulation was unnecessary. Since one of the routes of the proposed city railway was to run alongside the Danube Canal, there could be no question of a reliable service unless all risk of flooding was eliminated. This consideration, along with the endeavour to keep the waterway open to traffic irrespective of any variation in level between mainstream and canal, led to the construction between 1894 and 1898 of the Nussdorf Wehr, a dam combining weir and lock.[16] Three further dams were envisaged, but only one, the Kaiserbad, was put in hand and completed in 1908. Although fully up to specification, it was soon found to be unnecessary and fell into disuse. By the time the Danube Canal line was opened to traffic on 6 August 1901, the regulation of the waterway had largely been completed.

Another substantial undertaking was the regulation of the River Wien[17] which runs through the city. Rising in the Wienerwald, this river is unusual in that the volume of water it carries fluctuates alarmingly, the reason being that it runs for the most part through a zone of impermeable rock known as *flysch*. The nature of the Wien, then, is that of a torrent whose water level rises rapidly in wet weather and sinks during the dry season. Even after the work of regula-

15 Main Railway Customs House. 1899, photograph. Historisches Museum der Stadt Wien. The railways built between 1837 and 1881 were to exert a considerable influence on the city's subsequent social geography.

16 Westbahnhof. 1895, photograph. Historisches Museum der Stadt Wien.
Like almost all the other termini, the Kaiserin-Elisabeth-Westbahnhof, completed in 1858, was situated close to the Lines. The undoubted advantage of not laying tracks through built-up areas was offset by the drawback that Vienna never had a central station.

the Ostbahn. Dictated as they were by the nature of the terrain, the two lines bounded the southern sector of the city, while at the same time greatly enhancing its economic prospects. The Nordbahn, originally routed through more or less virgin territory, was to be largely responsible for the industrial development of an area on the left bank of the Danube. The Westbahn, which was brought in radially along the valley of the River Wien, did not materially hamper growth; rather it helped to stimulate the industries already established in that area. The same may be said of the Franz-Josephs-Bahn which ran close alongside the Danube Canal and parallel to Vienna's main artery to the north.

17 *Harbour in Winter* ('Winter-hafen'). *C.* 1905, photograph. Historisches Museum der Stadt Wien.
Between 1889 and 1902 one arm of the Danube, at the lower extremity of the Prater Island, was made into a harbour to protect vessels against ice-floes.

18 Nussdorf Dam. 1904, photograph. Historisches Museum der Stadt Wien.
The building of the dam (1894–8) by the architect Otto Wagner brought to completion the regulation of the Danube Canal by providing absolute protection against flooding.

19 Danube Canal. *C.* 1900, photograph. Historisches Museum der Stadt Wien.
Regulation work near the offices of the Danube Steamship Company. In the background the Giant Wheel, put up in 1897.

20 Ferdinand Weckbrodt: *Der Wienfluss unterhalb der Pilgrim-Brücke* ('The River Wien below the Pilgrim Bridge'). 1884, watercolour, 28 x 40.3 cm. Historisches Museum der Stadt Wien.
Flash floods, increasing pollution by the factories on its banks and, not least, the building of the *Stadt-bahn* (city railway), necessitated the regulation of the river (1894–9).

21 Johann Varrone: *Die Tegett-hoff-Brücke über dem Wienfluss* ('The Tegetthoff Bridge over the River Wien'). 1888, water-colour and gouache, 53.3 x 67.2 cm. Historisches Museum der Stadt Wien.
The regulation of the Wien deprived the river of its former picturesqueness. Here we have but one example of the many pastoral scenes which owed their charm not least to their urban setting.

Tegetthoff-Brücke

22 Regulation of the River Wien near the Margaretengürtel *Stadtbahn* (city railway) station. 1898, photograph. Historisches Museum der Stadt Wien.
A Wien valley line was included in the original plans for the *Stadtbahn* (city railway). Since the regulation of the waterway was an essential prerequisite for a reliable service, work on railway and river went hand in hand. By 1899 the whole line was in operation between Hütteldorf and the Main Customs House.

23 Regulation of the River Wien near the Secession Building. 1898, photograph. Historisches Museum der Stadt Wien.
The river, which formerly had flowed through a partially rural landscape, was transformed into an urban waterway, much of it arched over. Note the work in progress near the Secession building, erected by Joseph Maria Olbrich in 1897–8.

tion had been completed there was serious flooding, once in 1897 and again in 1899.

There was also another hazard associated with the Wien. When, in the first half of the nineteenth century, more and more factories, both large and small, were established along the valley, their effluent, together with the contents of domestic drains, was discharged into the river which, in consequence, became little more than an open sewer. Not only had the regulation work been excellently conceived, and so planned that some of the final operations could be safely left to the future, it also radically changed the nature of the Wien. What had been a more or less rural stream became an urban watercourse, canalized and, for much of its length, arched over. This gave rise to a number of problems, such as the design of the Karlsplatz, which were to remain unsolved for decades to come.

Hardly had the Lines been constructed than doubts began to be cast on their defensive merits. Hence there was little cause for surprise when, in 1873, work began on a boulevard, the Gürtelstrasse, that was to follow the course of these fortifications. The intention was to create a thoroughfare of the highest class which would greatly facilitate communications between the different parts of the city. As mentioned above, the Lines were handed over to the Municipality on 21 August 1893, thereby enabling work to be speeded up on the boulevard itself and a start to be made on the Gürtelline, the city railway's third route. While the Danube Canal line and the Wien Valley line derive their character from the waterways they follow, the architectonic solution of the Gürtel route was a response to the exceptionally hilly terrain through which it ran. The line, chiefly characterized by alternating stretches of underground and overhead track,[18] is an essay in railroad architecture and engineering that has set its stamp on that part of the city lying along the boundary between the inner and outer districts.

24 The *Stadtbahn* (City Railway) near Gumpendorferstrasse Station. *C.* 1900, photograph. Historisches Museum der Stadt Wien.
The Gürtel line, which runs along the boundary between the inner and outer suburbs, is chiefly remarkable for being both an underground and an overhead railway.

'Belt of woods and meadows'

With the incorporation of the outer suburbs, Vienna acquired not only additional built-up areas, but also the surrounding countryside and with it part of the Wienerwald, 'the chief jewel in Austria's crown'.[19] In 1873, after three years of tireless effort, Josef Schöffel, a parliamentary deputy, succeeded in saving the woods from deforestation. In 1905 the Municipal Council resolved unanimously to create a 'belt of woods and meadows'. In this way they not only acknowledged, but officially endorsed,

the importance of the Wienerwald as a lung for the city and a place of recreation for its inhabitants whose number, according to the demographers of the time, could be expected to rise to no less than four million by the mid-twentieth century. It is to these measures that the present citizens of Vienna owe their freedom of access to a green belt which has materially contributed to what is now so aptly described as the 'good life'.

Of all the lines built on the mountains in the neighbourhood of Vienna, the best known was the country's first cog railway, built in 1874, which linked Nussdorf with

25 Carl Schuster: *Stadtbahn* ('City Railway'). *C.* 1900, pen drawing, 26.5 x 34.6 cm. Historisches Museum der Stadt Wien.
The Vienna *Stadtbahn* was built between 1894 and 1900. Owing to the nature of the terrain, the railway ran both underground and overhead. Otto Wagner was responsible for its architecture, some of which is of a striking, not to say grandiose, nature.

26 Sunday Walk in the Wienerwald. *C.* 1900, photograph. Historisches Museum der Stadt
Wien.
At the height of the *Gründerzeit,*
the Wienerwald was under threat
of deforestation and industrial
development. That threat was
averted and in 1905 the region was
officially designated a 'belt of
woods and meadows', thus assur-
ing the continued existence of
pure air for the metropolis and a
recreational area for its citizens.

27 The Kahlenberg Cog
Railway. *C.* 1900, potograph.
Historisches Museum der Stadt
Wien.
The building of Austria's first cog
railway followed the opening up
of the Wienerwald to tourism.
From 1874 to 1920 it ran between
Nussdorf and the hotel on the
Kahlenberg.

the hotel on the Kahlenberg.[20] This jolly symbol of *Gründerzeit joie de vivre* was short-lived, for in 1920 it fell victim to the post-war economic catastrophe.

Though the existence of a conservation area on the periphery of the Wienerwald restricted the city's expansion northwards and westwards, the creation on 28 December 1904 of Floridsdorf (21st District), on the left bank of the Danube,[21] provided a development area capable of accommodating over a million inhabitants, as well as an extensive industrial and commercial centre that was also to comprise a port. Its integration, which brought the total area covered by Vienna up to 273 square kilometres, was a far-sighted measure, the benefits of which would not begin to make themselves felt until some time in the future. However, before World War I the 21st District provided the site for one noteworthy public undertaking, namely the construction of the Leopoldau gasworks which came into service in 1911. This formed part of the series of public works which mark the course of the Christian Socials' deliberate communalization of Vienna's infrastructure.

The extent to which the city, though untouched by the actual fighting, was affected by the Great War is discussed elsewhere in this book. Topographically speaking, there were no changes of note, save for the military works and installations put in hand to safeguard the 'Vienna bridgehead'[22] after the Russians' victories in Galicia in the late summer and autumn of 1914 had brought them within striking distance of the city.

Yet the conflict ushered in a development culminating in the socialist concept of communal housing, a concept which, as realized in Vienna, was to make that city a general cynosure between the two wars. In common with nearly all other European countries, whether belligerent or neutral, Austria was constrained by social and economic pressures to introduce controls on rent and the right of eviction. These were subsumed under the imperial 'Ordinance for the Protection of Tenants'[23] promulgated in January 1917. Unlike other states, however, Austria did not revoke that ordinance after the end of the war. Indeed, the principles it embodied were scrupulously adhered to, particularly in Vienna where, in the elections of 4 May 1919 – the first to be held after the introduction of universal and equal suffrage for men and women alike – the Social Democrats had secured 100 seats out of 165 on the Municipal Council. In 1922 the ordinance was made law. These were unquestionably restrictive measures so far as property owners were concerned and tended to discourage the investment in new housing schemes of such little capital as remained in those inflationary times. Accordingly, the municipal authorities assumed responsibility for that task. With the advent of the Social Democrats it became possible to regard as a common aim the construction of new housing financed by taxes levied on all. Hence the dwelling became a social product which must be available to all. A beginning was made with the Metzleinstaler Hof, erected between 1919 and 1923; it is the symbol of the changes in the social aspect of Vienna which were to find architectural expression in the communal housing projects of the inter-war years.

28–9 The Metzleinstaler Hof. 1923, photographs. Historisches Museum der Stadt Wien. Designed by Hubert Gessner and built between 1919 and 1923, the Metzleinstaler Hof in the 5th District was the first tenement block put up by the Vienna Municipality.

1   Eugen Guglia, *Wien. Ein Führer durch Stadt und Umgebung*, Vienna, 1908, p. XLIV.

2   The *Gründerzeit* was, strictly speaking, a brief period of wild financial speculation which came to an end with the crash of 1873. Here it is used to denote more or less what in England would be called the Victorian era.

3   In 1694, 34 of the outlying localities were brought within the jurisdiction of the city.

4   Cf. Felix Czeike, *Geschichte der Stadt Wien*, Vienna, 1981, p. 233.

5   Cf. Wolfgang Mayer, *Die städtische Entwicklung Wiens bis 1945*. Catalogue of the exhibition mounted by the Geschäftsgruppe Stadtplanung and the Wiener Stadt- und Landesarchiv, Vienna, 1978, p. 19.

6   *Wiener Communal-Kalender und Städtisches Jahrbuch,* Vol. 8, N. S., Vienna, 1880, p. 357.

7   Cf. Felix Czeike (cit. Note 4), p. 233.

8   Districts:
 1 Inner City
 2 Leopoldstadt
 3 Landstrasse
 4 Wieden
 5 Margarethen
 6 Mariahilf
 7 Neubau
 8 Josefstadt
 9 Alsergrund
 10 Favoriten
 11 Simmering
 12 Meidling
 13 Hietzing
 14 Rudolfsheim
 15 Fünfhaus
 16 Ottakring
 17 Hernals
 18 Währing
 19 Döbling
N. B. While the names of the districts have remained the same since 1890–2, some of the boundaries have been altered.

9   *Wiener Communal-Kalender und Städtisches Jahrbuch,* Vol. 20, N. S., Vienna, 1892, p. 390.

10   *Wiener Communal-Kalender und Städtisches Jahrbuch,* Vol. 21, N. S., Vienna, 1893, p. 465.

11   Cf. Hans Bobek and Elisabeth Lichtenberger, *Wien. Bauliche Gestalt und Entwicklung seit der Mitte des 19. Jahrhunderts*, Graz-Cologne, 1966, pp. 103 ff.

12   Ibid., p. 113.

13   1837/8: Nordbahn (Kaiser-Ferdinands-Nordbahn)
1841: Südbahn (Wien-Gloggnitzer-Bahn)
1846: Ostbahn (Wien-Raaber-Bahn; Staatsbahn)
1851: Verbindungsbahn
1857/8 Westbahn (Kaiserin-Elisabeth-Westbahn)
1870: Franz-Josephs-Bahn (Kaiser-Franz-Josephs-Bahn)
1880/1: Aspangbahn

14   Cf. Hans Bobek and Elisabeth Lichtenberger (cit. Note 11), p. 42. In 1910 Strebersdorf was combined with Floridsdorf. In 1938 the south-eastern portion of the 21st District was detached to become the 22nd District (Donaustadt).

15   Martin Paul, *Technischer Führer durch Wien*, Vienna, 1910, p. 205.

16   Ibid., pp. 206 ff.

17   Cf. Günter Düriegl, *Wien auf alten Photographien*, Vienna-Munich, 1981, pp. 141 ff.

18   Renata Kassal-Mikula, *Otto Wagner (1841–1918). Die Wiener Stadtbahn*, Vienna, 1982, p. 6.

19   Archduke Rudolf, 'Der Wienerwald', in *Die österreichisch-ungarische Monarchie in Wort und Bild. Wien und Niederösterreich*, 2. Abteilung: *Niederösterreich*, Vienna, 1888, pp. 3 ff.
The Wienerwald is bounded to the north by Tulln basin and the Danube, to the east by the Wien basin, to the south by the river Triesting and the Gölsenbach, and to the west by the river Traisen.

20   For railways cf. Günter Düriegl (cit. Note 17), p. 144.

21   Felix Czeike (cit. Note 4), p. 250.

22   Walter Hummelberger and Kurt Peball, *Die Befestigungen Wiens. Wiener Geschichtsbücher*, Vol. 14, Vienna-Hamburg, 1974, pp. 95 ff.

23   *Reichsgesetzblatt für die im Reichsrate vertretenen Königreiche und Länder*, 1917, No. 34.

II POLITICS IN VIENNA BEFORE AND AFTER THE TURN OF THE CENTURY

Robert Waissenberger

Mass parties

Many of the problems which beset the world today can, on reflection, be identified with those that confronted Austria in the period under discussion. After the fall of the Danubian Monarchy, the successor states gradually came to realize that an attempt to iron out the differences between the nations would have been preferable to a general free-for-all in pursuit of autonomy and independence. For it was also becoming apparent that small nations ran a very real risk of becoming, sooner or later, the satellites of larger ones.

At the turn of the century Vienna saw an intellectual ferment which not only stimulated a wealth of new political, scientific and cultural ideas, but also, and as a natural consequence of her position as the hub of Austria-Hungary, extended far beyond the city's confines. National awareness which, during the nineteenth century, had been growing among the Monarchy's ethnic groups was now beginning to exacerbate their mutual rivalry. Detrimental though this was to the survival of the state, it was to prove fruitful in a number of other spheres.

To a large extent culture is the product of resistance to the *status quo* and the impulse man feels to oppose it. The forces that effectively influenced events in Vienna were of various kinds, some deriving from the past, others pointing to the future. And here the stratification of society – nobility, middle classes and proletariat – played a decisive role. The aristocracy had long since lost much of its eighteenth-century lustre. As in the past, however, many of its members occupied senior posts in politics and the army. In the sphere of business, on the other hand, the nobility had for some time been relegated to second place. Indeed, the nineteenth century was the heyday of the bourgeoisie which had successfully survived the revolution of 1848 and the trial of strength it represented. True, the rising had been put down by military force, but the victory was not to prove enduring. For the men destined to wield political power in the latter part of the century were none other than those same 'forty-eighters'.

On the other hand, the time of the Fourth Estate had not yet come. Here again, the bourgeoisie had consolidated its position during the 1848 revolution, foiling all attempts on the part of the proletariat to attain political power. In the post-revolutionary period, it was the liberals who predominated in politics. For the reverse suffered by absolutism in its encounters with foreign foes had affected the stability of the régime which therefore needed allies rather than opponents at home. Yet the liberal victory was by no means complete; while certain goals such as constitutional government had been attained, the franchise was still restricted and Imperial bureaucracy remained firmly entrenched. Nevertheless, having once gained a foothold in politics, the erstwhile revolutionaries continued to adhere to their principles for another two decades (1860–80). To that extent the old ideas had succeeded in holding their own.

By 1880, however, other social groups were demanding a say in Austrian politics – not only, as might have been expected, the industrial workers in the larger cities, but also the owners of small businesses, the peasants and, to an increasing extent, the Slav nations of the Monarchy.

The years prior to 1890 are of particular importance, since they saw the emergence of the German national movements and of the Christian Social and Social Democratic parties. Among the crucial problems which then dominated the political scene we should cite the stark contrast between the new plutocracy and the urban poor, the activism of the German Nationalists, the growing tension between the nationalities and, last but not least, anti-Semitism. It is difficult to underestimate the importance of the latter in the Old Austria where it was exceptionally rife – so much so that, among wide sections of the population, a politician could only succeed by professing some degree of anti-Semitism.

The Social Democratic Party was founded in late 1888 in the small Lower Austrian village of Hainfeld. From the very outset the party strove to show that its policy was not directed against the state, to which it remained loyal. Nevertheless, political opponents endeavoured to make a bogey of Social Democracy by presenting it as an exponent of anarchism. When the workers announced that they were to stage a demonstration on 1 May 1890, the bourgeoisie interpreted this to mean a sort of popular uprising. Some took fright; others, like the young Hofmannsthal (cf. Chapter 8), simply expressed revulsion. However, the demonstration in the Prater (an amusement park) was perfectly orderly and no clashes whatever occurred. That respected journal, the *Neue Freie Presse,* carried a highly laudatory report of the event, commending, in particular, the discipline of the workers. They had taken care not to offend other sections of the community, nor had there been any confrontations with the police. The march was intended to provide a

contrast to the 'Procession of Flowers', a middle- and upper-class gathering which took place every May Day in the Prater.

During this period the workers were not solely concerned with the struggle for their rights, for they sought above all to draw attention to the trials and hardships they suffered. Wages were low and hours of work (12–14 a day) long, despite the statutory regulations then existing in Imperial Austria. For example, leave of absence and holidays were virtually unknown. Sundays were free but in many cases this meant only Sunday afternoons, since those workers employed in the service industries were required as a matter of course to make themselves available on Sunday mornings. This is not to imply that society was unaware of the misery, destitution and social grievances of the people. Yet social ills were far from being the main object of that society's concern. This was still a time when poverty was regarded as wicked and despicable, a condition for which the sufferers alone were to blame. That there should have been considerable tension between the various social strata is not surprising, given the abject poverty of the proletariat at one end of the scale and the enormous wealth, particularly of the com-

mercial classes, at the other. One glaring example is provided by the brick-makers who lived in wretched hovels near the Wienerberg brick-fields. Most of these workers had come from Bohemia and Moravia and had been only too pleased to find jobs in Vienna. Their plight was denounced in a pamphlet by Viktor Adler who, however, did not go so far as to impugn a system he had repeatedly and explicitly endorsed.

Adler, a politician and doctor of medicine from Prague, had once supported the German Nationalists and had been impelled by the latter's increasingly strident anti-Semitism to transfer his allegiance to the Social Democrats, whose ranks he joined in 1881. At this time the party, then in its formative, proselytizing stage, was attracting some of the ablest and most creative proponents of socialism, among them Otto Bauer and Karl Renner. However, it was largely thanks to Adler, the most eminent of them all, that the various tendencies within that party were brought under one umbrella during the Hainfeld Congress. Karl Renner, a Moravian by birth, was, like Adler, an early arrival in Vienna, where he obtained a

post in the parliament library. He joined the labour movement in 1893. A moderate who favoured compromise, Renner became Chancellor in 1918 and, in 1945, the first President of the Second Federal Republic of Austria. After the First World War Otto Bauer, who had first made his name with his treatise, *The Nationality Question and Social Democracy,* became the chief exponent of Austro-Marxism, the policy of which, despite certain radical tendencies, had always been one of moderation and gradual progress. In other words, the aim was to reform rather than subvert the existing order. Another goal was better education for the working class, based on the premise that it was less easy to exploit an intelligent than an uneducated worker. Far from being an anarchist bogey, as some sections of the population had supposed after the founding of the party at Hainfeld, the Social Democrats sought to combat what was an infinitely greater and more real danger, namely the rivalry between the nationalities. At a time when national dissension was becoming ever more acute, this was, to say the least, a problematical task, in-

32 Wood-engraving from the *Illustriertes Wiener Extrablatt* of 13 April 1890: 'Picture of the Brawls in Neulerchenfeld'. Strikes were frequent in Vienna at this time, for the workers were dissatisfied with their living and working conditions. The fighting that broke out in Neulerchenfeld (Hernals) between strikers and non-strikers in the building trade was eventually suppressed by the military.

33 '1 May in Vienna'. Wood-engraving from the *Extrablatt* of 4 May 1890.
Part of the caption reads: 'Between one and four o'clock, the workmen continued to converge on the Prater. As had been previously arranged, they then dispersed to various inns to spend the rest of their holiday drinking beer and singing, having devoted the morning to the more serious business of the rally. At half past five the first contingents, shepherded by stewards, set off on the homeward march.'

34 Maximilian Lenz: *Praterfahrt* ('Driving in the Prater'). 1900, oil on canvas, 73 x 160 cm. Historisches Museum der Stadt Wien. On Sundays and holidays, especially, the Viennese nobility in elegant attire would parade in cabs down the main avenue of the Prater. This was the scene of the first 'Procession of Flowers' on 1 May 1886, when special finery was worn in honour of spring.

volving as it did a clash with vested interests, and the consequent risk of falling foul of both Left and Right. The *Reichsrat* (Imperial Parliament) became the scene of furious exchanges in the course of which the national minorities clamoured for their rights.

In seeking to segregate themselves in Vienna the various national groups came to be associated with this or that part of the capital. German was their *lingua franca*, not because it was spoken fluently by all, but rather because it was the language of the nation which laid claim to political leadership – a claim which would, if necessary, be vindicated by force of arms.

Badeni ordinances

In 1897 the minister-president, Count Badeni, promulgated language ordinances which inflamed national sentiment to the extent of provoking riots. The count, a big landowner in Poland, had always been at pains to achieve a compromise between federalism and centralism in the country of his birth as, by his ordinances, he now

hoped to do throughout the Monarchy. The new regulations, which were to come into force in 1901, required officials in the Sudeten territories to give proof of their ability to speak both German and Czech. This seemed reasonable enough and would enable people in those areas to use their mother tongue in court or on other official occasions. But the officials concerned were dismayed and outraged – indeed, so inflated did the whole business become as almost to attain the dimensions of a political crisis. Count Badeni had doubtless underestimated what was at stake and had thought in terms of conditions at home in Poland between which and the now increasingly explosive situation there could be no real comparison.

The ordinances aroused a storm of protest, first in the Press and, later, in the *Reichsrat*. Matters came to a head with the emperor's request for Badeni's resignation, after Karl Lueger, the mayor of Vienna, had declared that he could no longer guarantee to maintain law and order. And, in fact, there had already been fighting in the streets of Vienna, sparked off by an unseemly rum-

35   The *Glühlichter,* a 'humorous and satirical working men's paper'. Issue of 1 May 1891. The title-page depicts working men demonstrating for their rights on 1 May 1891. The paper, which first appeared in 1889, ceased publication in 1915.

36   Brick-makers. Photograph. Dr-Karl-Renner-Archiv, Vienna.
Workers from all parts of the Monarchy flocked to Vienna where many of them were doomed to live in wretched circumstances. The brick-makers in particular were badly housed and poorly paid. Their plight was high-lighted in a political pamphlet written by the Social Democratic leader, Viktor Adler.

37   Alexander Demetrius Goltz: *Viktor Adler.* 1919, oil on wood, 62 x 51 cm. Historisches Museum der Stadt Wien.
Of Jewish origin, Viktor Adler at first supported the German national movement but was driven by the latter's increasingly virulent anti-Semitism to associate himself with the Social Democrats. A moderate, he eventually became their undisputed leader.

38   Dr Karl Renner. Photograph. Dr-Karl-Renner-Archiv, Vienna.
Renner was a leading figure in Austrian Social Democracy. He was also one of the architects of the new Austria, having been Chancellor and second President of the Parliament in the First Republic, the first Chancellor and, subsequently, President of the Second Republic.

39   Moriz Jung: *Die rote Bestie* ('The Red Monster'). Pen-and-ink, coloured wash, 24.4 x 18.7 cm. Historisches Museum der Stadt Wien.
To the citizens of Vienna the rise of organized labour and the growing strength of the Social Democrats portended, as it were, the end of the world. Not surprisingly, the mood was seized upon by cartoonists.

pus in Parliament where the filibustering tactics of the German deputies had been promptly aped by the deputies of the other nations. Finally, on 28 November 1897, the dispute reached a climax in a confrontation between workers and nationalist students during which one side sang the 'Song of Labour' and the other the 'Watch on the Rhine'. About midday mounted police arrived on the scene and proceeded to lay about them with a will. However, it was not until cavalry had been brought up to reinforce the police that the demonstrators were dispersed. Badeni was forced to hand in his resignation, whereupon a number of his ordinances were rescinded. Nevertheless, the problem of the nationalities became ever more acute, along with the intensification of national sentiment. No one was in any doubt that a situation such as this must sooner or later end in disaster. In the meantime there was a short breathing-space dur-

ing which any suggestion that happened to be put forward was eagerly seized upon. But a solution to the problem as a whole failed to present itself.

It was a situation which, in many respects, was gratifying to the opponents of parliamentary government and perhaps even to the monarch himself, who is said to have remarked on more than one occasion that Austria was ungovernable under such a system and that events had proved him right. Although the problems debated in the *Reichsrat* were of a different order from those dealt with by the Municipal Council of Vienna, both reflected the national conflicts.

The political changes now taking place within the Municipal Council were marked by the defection of liberals to the Christian Social Party, a bourgeois-inspired mass movement. For the true liberals, the generation of 'forty-eighters', had been gradually withdrawing from the political scene.

Karl Lueger

Two figures of that period are noteworthy by reason of the exceptional influence they exerted on the politics of the capital, namely Georg von Schönerer and Karl Lueger. Initially both had expressed sentiments that were wholly in favour of liberalism, but in the course of time they turned their coats, eventually becoming its most bitter opponents.

Schönerer, the 'Knight of Rosenau', an uncompromising nationalist and anti-Semite, was elected to the *Reichsrat* in 1873.

There his main concern was to safeguard the interests of the farming community, a policy which quickly brought him into conflict with the liberals. He also put forward demands for a customs union with Germany. His political pronouncements soon betrayed a marked anti-Semitic tendency and, indeed, he was gradually to become 'the strongest and most thoroughly consistent anti-Semite that Austria produced' (Schorske). Yet his conduct, like his aspirations, proved in the event to be so ill-considered that there was little prospect of organizing his supporters into a mass party, as Adolf Hitler was to do half a century or so later.

Karl Lueger was a politician of quite a different breed. He was a thoroughgoing pragmatist with a keen ear for slogans that would catch the fancy of the masses. The son of a minor official at Vienna's Polytechnic Institute, he came from a relatively humble background or, as the Viennese would say, *aus kleinen Verhältnissen*. He was educated as a day-boy at the Theresianum, a school which in general only accepted children from upper-class families. Later, he read law at Vienna University and became a wholehearted advocate of democratic ideals, a self-confessed Prussophil and an opponent of the *kleindeutsch* solution, namely a united Germany from which Austria would be excluded. In pursuit of success in local politics, he declared war on corruption. Ultimately he was to enter the *Reichsrat* as a democrat. An increasingly radical attitude, however, led him to divert his attacks from corruption to capitalism, the chief representatives of which, he claimed, were the Jews. From here it was only a short step to anti-Semitism as such, a step which won him more supporters than ever before since, as mentioned above, aversion to the Jews had always been rife in Vienna. But radical though he was, Lueger never renounced his allegiance to the Habsburg Monarchy, and continued to regard liberalism as the real enemy. A factor common to all the anti-liberal elements was Catholicism, to which Lueger also subscribed as providing an unmistakable badge of allegiance.

Democracy, social reform and anti-Semitism – such was the banner under which the Christian Social Party was founded in 1889, at almost the same time as the Social Democratic Party. It was Lueger who succeeded in welding into a single whole a number of different tendencies – Catholic, democratic and social. His activities were centred almost entirely on the Municipal Council over which he was determined to preside. Yet several years were to elapse before he could overcome the obstacles that were placed in his way, notably by the emperor and his advisers. The success of the Christian Socials was, in large measure, a personal triumph for Lueger himself who, as a true tribune of the people, was adept at striking the right note vis-à-vis the electorate. In general his attitude was cool and reserved, commanding the respect due to a leader. But at the appropriate moment, and given the right audience, he would relapse into Viennese dialect, an astute political approach which won over an ever greater proportion of the electorate. Eventually he obtained the majority required for his appointment as mayor, but failed to secure the consent of the emperor, no doubt because of the opposition of his arch-enemy, Count Badeni, whose hostility he had aroused by his vehement tirades against the Jews, the established authorities and Hungary. Lueger was also opposed by the upper middle classes who threatened to leave Vienna in the event of his becoming mayor. The Hungarians, for their part, let it be known that his appointment would be regarded as a hostile act in view of his perpetual outbursts against their country. On 29 October 1895 Lueger again ran for mayor, obtaining 93 out of 137 votes. Neither his appeal to the governor of Lower Austria, Count Kielmannsegg, nor the support of the heir apparent, Francis Ferdinand, were of any avail, for Badeni, fearing for the success of his policy, yet again advised the emperor not to ratify Lueger's appointment.

In the course of a subsequent meeting which took place between Badeni and Lueger, the latter undertook to refrain from serious criticism of the government should he be appointed mayor. When a further poll gave him an overwhelming majority in the Municipal Council, it was agreed that, ini-

43 Franz Alt: *Neues Rathaus* ('The New Town Hall'). 1882, water-colour, 24.9 x 37.7 cm. Historisches Museum der Stadt Wien.
The town hall was designed by Friedrich von Schmidt and officially opened in 1883. An opulent neo-Gothic building in the Ringstrasse, it symbolized the bourgeoisie's heightened sense of its own importance.

44 Friedrich von Schmidt: *Innere Ansicht des Gemeinderatssitzungssaales im Wiener Rathaus* ('Interior of the Municipal Chamber in Vienna Town Hall'). Pen and brush, coloured wash, 39.9 x 47.9 cm. Historisches Museum der Stadt Wien.
In accordance with the wishes of the architect, the walls of the municipal chamber were adorned with numerous paintings depicting Vienna's history in terms of the Austrian dynasty. Like Parliament, the chamber witnessed heated debates which often echoed national sentiment.

Lueger was a skilled tactician, able to take advantage of the weak spots of his opponents, with whom he would not hesitate to walk arm-in-arm, however, should he deem it opportune. He was a tribune of the people, not only in manner but also in person, having by his good looks earned the sobriquet 'Charles the Handsome'. In many ways his popularity eclipsed that of the old emperor, which may perhaps help to explain the latter's reservations towards him.

The years he served as mayor of Vienna undoubtedly brought many benefits. His policy was tailored to the needs of the people. When Lueger took over, public transport, as well as the supply of gas and power, were still in the hands of private undertakings which were at liberty to dictate prices, a situation that was clearly not in the interests of the consumer. One of the principal aims in the programme laid down by Lueger and his Christian Socials was to find a remedy for this state of affairs.

Publicly owned gasworks were built in Simmering in 1899, and about this time work also began on a power station, again in Simmering, closely linked with the electrification of the tramway system. At the time when Lueger became mayor, the city's tramways were operated by two private concerns. The prospect of their being taken over by the authorities seemed remote, but after much political manœuvering this was successfully achieved. Indeed, within a few years Vienna found herself in possession of the world's most extensive electric tramway system.

Lueger's plans for Vienna were farsighted, and the policy he pursued was in keeping with them. Not a little prescience is apparent in the advocacy of a 'green belt' round the city, as also of a number of green zones, all of which contributed materially to the health of Vienna's citizens. The above-mentioned projects went hand in hand with the construction of a new conduit for the conveyance of pure drinking-water from the Hochschwab region, the intention being to reduce the load on the existing supply, whose source was likewise in the Alps.

Obviously none of these municipal undertakings, which followed one another

tially, Dr Joseph Strobach should be made mayor and Lueger deputy mayor, an appointment that did not call for royal assent. However, after another major victory on 4 April 1897 he was finally appointed mayor, and confirmed in that office by the emperor a few days later.

Anti-Semitism, clericalism and a pronounced tendency towards non-Marxist socialism had ensured his resounding success, a success which consolidated his position in the eyes of the electorate, notably the petty bourgeoisie. In his speeches Lueger resorted to crude generalizations in order to make himself more readily understood by the mob. 'Saving the little man's livelihood', 'Jewish big business' and 'bringing the people back to the churches' – such were the terms he employed. His anti-Semitism had widespread repercussions, not least upon the young Adolf Hitler, most of whose political views had taken shape during the time he spent in Vienna. Later he was to describe Lueger in *Mein Kampf* as 'the most powerful mayor of all time', whose chief misfortune it had been to 'live and work in such an impossible country'.

46 A. Mayerhofer: *Bürgermeister* (Mayor) *Dr Karl Lueger.* 1902, oil on canvas, 90 x 75.2 cm. Historisches Museum der Stadt Wien. Lueger, leader of the Christian Social Party, was one of the most able local politicians of his day. The great popularity he enjoyed among the electorate ensured the success of his movement. The petty bourgeoisie, in particular, tended to identify with his innovative social policy in the municipal sphere.

in rapid succession, could have been started without the help of substantial loans. However, the servicing of these loans placed a considerable burden on the city's finances. When, after the First World War, the Social Democrats came to power in Vienna, they maintained – not without some justification – that they had inherited a totally bankrupt administration.

Attention was also paid to the education and welfare of the young. A number of charitable schemes were introduced with the aim of solving the problem of indigence and want. The same period also saw the building of hospitals and homes for the aged. These institutions, which were open to all, have, in many ways, served as a blueprint for the urban administrators of today. Finally, mention should also be made

of the rights gained by the Municipality's manual and office workers, who were now enjoying the benefits of a substantial improvement in their terms of service.

Welfare schemes were often introduced with an eye to the trial of strength which, sooner or later, was bound to take place between Christian Socials and Social Democrats. In the meantime the former were able to extend and consolidate their position and thus become the most powerful political factor in Austria. Their rise may largely be attributed to the role played by municipal politics, a sphere in which Lueger excelled, thanks to his charismatic personality.

The above-mentioned measures were welcomed by large sections of the population. However, the workers soon perceived

47 Gasworks, Simmering. Photograph. Historisches Museum der Stadt Wien.
Vienna's gas supply had long remained in the hands of private companies whose contracts were not due to expire until the end of the century. After attempts at their renegotiation had proved fruitless, the Municipality decided to build its own gasworks in Simmering. Completed in October 1899, it was the first of the major projects undertaken during Karl Lueger's mayorship.

48 Construction of the new drinking-water conduit. Photograph. Historisches Museum der Stadt Wien.
In the interest of public health, one conduit had already been constructed to supply the city with pure drinking-water from the neighbourhood of the Schneeberg. To meet an ever-increasing demand, the Municipality, under Karl Lueger, decided to build a second conduit with its source in the Hochschwab region.

that the Social Democrats, being of a Marxist complexion, would be better able to serve their cause than the Christian Socials, who now stood revealed as the party of the middle and lower middle classes. So far as further concessions to the workers were concerned, that party had clearly reached the end of the road. Neither the Christian Socials nor the government could, of course, fail to be aware of the implications of such a trend, but they did nothing to counter it, and this despite the constant defections from the ranks of the Christian Socials to those of the Social Democrats.

Anti-Semitism

It so happened that, between 1909 and 1911 – the time of the Christian Socials' triumphal progress under Karl Lueger – Adolf Hitler was living in Vienna. He had just turned twenty when, shortly after his arrival, he sought to gain admission to the Academy of Fine Arts and, having been rejected, proceeded to earn his living as a building labourer and draughtsman. During this period he learned to set his political sights on the middle classes, but what impressed him most was the local brand of anti-Semitism which, as understood by the Christian Socials, did not appeal to him because it was based on religion rather than race. In fact he dismissed it as 'bogus' since, 'if the worst came to the worst, a sprinkling of baptismal water would suffice to save business and Judaism at one blow'. To Hitler anti-Semitism was always a matter of race and, since the distinction lay in the blood, the convert to Christianity was no less a Jew than he had been before. Compared with this radical attitude, Lueger's anti-Semitism possessed features that were positively humane.

But anti-Semitism as such was also responsible for evoking a reaction in the form of Zionism as evolved by Theodor Herzl. For the gradual decline of liberalism tended, not altogether without reason, to be laid at the door of emancipated Jewry. Herzl's idea of a Jewish state was to a large extent the product of his liberal opinions and was of course

understandable if we consider his origins. Educated initially in Budapest, he had encountered anti-Semitism while still at school. Later on, in Vienna – the only place in which he really felt at home – he came to realize that the education accorded by many Jews to their sons was calculated to cut them off from wide sections of uneducated Jewry. Commercialism was the gibe often thrown at the Jews who, in order to rid themselves of that stigma, would send their sons to university where they graduated, as often as not, in medicine or law.

A noteworthy feature of the younger Jewish generation was the marked interest they showed in German literature. Indeed, there is no denying that it was this group of assimilated Jews who lent exceptional intellectual lustre to the Vienna of that day. An essential part of the make-up of men such as Viktor Adler, Sigmund Freud, Arthur Schnitzler, Arnold Schoenberg and Ludwig Wittgenstein was their unparochial, wholly cosmopolitan outlook. In no way could they be described as mere local celebrities. Thus it was largely thanks to them that Vienna attained such eminence in the scientific and cultural spheres. Unlike many other highly respected figures in these fields, they succeeded in divesting themselves of the narrow 'Victorian' outlook that had prevailed until then. Inevitably, large numbers of people regarded the liberal assimilated Jews of the upper middle class as serious competitors who must be opposed. The latter, in their turn, who led an opulent cultivated existence, looked with distaste upon the orthodox Jewry of the ghetto. This attitude, tantamount to anti-Semitism, was directed primarily at the immigrants who continued to flow in from the east. These people, it was alleged, had been mentally and physically deformed by segregation, while inbreeding had rendered them incapable of further development. Such was the opinion, not of some insignificant anti-Semite, but of no less a man than Theodor Herzl at an early stage in his career. Initially, he had been in favour of assimilation, yet from episodes such as the expulsion of young Jews from students' associations it soon became evident that, far

from promoting the cherished aims of eliminating anti-Semitism, assimilation would prove a stumbling-block.

Considerations of this kind finally induced Theodor Herzl to take up the cudgels on behalf of Jewry and, in particular, to canvass the idea of a Jewish state. This is not to say that he wholeheartedly espoused that cause from the outset. But the day came when he suddenly realized that, in the debate on anti-Semitism, reason would never prevail. Hence his misgivings about the efficacy of, for example, the Society for the Prevention of Anti-Semitism, an organization set up by Austrian intellectuals. Some of his own solutions were very different, among them his proposal to challenge anti-Semitic politicians to a duel, or to secure the wholesale conversion of Vienna's Jewry to Catholicism. Finally, having in the course of several formative stages drawn some painful conclusions, not least from the Dreyfus affair in France, he became obsessed with the notion of a Jewish state. It is somewhat ironic that the idea should have come to him during a performance of *Tannhäuser.* Yet Wagner's opera and the concept of a mass exodus to a foreign land are both, after all, essentially romantic.

The press

Very soon after this experience, Theodor Herzl brought out his first Zionist book, *Der Judenstaat* ('The Jewish State'). The place and date (Vienna, 1896) of its publication could not have been more apt, for at the turn of the century journalism played a considerable role in the city. Nor was the Viennese press in any way provincial; indeed, it could boast a number of first-rate journalists as well as several highly esteemed newspapers, notably the *Neue Freie Presse,* the mouthpiece of the literary world, and the *Wiener Zeitung* which, as an official organ, was necessarily somewhat guarded where politics was concerned. The press was, of course, subject to censorship, the application of which was most often rigorous but also at times exceedingly lax. Sometimes an issue might be confiscated or else appear with blank spaces. Again, editors might be informed in advance of certain matters that must not be alluded to in the press. The sale of newspapers was subject to a licence issued by the censor.

The *Neue Freie Presse,* which demanded of its readers a reasonable degree of education, was a paper of considerable influence. Its editorial department comprised a team of first-class journalists specializing in politics, business and the arts. The main credit for this happy state of affairs must go to Moriz Benedikt, its editor-in-chief, who had a flair for choosing the right men. From 1881 to 1908 he was co-publisher and thereafter sole proprietor of the paper, which enjoyed a steadily growing international reputation. Its theatre critic, Hugo Wittmann, was himself a well-known writer of operatic libretti and a shrewd observer of the Viennese theatrical scene. Ludwig Speidel, the feuilletonist, enjoyed a renown extending far beyond the confines of the city, while Eduard Hanslick, passionate admirer of Brahms and implacably hostile to Wagner, Bruckner, Mahler and Wolf, was the paper's much-feared music critic. Lastly, Daniel Spitzer, who died in 1893, contributed a witty and racy feature entitled *Strolls around Vienna,* which placed him among the truly great satirists of Viennese cultural life.

DER

JUDENSTAAT.

VERSUCH

EINER

MODERNEN LÖSUNG DER JUDENFRAGE

VON

THEODOR HERZL

DOCTOR DER RECHTE.

LEIPZIG und WIEN 1896.

M. BREITENSTEIN'S VERLAGS-BUCHHANDLUNG

WIEN, IX., WÄHRINGERSTRASSE 5.

However, the *Neue Freie Presse* faced competition in the shape of the *Wiener Zeitung,* for under its editor-in-chief, Friedrich Uhl, that paper's cultural section had begun to acquire considerable importance.

The changes that were gradually transforming the domestic political scene were necessarily accompanied by similar changes in the press. The year 1894, for instance, saw the appearance of the *Reichspost,* aimed chiefly at Christian Social readers. It was the most important of all the party journals founded at this time, among them Social Democratic organs such as the *Volksstimme,* the *Volkswille,* the *Gleichheit* and, later, the *Arbeiter-Zeitung.* Needless to say, these opposition papers were constantly under threat of confiscation.

Newspapers were either sold at kiosks or mailed direct to subscribers. They were also made available in coffee-houses which, at this time, became centres of what can only be described as a newspaper cult, a trend that could not but be beneficial to the quality of the press. For here the customers were able to linger over their reading and thus savour to the full the excellence of the reviews and well-considered commentaries.

51   Theodor Herzl, *The Jewish State,* 1896.
Having finally realized that assimilation could not provide the solution to the Jewish question Herzl wrote a pamphlet entitled *The Jewish State* in which he advocated the founding of a new homeland for the Jews.

52   Theodor Herzl. Photograph. Theatersammlung, Österreichische Nationalbibliothek, Vienna.

Emperor Francis Joseph

Many aspects of Austrian politics are comprehensible only when considered in conjunction with the long reign of the Emperor Francis Joseph. Initially, after the revolution of 1848, he had met with opposition from many quarters but, having successfully overcome these and other obstacles arising from the profound changes undergone by Austria, he had, by 1890, become a revered sexagenarian whose *raison d'être* was no longer subject to debate.

On his accession he left no room for doubt that he ·was a champion of absolutism, a principle which at that time had fallen into disrepute and which he was determined to reaffirm, if not reinstate. He unequivocally ruled against constitutional government, despite the fact that public opinion was in favour of a constitution. There was never any serious demand for the abolition of the monarchy in Austria where trepidation was aroused by anything that smacked unduly of revolution. The Emperor Francis Joseph, at any rate during the early years of his reign, had had to contend, not only with the revolutionary ideas of 1848, that is to say with a liberal opposition, but also with the enmity, national in origin, of the Hungarians who were seeking a large measure of independence and autonomy. It has often been said that, in the Old Austria, nothing was tackled save the most essential tasks, and then usually on a makeshift basis. That mentality was largely shared by Francis Joseph himself whose total lack of sympathy with reform went hand in hand with a profound mistrust of innovation. That these views should have become more deeply ingrained as he grew older is hardly cause for surprise. His innate inflexibility was now compounded by the obstinacy of old age.

Whereas in his youth the monarch had been known, indeed hated, as the suppressor of the revolution and enslaver of nations, especially Hungary, in old age he became, as it were, the symbol of his empire. So long as he was alive there was no danger that that empire would crumble. His regal bearing and the respect in which he was held were sufficient safeguards. And a regal bearing was for him a lifelong preoccupation. For he had been well prepared for his high office. The imperial house and, more notably, his ambitious mother the Archduchess Sophie, had educated him as a sovereign who would sustain the empire in accordance with 'the principle', in other words the conservative tradition. It was an empire he was to rule for sixty-eight years. Indeed, one of the things that singled him out was his survival at a time when his foes, notably the revolutionaries of 1848, were

49

long since dead. Yet, as the years went by, even he was forced by circumstances to depart in many respects from 'the principle'. Moreover, the Hungarians, who had been the real losers in the revolution of 1848, had been granted a state of their own, a state linked with Austria primarily through the person of the emperor-king.

To the peoples of the empire, as to individuals in general, the monarch was a model of excellence. And just as Francis Joseph set an example of honesty, rectitude and dignity, so the high aristocracy and the court acted as a kind of lode-star to those lower down the social scale. The latter, who depended for their information on the daily press, with its sparse and highly filtered court news, inevitably drew on their imagination to complete what was often a somewhat inaccurate picture. The empress, a beautiful, unworldly and unhappy woman, remained for the most part shrouded in mystery, but there could be little doubt that her life was one of boredom, tied as she was

to a man whose nature was quite foreign to her own. Reading, collecting objects that caught her fancy, and writing poetry in which she herself was the principal figure – such were the occupations that went to make up her days, to the detriment, be it said, of her role as empress and consort. Court receptions she habitually eschewed, save for an occasional fleeting appearance. Such behaviour was undiplomatic, to say the least; nor can she, as a 'reluctant empress', be exonerated from the charge of having neglected duties that were plainly incumbent upon her. But there was also another aspect of the matter and one which was not without significance. For she was one of those figures whom people tend to idolize and adore, regarding their way of life as something altogether out of the ordinary. As an example, we might cite Gabriele d'Annunzio's elegy in which the empress is accorded almost divine honours. Eventually, thanks to her aloofness, she became a symbol of something which also finds expression in the works of the *Jugendstil**, namely a tendency to exaltation which removed her far from the common run and took her, as it were, into another world that bore little relation to our own.

On 10 September 1898, when about to board a steamer at Geneva, the sixty-one-year-old empress was assassinated by Luigi Luccheni, a young building worker and 'lone' anarchist. However, as is usually the case in incidents of this kind, no one ever discovered what had induced him to perpetrate the deed; that he was mentally unbalanced is not in doubt. He later declared that, in his view, life had no meaning – a view that may have been conducive to the suicide that followed his sentence to life imprisonment.

Every community experiences times of greatness and times of prostration. So far as Vienna was concerned, the turn of the century was one of the city's high-water marks. Yet the different branches of art, discussed

---

*The German equivalent of Art Nouveau (translator's note).

54 Emperor Francis Joseph and the Heir Apparent Archduke Francis Ferdinand. Photograph. Historisches Museum der Stadt Wien.
It was common knowledge that the emperor and the heir apparent were not on the best of terms and that the latter had set up in his residence, the Belvedere, what might almost be described as a shadow government. Nevertheless the two men concealed their differences, Francis Ferdinand being fully aware of the duty he owed the emperor as his monarch and supreme commander.

elsewhere in this book, all had one thing in common in that they were all inspired, as it were, at one remove. By this we mean that the literature, music, painting, sculpture and applied arts of the day necessarily presupposed a high standard of education for, to the creative mind, a knowledge of the arts of the past was an indispensable adjunct. In this respect the art of the *fin de siècle*, despite its wider horizons, bore a close resemblance to that of historicism or eclecticism. Since far more was known than hitherto about the art of other countries, artists were subject to a wide variety of influences and were quick to assimilate new techniques and seize upon any new materials. However, as pointed out elsewhere, the basic tendency was towards refinement, and was to prove so enduring as to give rise here and there to a counter-movement.

Political changes

In politics an increasingly harsh note was making itself heard, while in the press kid gloves had been virtually discarded. This situation is summed up by no less a writer than Robert Musil in his short essay *Politik in Österreich 1913* ('Politics in Austria 1913'). 'There are few countries', he writes, 'in which politics are conducted with such passion and none in which politics, given a like degree of passion, are a matter of such indifference as here; passion as pretext. Outwardly everything is so parliamentary that more people are shot dead than anywhere else, and at any moment everything may be brought to a standstill by this or that party's reversal of opinion; high officials, generals, privy counsellors – none are immune from insult, a man can frighten his superior with a threat of exposure in parliament, or make politics pay, or box his opponent's ears. It is a convention, no more and no less, a game played in accordance with set rules.'

As things turned out, that game was unfortunately not always played in accordance with set rules, although these may still have applied here and there in the Monarchy. As an example we might cite the Sunday morning demonstrations in Wenceslas Square in

Prague, an activity which had become almost a ritual. On these occasions minor skirmishes would occur between Czech and German students who might consort quite amicably the same afternoon when engaged in some other sport, such as skating.

Elsewhere, however, disputes were not always settled in such a relatively harmless and bloodless manner. Nor did observers with a real grasp of the political situation entertain any doubt that matters were approaching a crisis, and that rivalry among the nationalities would sooner or later put the cohesion of the monarchy to the test. So long as Lueger controlled the fortunes of the party, its position remained virtually impregnable. But this of itself presented certain problems, for the more entrenched that

party became, the more hidebound it tended to grow. At the same time, however, it succeeded in establishing closer ties with the nobility and the court. For the adherence of the clerical faction to the Christian Socials had earned them not only the approval of the emperor but also, and in particular, that of the Crown Prince, Francis Ferdinand. Their fortunes remained in the ascendant until the introduction of universal suffrage in 1907, but thereafter entered into a decline. This process was accelerated by Lueger's death in 1910, when the Christian Social Party lost its impetus and, on the local level, ceased to concern itself with communal schemes. It was evidently content to rest on its laurels, an attitude to which the electorate not unnaturally responded by

57 Wilhelm Gause: *Kundgebung für das allgemeine Wahlrecht vor dem Parlament in Wien 1907* ('Demonstration in Favour of Universal Suffrage outside the Parliament Building in Vienna in 1907'). 1908, chalk drawing, 36 x 53 cm. Historisches Museum der Stadt Wien.
On 26 January 1907 Emperor Francis Joseph gave his assent to the introduction of universal, equal, direct and secret suffrage for men in Austria.

58 Felician Freiherr von Myrbach: *Rückkehr der Arbeiter von einer Demonstration am 1. Mai 1899* ('Workmen Returning from a Demonstration on 1 May 1899'). 1899, pencil drawing, 37 x 26 cm. Historisches Museum der Stadt Wien.

Vienna was to experience an increasing number of demonstrations, some peaceful, others less so.

withdrawing its support. Thus, in the *Reichsrat* elections of 1911, the Christian Social Party suffered its first resounding defeat. Moreover, as time went on, its character acquired a new facet with the accretion of nationalist elements. Meanwhile the popularity of the Social Democrats had steadily increased. They could now count on the support, not only of the trade unions, but also of the working class as a whole. Their campaign for workers' rights continued to gain momentum until halted by the outbreak of the First World War.

War-time Vienna

The news that the heir apparent, Archduke Francis Ferdinand, and his wife, Sophie von Hohenberg, had been assassinated in Sarajevo on 28 June 1914 was as shattering as it was unexpected. From then until the outbreak of war the atmosphere remained extremely tense. With the expiry of the ultimatum presented by the government in Vienna to Serbia, it became clear to all that war was inevitable. To keep readers *au fait* with the political situation, special editions

of the newspapers continued to appear during the night of 26 July. The following morning the first mobilization papers were sent out and, on 28 July, it was announced that Austria-Hungary had formally declared war on Serbia. Soon fighting broke out on all fronts, notably in the Russo-German theatre. On 2 August, a Sunday, the half-holiday was abolished. People swarmed through the streets of Vienna, while the authorities were inundated with anxious enquiries. The response to mobilization was, on the whole, enthusiastic. However, it was with growing misgivings that a small, if better-informed, minority reflected upon the possible consequences of the war.

Anyone seeking to form an image of the mood of Vienna, and of war-time events generally, should read Karl Kraus's magnificent literary collage, *The Last Days of Mankind*, perhaps the most memorable document on the mood of the city at that time. For its inhabitants were possessed by what can only be described as war fever. Initially the enthusiasm was so great that even the leaders of the Social Democratic Party – if not altogether unanimously and doubtless against their better judgement – resolved to adopt an affirmative stance. However, that enthusiasm was short-lived and soon gave way to a more sober attitude. Contrary to expectations, the war failed to bring a succession of victories; instead, news of reverses soon began to trickle in, while casualty lists grew ever longer. At the outset the army had advanced into Russian Poland, only to suffer substantial losses, with the result that it was ordered to withdraw. The surprise effect of the heavy counter-attacks subsequently delivered by the Russians was such that fears arose for the safety of the capital. Accordingly a start was made on the erection of defense works around the city, along the Ostbahn and in the Wienerwald. Barbed-wire entanglements and concrete gun emplacements made their appearance, while villages, previously fortified to resist the Prussians in 1866, were again placed on a defensive footing. Fortunately, however, these precautions proved unnecessary, for the Russian advance was halted.

Extra-Ausgabe

ber

Wiener Zeitung.

Nr. 174.   Dienstag, den 28. Juli   1914.

Amtlicher Teil.

Kriegserklärung.

Auf Grund Allerhöchster Entschließung Seiner k. u. k. Apostolischen Majestät vom 28. Juli 1914 wurde heute an die königl. serbische Regierung eine in französischer Sprache abgefaßte Kriegserklärung gerichtet, welche im Urtext und in deutscher Übersetzung folgendermaßen lautet:

„Le Gouvernement Royal de Serbie n'ayant pas répondu d'une manière satisfaisante à la Note qui lui avait été remise par le Ministre d'Autriche-Hongrie à Belgrade à la date du 23 juillet 1914, le Gouvernement I. et R. se trouve dans la nécessité de pourvoir lui-même à la sauvegarde de ses droits et intérêts et de recourir à cet effet à la force des armes. L'Autriche-Hongrie se considère donc de ce moment en état de guerre avec la Serbie.

Le Ministre des Affaires Etrangères d'Autriche-Hongrie Comte Berchtold."

„Da die königl. serbische Regierung die Note, welche ihr vom österreichisch-ungarischen Gesandten in Belgrad am 23. Juli 1914 übergeben worden war, nicht in befriedigender Weise beantwortet hat, so sieht sich die k. u. k. Regierung in die Notwendigkeit versetzt, selbst für die Wahrung ihrer Rechte und Interessen Sorge zu tragen und zu diesem Ende an die Gewalt der Waffen zu appellieren. Oesterreich-Ungarn betrachtet sich daher von diesem Augenblicke an als im Kriegszustande mit Serbien befindlich.

Der österreichisch-ungarische Minister des Äußern Graf Berchtold."

59 Special edition of the *Wiener Zeitung* of 28 July 1914 announcing Austria-Hungary's declaration of war on Serbia. Both the government and the public believed that the war would be over within a few months and that the sanctions to be imposed on the small state of Serbia would quickly solve all problems.
Declaration of War.
In pursuance of the Resolution of His Imperial and Royal Apostolic Majesty of the 23rd of July 1914, a Declaration of War, conveyed in the French language, was this day placed in the hands of the Royal Serbian Government. The wording of the original text of the said Declaration and of the German translation is as follows:
'Le Gouvernement Royal de Serbie n'ayant pas répondu d'une manière satisfaisante à la Note qui lui avait été remise par le Ministre d'Autriche-Hongrie à Belgrade à la date du 23 juillet 1914, le Gouvernement I. et R. se trouve dans la nécessité de pourvoir lui-même à la sauvegarde de ses droits et intérêts et de recourir à cet effet à la force des armes. L'Autriche-Hongrie se considère donc de ce moment en état de guerre avec la Serbie.
Le Ministre des Affaires Etrangères d'Autriche-Hongrie Comte Berchtold.'
'Since the Royal Serbian Government has failed to respond in a satisfactory manner to the Note placed in its hands on the 23rd of July 1914 by the Austro-Hungarian Ambassador in Belgrade, the Imperial and Royal Government finds itself obliged to safeguard its rights and interests, and to that end to resort to force of arms. As from this moment, therefore, Austria-Hungary considers herself as being at war with Serbia.
The Austro-Hungarian Minister for Foreign Affairs Count Berchtold.'

By now, anti-war sentiment was on the increase. Throughout the belligerent countries Social Democrats reverted to their pacifist views and rallied to the International which, at the outset, had proved itself a broken reed. In Austria they encountered exceptional difficulties, because the constitution had been suspended in favour of the notorious emergency decrees, thus eliminating the possibility of effective opposition.

One of the more vocal opponents of the war was Friedrich Adler, son of the Social Democratic leader. He made a speech denouncing the government for its failure to convene parliament and deploring the continued 'incarceration of the nations'. However, having elicited no response, he resolved to draw attention to the injustice by committing a political assassination. He chose for his victim the minister-president, Count Karl Stürgkh, whom he shot and killed on 16 October 1916. Needless to say, the incident created a considerable stir, without, however, exerting any particular influence on political events.

It was not until May 1917 that the *Reichsrat* was again convened. After the death of the Emperor Francis Joseph in the preceding year, the days of the Monarchy were clearly numbered. His successor, the Emperor Charles I, was an avowed peace-

60 War Fever in Vienna.
Photograph. Historisches Museum der Stadt Wien.
When war seemed inevitable, following Archduke Francis Ferdinand's assassination by Serbian nationalists, the populace was gripped by an unprecedented enthusiasm. The authorities were counting on a short war, while the troops expected to be back home by Christmas 1914 at the latest.

lover who took the view that the war was not of his making. But he proved too weak either to play a part in terminating hostilities or, despite his patently good intentions, to effect a reconciliation between the nationalities and the Monarchy – in any case an impossible achievement, given the degree to which national sentiment had become inflamed.

By 1917 the Social Democrats had ceased to give their tacit support to the government's war effort and, mindful of their pacifist views, began to demand peace at any price. These representations naturally found favour with the populace, for the general situation was deteriorating and, worse still, there was a serious food shortage. Although the government had long been convinced of the inevitability of war, they had rashly assumed that little or no forward planning would be necessary to ensure an adequate supply of armaments, comestibles and raw materials. For they had thought – and this was their gravest miscalculation – that the war would be over in a few weeks and that there was therefore no need to take extensive precautions. At the outset enthusiasm had been fanned by popular slogans such as 'Death to all Serbs' and 'One round, one Russian'. But as losses in men and equipment continued to mount, so did the need for their replacement, which in turn called for a wholesale reorganization of the country's economy. Only now, when

it was already too late, were attempts made to put matters right.

Needless to say, the shortage of foodstuffs hit the inhabitants of Vienna particularly hard, the more so since poor harvests had caused an enormous rise in prices. Various palliatives were tried – for instance the provision of communal kitchens – but with little or no success. As food supplies continued to dwindle, the prospect of famine loomed ever larger.

In an attempt to cope with this situation price controls were imposed, only to lead to a flourishing black market. Towards the end of May 1915 ration cards were issued for bread and flour, while white flour was banned outright. In 1916 rationing was introduced, not only for milk, coffee, sugar, fats and potatoes, but also for clothing, footwear and tobacco.

The shortage of raw materials told mainly on the armaments industry. Hence all objects of copper, brass, pewter or bronze – from church-bells to beer-mugs – had to be surrendered in the interests of the war effort. Specie was withdrawn from circulation and replaced by paper money and an iron coinage. Undernourishment was rife, especially among children, and people fainted from hunger in the streets. Understandably enough, a reaction to this state of affairs was not long in coming. As early as May 1917 the first strikes broke out in the capital's munitions factories, though these were quickly settled. Eight months later, however, the authorities were compelled to reduce the bread and flour ration, to general consternation.

Meanwhile in Russia, where the Bolsheviks were now in power, a peace conference was in progress at Brest-Litovsk. When its delegates called on the belligerents to put an end to the slaughter, President Wilson responded by propounding fourteen points for world peace, one of the requirements being autonomy for the nations of Austria-Hungary.

On the same day as the bread and flour ration was reduced, the papers reported that the Brest-Litovsk peace negotiations were being jeopardized by Germany's excessive territorial demands on Russia. These two

61 Karl Graf Stürgkh, the
Minister-President. Photograph.
Historisches Museum der Stadt
Wien.
Count Stürgkh suspended the
Austrian *Reichsrat* (Imperial
Parliament) in March 1914, and
thereafter stubbornly opposed its
recall. For this reason he was shot
by the Social Democrat Friedrich
Adler on 21 October 1916.

62 The Emperor Francis Joseph lying in state in Schönbrunn. Photograph. Historisches Museum der Stadt Wien.

So long as the old emperor was alive, there seemed little danger of the Austro-Hungarian Empire collapsing. His death during the war was seen by many people as marking the beginning of the end.

63 Off to Serbia! Photograph. Historisches Museum der Stadt Wien.

The origins of the First World War must be traced back to Serbia and the nationalist conspirators responsible for the assassination of the Austrian heir apparent. For the punitive expedition subsequently undertaken against that country sparked off the conflict which was eventually to attain the dimensions of a world conflagration.

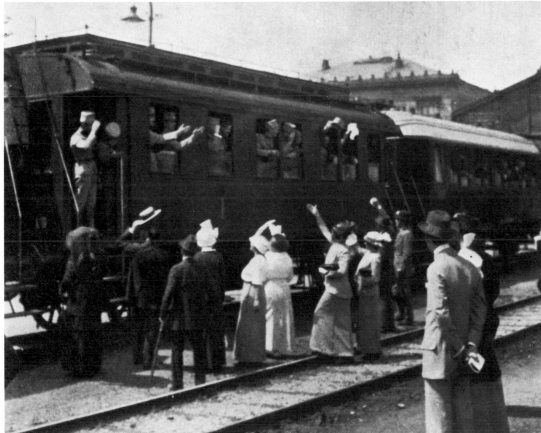

announcements were largely instrumental in sparking off a strike by the Daimler workers in Wiener Neustadt, an action which quickly spread to Vienna, notably to the factories in Floridsdorf and the Arsenal. The Social Democratic leaders, who initially had not been involved, helped to bring about a settlement by securing from the government an assurance, first that negotiations at Brest-Litovsk would not be allowed to founder as a result of territorial demands; second, that larger consignments of foodstuffs be brought in from Hungary; third, that municipal suffrage be reformed; and, lastly, that the war industries be demilitarized.

In April 1918, when arrangements for the supply of bread again broke down, the government considered the possibility of requisitioning several consignments of maize then on their way up the Danube from Romania to Germany. Supplies of gas and electricity had been cut off with the result that, at night, the streets of the city were plunged in darkness. Economy measures had brought traffic virtually to a standstill. Fuel was so short that the inhabitants, already starving, were now compelled to freeze as well. The sparkle and *joie de vivre* which had once characterized the city increasingly gave way to an atmosphere of desolation and misery.

In such adverse circumstances Austria-Hungary could hardly hope to last out for more than another month. Her eventual collapse was due not so much to military reverses as to failure on the home front, where the shortage of essential commodities was assuming catastrophic proportions. The armistice – notably with Italy, which seized on the occasion to push her frontier up to the Brenner – spelt the end, not only of the war, but also of the Monarchy. On 11 November 1918 the Emperor Charles I renounced all share in matters of government and, on the following day, the Republic of German Austria was proclaimed. The partition of the Monarchy into six nation states left Austria a mere rump, with a population of only seven million, of which almost a third lived in Vienna, and its very survival seemed questionable.

The post-war period

The immediate post-war period was one of untold misery. Nor could the consequences of the war be rapidly overcome, for the appalling shortage of foodstuffs and other essentials still continued unabated. Many people, especially the young, whose resistance to disease had been greatly lowered, succumbed to the influenza epidemic of 1919.

Some curious remedies were proposed for these deplorable conditions, among them the sale of the imperial art treasures to foreign collectors, in order to procure the wherewithal for food. But this was merely an outward and visible manifestation of the country's plight. Less publicized was the fact that people would often dispose of their personal possessions, their jewellery and works of art, in the hope of being able to pay the exorbitant prices then being asked for the necessities of life.

The political situation was such that the two main parties, Social Democrats and Christian Socials, treated one another with some degree of consideration. But this period of relative harmony soon came to an end with their assumption of diametrically opposed positions. At that time the Christian Socials controlled the countryside, while the Social Democrats held a majority in the city. In 1921 Vienna became an independent federal province, which meant that the Social Democrats had little or no hope of securing a majority in the rural areas of Lower Austria.

One of the chief aims of the Vienna Municipal Council was to remedy the housing shortage and, at the same time, provide a decent standard of accommodation. Cash for the scheme was raised by the so-called Breitner levy, named after the Social Democratic councillor responsible for finance, with the result that, in the course of the next few years, the Municipality was able to build some 75,000 new apartments. The war-time regulations protecting tenants against eviction and excessive rent increases had remained in force, if only for economic reasons. For any increase in rent would inevitably have led to a correspond-

64 Our Army Needs Metal. 1915, poster by Rudolf Geyer, 126 x 95 cm. Wiener Stadt- und Landesbibliothek.
Austria-Hungary had made inadequate preparations for war, the result being that by 1915 at the latest there was an acute shortage of raw materials. In 1916 the authorities attempted to remedy this state of affairs by requisitioning all articles made of metal.

65 Against the United Front of Capitalism. 1920, poster by Michael Biró, 122 x 95 cm. Wiener Stadt- und Landesbibliothek.
To the Social Democrats Parliament was an institution essential to the attainment of their aims, yet difficult of access because of the strength of the Christian Social and Pan-German parties. At the 1920 elections they sought to woo the electorate by adopting a militant stance against the clergy, military, big landowners and *entrepreneurs*.

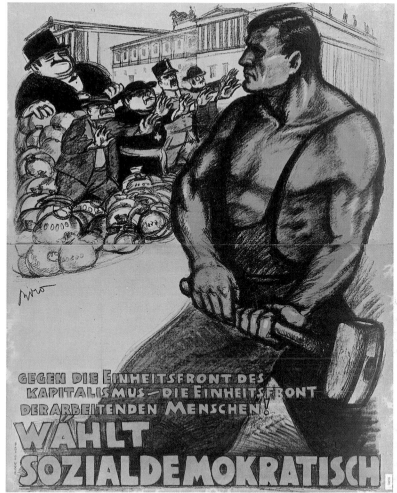

66 Gathering Wood in the Wienerwald. Photograph. Historisches Museum der Stadt Wien. For some time after the end of the war necessities of life were virtually unobtainable in Vienna, fuel being in particularly short supply. Hence the people went wood-gathering in the Wienerwald, much to the forest's detriment.

67 Proclamation of the Republic on 12 November 1918. Photograph. Historisches Museum der Stadt Wien. The Republic of German Austria, all that now remained of the Danubian Monarchy, was proclaimed after the Emperor Charles I had handed over the reins of government to the venerable leader of the Social Democrats, Viktor Adler.

68 Hugo Breitner. Photograph. Historisches Museum der Stadt Wien.
The Social Democratic administration of Vienna pursued a policy aimed at the elimination of poverty and want. So successful were their efforts that the term 'Red Vienna' became familiar far beyond the confines of the city. Hugo Breitner's method consisted in squeezing the well-to-do so as to finance the Municipality's social schemes.

69 Julius Tandler. Photograph. Historisches Museum der Stadt Wien.
Julius Tandler, university professor and municipal councillor, was active in promoting Vienna's progressive social policy. His chief concern was the prevention of tuberculosis, a disease which had assumed the proportions of an epidemic and to which large numbers of young people were falling victim.

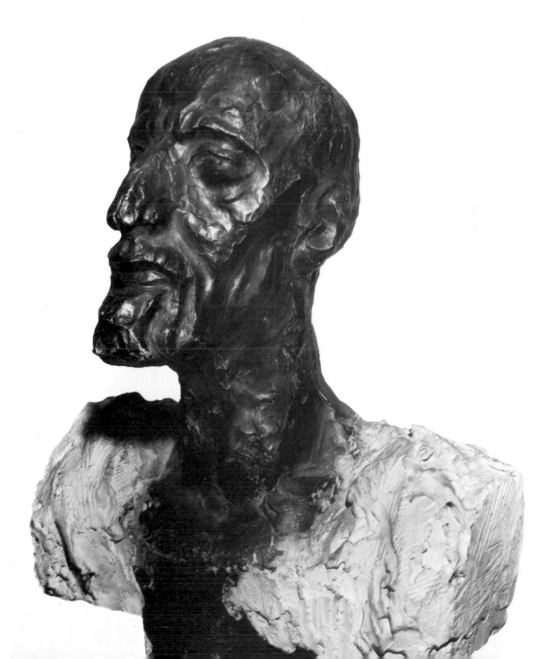

70 Anton Hanak: *Bürgermeister* (Mayor) *Karl Seitz*. Plaster-bronze, H. 70 cm, W. 48 cm. Historisches Museum der Stadt Wien.
During the 1920s reforms were introduced slowly but surely under the leadership of Karl Seitz.

ing increase in wages, which in turn would have put up production costs, thereby making it harder to sell Austrian manufactures in foreign markets.

Slowly the city began to recover from the effects of the war, though at first there was little to show for it. The fact that democratic procedures had yet to become generally accepted continually gave rise to complications that were further compounded by the onset of the slump at the end of the 1920s. The collapse of the old pre-1914 social order naturally had widespread repercussions in the cultural sphere. Instead of being the hub of a large empire, Vienna was now the somewhat forlorn capital of a little state, a circumstance which impoverished her still further by putting an end to the influx of intellectuals from neighbouring countries. It was during this period that the social policy of Mayor Karl Seitz and his predominantly Social Democratic Municipal Council built up Vienna's reputation as a socially progressive city.

SELECT BIBLIOGRAPHY

Anatols Jahre, Beispiele aus der Zeit vor der Jahrhundertwende, Katalog zur 71. Sonderausstellung des Historischen Museums der Stadt Wien in der Hermesvilla, Vienna, 1982.

Czeike, Felix, *Das grosse Groner-Wien-Lexikon*, Vienna–Munich–Zurich, 1974.

Johnston, William M., *Österreichische Kultur- und Geistesgeschichte, Gesellschaft und Ideen im Donauraum 1848 bis 1938*, Vienna–Cologne–Graz, 1972.

Kaufmann, Fritz, *Sozialdemokratie in Österreich – Idee und Geschichte einer Partei, Von 1889 bis zur Gegenwart*, Vienna, 1978.

Kralik, Richard, *Geschichte der Stadt Wien und ihre Kultur*, 2nd ed., Vienna, 1926

Mikoletzky, Hans Leo, *Österreich – das entscheidende 19. Jahrhundert, Geschichte, Kultur, Wirtschaft*, Vienna, 1972.

Schorske, Carl E., Fin de siècle *Vienna. Politics and Culture*. London, 1979, New York, 1980.

Walter, Friedrich, *Wien, Geschichte einer deutschen Grossstadt an der Grenze*. Vol. 3, *Die neueste Zeit*, Vienna, 1944.

III THE TWO FACES OF VIENNA

Reingard Witzmann

Magnetism of the metropolis

The demolition of Vienna's old fortifications in the early 1850s marked the first step in the city's progress towards metropolitan status. The population increased by leaps and bounds, not only as a result of the high birth-rate, but also because of the heavy influx of immigrants from all parts of the Monarchy. The latter process went hand in hand with the growth and consolidation of a highly industrialized society whose hierarchical structure became ever more clearly defined. A symbol of the new affluence was that splendid urban boulevard, the Ringstrasse, most of which came into being during the last quarter of the century.

Like many other events of importance, the creation of 'Greater Vienna' by the incorporation of the outer suburbs was celebrated in a waltz of the same name, specially composed for the occasion by Johann Strauss (op. 440). The piece, whose opening words are 'Let us sing thy praises, Vienna of the future', called for a vast orchestra and male voice choir, in stark contrast to the modest bands which, under the composer's father, had played in coffee-houses and taverns more than half a century before. The enthusiasm and optimism exuded by its text reflect the aura of prosperity which surrounded the *fin de siècle* and which is still perceptible today in the faded sepia photographs, taken against a studio background, of ladies and gentlemen in garments of such splendour as almost to suggest theatrical costume. Their sophistication exemplifies the contemporary obsession with the urban scene from which nature was rigorously excluded. Indeed, the meadows which surrounded the suburbs were rapidly succumbing to development – while little remained of the immense expanse of the former glacis save for a few enclosed parks.

Though they elicited expressions of nostalgia from writers such as Ferdinand von Saar and Alfons Petzold, these changes acted as a stimulus to the poet Anton Wildgans, born in Vienna in 1881, not to mention others. In his poem 'I am a Child of the City', he testifies to the new spirit pervading the metropolis at that time, and expresses a no less novel concept of 'home', when he describes himself as 'Part of the crowd that swarms along / Your streets, of the fluid, nameless throng, / I, a mere speck ignored by you…' The words reflect a process of change and upheaval in which great importance is attached to self-discovery and self-identification. This acceptance of the new outward manifestations of city life, involving as it did a fresh image of urban man, evoked a reaction in favour of the 'good old days'. For many local patriots feared that the archetypal Viennese, together with his idiosyncrasies, would be submerged by the influx of extraneous elements. The result was a kind of hot-house cult of all things Viennese – Viennese air, Viennese humour, Viennese stock, and so forth. Such catchwords found particular favour among folksingers.

71   Wilhelm Gause: *Ball der Stadt
Wien* ('Municipal Ball'). 1904,
water-colour and oil on canvas,
62 x 88 cm. Historisches Museum
der Stadt Wien.
The municipal ball was the
counterpart of the court ball at
the Hofburg. An annual event, inaugurated in 1890, it was held in
the newly-built town hall. Here it
is presided over by Mayor Karl
Lueger (centre left); beside him
stands Deputy Mayor Josef
Strobach.

72 Anton Romako: *Herr und Dame in einem Salon* ('Lady and Gentleman in a Drawing-Room'). 1887, oil on wood, 48.5 x 62.5 cm. Historisches Museum der Stadt Wien.

Amidst the clutter of a 'Makart' drawing-room, the artist has placed two puppet-like figures, a man pleasurably contemplating a glass of wine, and a woman holding a letter. The irony with which the hedonistic and eccentric life-style of that class is portrayed turns this painting into a universal symbol of the *fin-de-siècle*.

In *Die österreichisch-ungarische Monarchie in Wort und Bild* ('The Austro-Hungarian Monarchy in Word and Picture') (1886), Friedrich Schlögl discusses the tremendous changes wrought in the capital by the developments touched upon at the beginning of this chapter. 'For no matter where you look', he writes, 'Vienna has, willynilly, undergone drastic modification. It is not only in architecture that, after a long period of stagnation, not to say ossification, the city has, within a few decades, become quite different; the ways of life, the manners and customs, the needs and habits of a population enormously swollen and completely disorientated by the most unexpected events, have changed almost beyond recognition.'

Social composition

These far-reaching modifications of the social structure must largely be attributed to industrialization, although the preponderance, until well into the twentieth century, of small and medium-sized businesses prevented Vienna from becoming a typical industrial city. Nevertheless, thanks to its building programmes and the establishment of pioneering enterprises financed by foreign capital, the metropolis evolved more dynamically than did industrial regions elsewhere.

In 1890 rather more than half the population consisted of immigrants from the overpopulated agrarian districts of southern Bohemia and Moravia. Labourers, domestic servants and the younger sons of peasants and craftsmen – such were the people who, during the second half of the nineteenth century, came flocking to the capital in the hope of finding regular work and cheap entertainment. The proportion of Czech immigrants was much larger than any other. By 1900 Slav-speakers accounted for 7.1 per cent of the population, as opposed to 0.1 per cent for the other nationalities. Jewish immigrants from the Sudetenland, Hungary and Eastern Galicia also made their mark in the city and, by the turn of the century, had become a factor of vital importance in the commercial and, above all, the cultural sphere. The proportion of Jewish inhabit-

73 Franz von Persoglia: *Volkssänger im Wiener Prater* ('Folk-Singers in the Prater'). C. 1890, water-colour on pencil, 19.3 x 27.5 cm. Historisches Museum der Stadt Wien. The songs of these 'untutored singers' belong to the same tradition as the music-hall ditties of the Biedermeier period. Usually dressed as laundry maids and cabbies, the folk-singers fostered the cult of things Viennese, a cult epitomized in the phrase, 'you'll never put a Viennese down'.

74 *Aussenseiter im Wurstelprater* ('Lookers-on in the Wurstelprater'). C. 1908, photograph by Emil Mayer, postcard. Historisches Museum der Stadt Wien. 'Here, crowding outside the trellis, is an eager, undemanding audience: schoolboys, apprentices, schoolgirls, adolescents of all kinds, unnoticed and at leisure. True, it is not a paying audience, nor would it want to be. But what it tenders is veneration, respect and enthusiasm... The young of the Wurstelprater worship their acrobats, contortionists, clowns and athletes.' (Felix Salten.)

75 *Wiener Strassenbilder* ('Street Scenes in Vienna'). C. 1880–90. Photographs by Emanuel Wähner. Historisches Museum der Stadt Wien.

Amateur photographers were the first to take realistic pictures of people in the street. Here Wähner has not succumbed to the sentimentally stylized image of the lower classes prevalent at the time.

ants rose from 0.3 per cent in 1800 to 3 per cent in 1850 and 10 per cent in 1900.

The growth of the city that resulted from these major population movements was not without its darker side. For most of the immigrants, coming as they did from agrarian or small-town backgrounds in which tradition was paramount, had to adapt themselves to the rapid pace of an industrial world and to a style of life with which they were wholly unfamiliar. Nor were they in a position to pick and choose when it came to finding jobs or lodgings.

It was a period of glaring contrasts, unparalleled in the history of Vienna. On the one hand, town-planning on a grandiose scale, immoderate wealth, and a strict moral code; on the other, inadequate provision for

the homeless, abject poverty, and a high rate of illegitimacy. The customary division of the social structure into upper, middle and lower classes is not entirely applicable to the more complex circumstances then prevailing. We shall therefore consider the various strata, beginning at the top. However it should be remembered that the relatively monolithic upper class represented no more than the tip of the social pyramid, the base of which was continually expanding as a result of the disproportionately rapid growth of the middle and lower classes.

The Imperial family constituted a category of its own, wholly divorced from any other. Social intercourse between the Hofburg and the outside world was nonexistent, for the court was completely barred to such people during Francis Joseph's reign. It was also barred to those of his own relatives who married 'beneath' them. Thus three archdukes in quick succession forfeited their hereditary titles to become, respectively, plain Mr Orth, Mr Burg and Mr Wölfling. In his memoirs the latter, once Archduke Leopold Ferdinand von Habsburg-Toskana, cynically comments on the emperor's omnipotence. 'Not a sparrow', he writes, 'might fall from the Hofburg roof without his knowledge.'

The Viennese court was one of the few in Europe in which birth was regarded as paramount. The hereditary aristocracy numbered some three hundred families. Their intercourse with the Imperial family was restricted to certain court banquets or other grand public occasions, as noted in 1885 by a Russian diplomat, Count Vasili: 'The Imperial family does not mix with the aristocracy. The latter are summoned to banquets where they are seated strictly in order of precedence, but they are never received into the bosom of the Imperial family.'

In 1905 Felix Salten published a witty satire on the Viennese nobility. For the most part, he says, they had drawn in their horns and refrained from public indulgence in arrogant excesses. 'Nowadays they confine their high jinks to some officers' mess. Otherwise the bourgeoisie or, far more likely, the plucky… proletariat, would promptly administer rough justice.'

Meanwhile a new upper stratum had come into being. *Nouveau riche*, and in some cases ennobled, its representatives were drawn from the higher echelons of the civil service, finance and, in particular, industry. Since the 1880s this new moneyed aristocracy had stolen a march on the old nobility and it was chiefly to them that architects now turned for patronage.

Between this class and the middle class proper came the landlords, whose income was derived almost solely from rent. Their extraordinarily high opinion of themselves has been perpetuated in the eye-catching monuments with their pompous inscriptions that may be seen in so many Viennese cemeteries.

What was known as the middle class comprised on the one hand those with a higher education, such as managers, members of the liberal professions and public servants and, on the other, independent businessmen. Though less favoured by economic developments, the ratio of business men to the rest of the population – between 12 and 14 per cent – remained surprisingly constant, no doubt because their numbers were regularly replenished by new arrivals from the provinces. To survive in Vienna, such immigrants required two things – robust health and a modicum of capital. We possess virtually no accurate data relating to this group to whom, however, numerous feuilletons were devoted, notably by local writers such as Friedrich Schlögl and Vinzenz Chiavacci, in which they are presented in a rosy light as good bourgeois citizens living cosy comfortable lives.

The military cannot be said to have formed part of the city's social structure, for most of them were quartered in barracks. But when they appeared in public, either in the streets or in places of entertainment, their strict code of honour tended to give rise to fracas of various kinds.

The lowest stratum was made up of skilled and unskilled casual labour, along with domestic servants who, by reason of their occupation, formed part of the patriarchal microcosm represented by the household. Both labourers and domestics were usually immigrants who had left home without a penny to their name to seek their fortunes in the city.

Living conditions

The Viennese had coined a dialect term *entern* or 't'other side', originally to denote the districts beyond the Alser stream. Later this came to represent those parts of the capital that were cheaper to live in than, say, the Ringstrasse, and which, of course, possessed none of its cachet. It was a pattern that had been imposed during the *Gründerzeit* and which was to persist almost unchanged until the First World War. One third of the inhabitants of the Ringstrasse, or Greater

76 Leo Burger: *Auf der Strasse in einem Vorort* ('A Suburban Street'). 1885, water-colour, 90 x 120 cm. Hermesvilla, Vienna.
The artist depicts the street as a place of social intercourse. The fringe of the city was the habitat of the very poor. By 1890 half the dwellings in the suburbs were overcrowded.

77 Alois Schönn: *Obstmarkt am Schanzel* ('Am Schanzel Fruit Market'). 1895, oil on canvas, 143 x 240 cm. Historisches Museum der Stadt Wien.
The part of the Danube Canal embankment known as Am Schanzel served as Vienna's principal fruit market to which the produce was brought direct by barge.

78 Fritz Schönpflug: *Karikatur auf das Militär* ('Caricature of the Military'). 1918, postcard. Historisches Museum der Stadt Wien.

79 Karl Feiertag: *Auf der Ringstrasse* ('On the Ringstrasse'). C. 1900, water-colour, 29.1 x 18.3 cm. Historisches Museum der Stadt Wien.
One of the most frequented stretches of the Ringstrasse was the near, or city, side, with its fashionable coffee-houses. The stretch between the Kärntnerstrasse and the Schwarzenbergplatz was known as the Nobelring or Wiener Boulevard.

Vienna's 'aorta', as Ludwig Hevesi called it, were aristocrats, the rest being made up of industrialists, bankers and *rentiers*, who had built themselves elegant apartment houses in that thoroughfare. The smartest section, the Kärntner Ring, stretched from the Kärntnerstrasse to the Schwarzenbergplatz.

Here, sandwiched between the traditional aristocratic quarter in the Old City and Prinz Eugen's former summer palace, the Belvedere, lived the upper stratum, cheek by jowl with the tradesmen who served their manifold needs, the tailors, boot-makers, hatters and modistes.

It looks like a conspiratorial procession creeping through the dark, along the short stretch between the Kärntnertor and the Schwarzenbergplatz, but only on the near or city side, where every evening an unholy press builds up, a fashionable throng, all falling over each other's feet and perambulating up and down arm in arm... Whole files of two-legged beavers and sables jostle one another. At the appointed corner, everyone does an about-turn as though on a word of command, to produce a regular jam of knights of fashion, monocled nobles, members of the pressed-trouser brigade.

Once a week, however, on a Sunday afternoon, it was the people's turn to parade along the Kärntner Ring. Again Hevesi describes the scene:

Blanketed in a cloud of dust is the wide expanse of street, past the shuttered shops of which there slowly and inexorably winds a blackish, caterpillar-like procession, a host, as it were , of human larvae... the golden youth of more or less 't'other side' purlieus, striving with their clumpy boots to tread in the imprints made by the dainty, pointed shoes – soles blacked no less than uppers – of the 1st District. But there is one one thing the Sunday crowd can boast which is not possessed by the exquisites for whom every day is a holiday – and that is guts.

Just as the Kärntner Ring had become the habitat of the aristocracy, so the neo-Gothic town hall, completed in 1883, became a focal point, not only for the dwellings of the new rich, but also for those of academics and men of science. Adjoining the Ringstrasse was the so-called Postal Savings Bank district, after the name of the building put up there between 1904 and 1906 by the architect Otto Wagner. It became, as it were, an overspill for *rentiers* and members of the liberal professions who had been unable to obtain sites in the previously completed Ring. Here, lawyers and doctors, as also busines men, built themselves opulent houses and offices. Many of the *rentiers* were

At the turn of the century, this part of the Ring was known as the Wiener Boulevard and it was here that, of an evening, the rich and famous were accustomed to foregather. As Ludwig Hevesi somewhat ironically remarked in 1895:

80 Theo Zasche: *Beim Demel* ('At Demel's'). *C.* 1900, pen and ink, 21.8 x 30.5 cm. Historisches Museum der Stadt Wien. Demel's, the court confectioners, was a meeting-place where the *beau monde* indulged in polite conversation.

women who doubtless derived additional revenue from sub-letting or from other, perhaps less savoury, sources

Living conditions within the Lines were somewhat better than those in the outlying districts where much of the housing was deplorable. In what had once been open country there emerged a new type of building, the tenement block in which several hundred people would often live crammed together. Ever since the days of the liberals, housing had been left to the free play of market forces. The apartment had become a commodity, the tenant an object to be exploited by the landlord. As a result the general standard of accommodation in the pre-war years remained at a level unworthy of a great metropolis.

Within the space of a generation the face of the outer districts was transformed by a rash of building. 'Those ghastly tenement blocks, with their quadrangular, unlit courtyards, and their shocking inimicality to children, were still in the minority.' Thus Alfons Petzold in his childhood reminiscences. By the turn of the century, however, such housing had become the norm, thanks to speculators and property developers. Apartments consisting of one room and a kitchen gave on to long galleries with communal lavatories and water-taps. Barred windows often added to the gloom of already dreary kitchens. The façades, sparsely decorated with historicist motifs, generally concealed the sorry spectacle of a humanity jammed together like sardines in a tin. Since few could afford to pay the exorbitant rents, sub-letting – not only of living space, but of actual beds – became the rule in what were already overcrowded apartments. By 1890 'bed-hirers' constituted about one tenth of the working-class population in the outer districts, as compared with only 1.66 per cent in the area bounded by the Ringstrasse.

It was a problem with which the Municipality was totally unable to cope. Though the 1890 census had shown beyond all doubt

81 Maximilian Lenz: *Die Sirk-Ecke auf der Ringstrasse* ('The "Sirk-Ecke" on the Ringstrasse'). 1900, oil on canvas, 71 x 159 cm. Historisches Museum der Stadt Wien.
Over the way from the Opera House, at the junction of the Kärntnerstrasse and the Ringstrasse, was a piece of ground known as the 'Sirk-Ecke', for many years favoured as a meeting-place of high society. In Karl Kraus's tragedy, *The Last Days of Mankind*, written during the First World War, the 'Sirk-Ecke' constituted a 'cosmic point', the place where each act of the play began.

82 Ferdinand Kruis: *Neuer Markt am Abend* ('Evening in the Neuer Markt'). 1914, oil on canvas, 66 x 79 cm. Historisches Museum der Stadt Wien.

that over half the apartments in the sometime outer suburbs were grossly over-crowded, the gap between rent and wages proved impossible to bridge. Nor was the situation in any way improved by the building of yet more tenement blocks. When a man was in work he might, despite his low wage, just manage to scrape the rent together but, should he lose his job or fall ill, he would almost certainly find himself out on the street. Towards the end of the century there was a sharp rise in the number of such evictions.

As a result of the ordinances of 1879 and 1881, municipal welfare schemes were subjected to stricter controls and their administration made the responsibility of a Commission for the Poor and a team of unpaid visitors. Meanwhile the bourgeoisie had not been idle and a spate of philanthropic organizations made their appearance, among them the Society for Shelters for the Homeless (1870), the Vienna Soup Kitchen Society (1872), and the Society for the Erection and Maintenance of the Vienna Soup and Tea Institute (1875).

The role once performed by the family was now taken over by the community. Yet these well-intentioned schemes did nothing to improve the lot of the people concerned, being, in effect, no more than a form of charity, as is evident from the choice of the name 'Compassion' for a society founded in 1885. The provision of new shelters for the homeless made little impact and funds were also lacking – despite the generosity of men like the musician and composer Karl Millöcker who, out of his own pocket, paid for an extension to one such home.

In his autobiography Alfons Petzold relates from personal experience what it meant to be homeless. Again, in *Poverty and Crime in Vienna* (1908), Emil Kläger vividly describes the despair felt by outcasts whose only shelter was the warm, underground system of conduits leading into the now regulated River Wien, where they evolved a survival technique of their own.

Working conditions

In the metropolis the even tenor of everyday life was threatened by the wide gulf between haves and have-nots, and by the inhumane conditions in which the latter lived.

Of the many constituents which went to make up the mood of the *fin-de-siècle*, we shall here cite only two: first, the premonition of the Monarchy's impending doom, a theme frequently encountered in the literature of the period; second, the despair of the lower classes induced by poverty and an absence of social ties. 'What I longed for most was death', wrote Adelheid Popp, 'but I had to look for work.' She was the daughter of a Bohemian weaver and the life she describes in her autobiography, *Jugend einer Arbeiterin* ('Youth of a Working Girl'), must have been typical of that of many young women in Vienna in those days. In the 1890s she became an active member of the Social Democratic labour movement.

In 1890, 85 per cent of all paid female labour in Austria belonged to the working class, a higher proportion than in any other European country. Most of them were wretchedly housed and in a poor state of health, like the young needlewoman, an early love of Arthur Schnitzler's, who suffered, as he relates in his autobiography, from headaches, palpitations and a weak chest. She provided the inspiration for that archetypal character, the *süsses Mädel** (sweet girl) whom Schnitzler introduced into his plays and whose gentle vivacity still succeeds in moving us today.

According to Lily Braun, who championed female rights, women in 1901 were employed mainly as dress-makers, milliners, seamstresses, lace-makers, feather-workers and artificial flower-makers. Provided she did not fall ill, a woman could just survive on her wage, but there could be no question of her being able to support another member of her family.

Male workers also had their problems, not least the horse-drawn tram drivers, de-

---

* The Viennese equivalent of the *grisette*.

83 Karl Feiertag: *Burgmusik am Michaelerplatz* ('Military Band in the Michaeler Square'). C. 1900, water-colour, 18 x 29 cm. Historisches Museum der Stadt Wien. The changing of the Palace Guard, a popular attraction at the time, is described in a contemporary account: 'Outside the Inner City, where the Main Guard are already mustering in some barracks or other, a crowd of curious onlookers has collected…
With the band playing, the guard marches towards the city. The accompanying populace grows like an avalanche… The first arrivals consist for the most part of individuals at a loose end – penniless waiters, discharged commis, unemployed journeymen – who are later joined, in overwhelming numbers, by guttersnipes, your true Viennese urchin.' *(Wienerstadt.)* During the changing of the guard the band would play, thus treating the public to a free concert.

84 Wilhelm Gause: *Hernalser Kalvarienberg* ('Calvary at Hernals'). 1913, grisaille, 50 x 74 cm. Historisches Museum der Stadt Wien.
The pre-Easter festival had its origins in the procession of penitents which, starting at St Stephen's, made its way to the final station at Hernals parish church. The gaily coloured market with its drinking-booths and folk-singers tended to obscure the religious nature of the festival.

85 Felician Freiherr von Myrbach: *In der Blumenfabrik* ('In the Flower Factory'). 1892, pen-and-ink, 19.9 x 24.9 cm. Design for illustration to *Wienerstadt – Lebensbilder aus der Gegenwart*, Vienna, 1895. Historisches Museum der Stadt Wien.
In those days the artificial flowers made in Vienna were famed throughout the world. However, the pay and working conditions of the employees were so bad that the latter proved highly receptive to the new ideas on workers' rights.

86 Josef Gisela (Reznicek): *Näherinnen* ('Seamstresses'). C. 1890, oil on wood, 17 x 18.5 cm. Historisches Museum der Stadt Wien.
This attractive genre painting reflects the stereotype rather than the reality. The *süsses Mädel* (sweet girl), or *grisette,* pursued a trade in which wages were being forced down as a result of growing competition. Some earned their living in sweatshops, others as homeworkers for garment manufacturers and milliners. Dressmakers catered for a private clientele, while seamstresses and menders might work in their customers' houses.

87 *Am Naschmarkt* ('On the Naschmarkt'). *C.* 1910, photograph. Historisches Museum der Stadt Wien.
This large fruit and vegetable market owed much of its reputation to the female stall-holders who were renowned for their sharp tongues. The market was situated in front of the Freihaus opposite the Resselpark before being moved to the Wienzeile.

88 Felician Freiherr von Myrbach: *Die Büglerinnen* ('Women Ironing'). 1892, ink-and-brush, 29.4 x 20 cm. Design for illustration to *Wienerstadt – Lebensbilder aus der Gegenwart*, Vienna, 1895. Historisches Museum der Stadt Wien.
In many households women were employed to do the washing in return for a minute daily wage. They were gradually ousted by the laundries.

scribed by Viktor Adler in 1889 as 'the white slaves of the Vienna Tramway Company'. They worked anything up to nineteen hours a day and were held responsible for any damage suffered by the decrepit vehicles in their charge. When, on 4 April 1889, the drivers went on strike, the company was forced by public opinion to concede a twelve-hour day. Following Lueger's appointment as mayor, the city's transport system was taken into public ownership, as was the gas and electrical supply. Few firms in Vienna were comparable in size to the transport company with its 6,300 employees. In 1902 only eight concerns possessed more than a thousand workers, while 86 per cent of all businesses employed five people or less.

Small business men and their families numbered 803,000 out of a total population of 1,718,000. They constituted an amorphous, virtually unorganized mass that was,

on the whole, favourable to Lueger's new policies. For recreation they would repair of an evening to the Heuriger, to drink wine and enjoy the music of a Schrammel quartet. In one of his songs Johann Schrammel himself neatly encapsulates the type of person who frequented such places: 'I'm not real rich, I'm not real poor, my home's Vienna in Austria.'

Until the First World War most small and medium-sized businesses were able to hold their own, thus maintaining Vienna's position as a producer of consumer and luxury goods. There were, however, violent fluctuations in the numbers employed at any one time, for when business was slack many firms laid off their employees, while others closed their doors for good; sickness usually entailed dismissal. Workers might move from one employer to another offering slightly better pay, as did Petzold, who between the ages of fourteen and twenty-two

79

89 Work in progress on Vienna's gas supply. 1897, photograph. Atelier Nedomansky. Historisches Museum der Stadt Wien.
After the incorporation of the outer suburbs in 1892 the Municipality decided to build its own gasworks at Simmering, and four years later the work was put in hand. Previously most of the city's gas had been supplied by a British undertaking, the Imperial Continental Gas Association.

90 Vienna's first hostel for domestic servants. 1891, wood-engraving from the *Neuigkeits-Welt-Blatt* of 9 October 1891. Historisches Museum der Stadt Wien.
Domestic servants dismissed by their employers had little hope of finding accommodation. This, the first of a number of hostels for homeless girls, was founded in 1891; the establishments were largely supported by middle-class organizations.

went through more than twenty different jobs in as many different trades.

The mid-1890s marked the beginning of a period of vigorous industrial expansion. At the forefront were the factories producing electrical equipment, some of which, after the turn of the century, were to grow into concerns of considerable size. Since the work consisted of increasingly repetitive mechanized operations, skilled workers tended to be replaced by semi-skilled and un-skilled labour, in many cases female. In 1893 a young woman employed in a textile fac-tory, Amalie Seidel, called a strike, the first to be staged by women in Vienna, in which 700 workers took part. With the help of Adelheid Popp, now an active Social Democrat, they succeeded in obtaining shorter hours and better working condi-tions. Similar demands were beginning to make themselves heard among domestic ser-vants employed in 'good' middle-class districts. In 1890 maidservants constituted nearly 7 per cent of the city's population. On their arrival in Vienna – for most were of provincial origin – they were often obliged to turn for jobs to agencies of a somewhat dubious character. Indeed an enterprising girl who found herself thus stranded in a strange metropolis, with nowhere to lay her head, was in dire danger of succumbing to prostitution.

In 1891 some attempt was made to tackle this problem by setting up a hostel – the first of its kind – for sixty unemployed domestic servants. But even had its inmates succeeded in finding work, they would still have been grossly underprivileged. When, in 1893, domestic servants assembled for the first time to air their grievances, the meeting was dispersed by the authorities.

Leisure and pleasure

High in the calendar of public high days and holidays stood the seasonal festivals which we find enumerated in Hugo von Hof-mannsthal's late diary, *Ad me ipsum*, name-ly: 'Prater Parade, Corpus Christi and Im-perial funerals'. Many of the earlier festivals, such as the Brigittenau kermes, vintage and

91 Corpus Christi Procession in the Graben. 1909, photograph by R. Lechner. Historisches Museum der Stadt Wien.
The procession was one of the few annual events at which the emperor and his court appeared in public. A platform was provided for privileged onlookers, and windows overlooking the route were much in demand. The emperor with his entourage walk-ed immediately behind the canopy, preceding the heir ap-parent who led the next con-tingent.

81

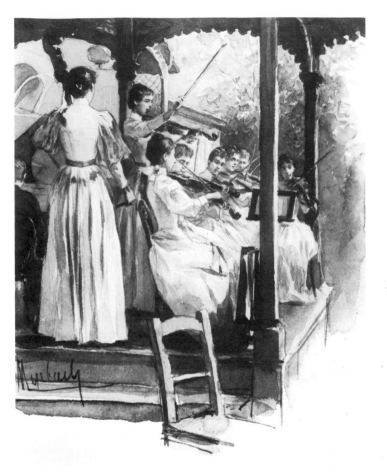

New Year celebrations, had been discarded, and there now remained only those more spectacular occasions for which the people formed the backdrop.

A favourite gathering-ground for all classes of the population was the Prater. The parades that took place there on Easter Monday and 1 May provided the upper classes with an opportunity for displaying themselves in all their finery. Or, as Friedrich Uhl put it in 1883: 'Everyone took part... The people lined the sides of the great avenue, awaiting open-mouthed the arrival of the fine gentlemen and beautiful ladies, who came gliding past in closed, luxuriously sprung carriages, each embellished with a coat of arms.' Legendary, too, was the spring festival instituted by Princess Metternich, the Procession of Flowers, which took place for the first time on 29 and 30 May 1886. One quarter of the population flocked to the Prater to watch the opulent procession, the proceeds of which went to charity.

The Prater also provided frequent Strauss concerts for the delectation of the *beau monde,* which also frequented certain of its coffee-houses, renowned for the quality and variety of their musical programmes. At a respectful distance from the tables, and too poor to join the audience proper, would stand a crowd of music-lovers, among them, perhaps, the young Arnold Schoenberg. For he is mentioned by David Josef Bach as one of a group of 'seventeen- and eighteen-year-olds (who) stood near the trellis to enjoy a free concert. In 1891 or 1892 the young military band-master – Grossmann by name, if I'm not mistaken – used to play excerpts from Wagner, and once, even, from the *Meistersinger.*'

Another favourite resort for the well-to-do was the Prater's pleasure park known as

92 Felician Freiherr von Myrbach: *Wiener Damenkapelle im Prater* ('Ladies' Orchestra in the Prater'). 1895, sepia, 20.5 x 15.2 cm. Historisches Museum der Stadt Wien. 'Generally young, sometimes even pretty, all uniformly dressed in white with coloured sashes, these girls are well trained and, above all, keep good time, and often display a genuine gift for music. Most of them have been driven by the loss of their parents or some other sad domestic circumstance to fend for themselves early on in life. They take their job seriously, regarding it neither as a brief for loose living nor as something to be ashamed of. What matter if popular wits sing jeering if innocuous songs about "them ladies' bands"?...' *(Wienerstadt.)*

93 Theo Zasche: *Hutschen-schleuderer im Wurstelprater* ('Swing-boats in the Wurstel-prater'). Sepia, 22.2 x 25.5 cm. Historisches Museum der Stadt Wien.
One of the earliest forms of amusement in the Prater, along with merry-go-rounds, were the swings which feature so largely in Ferenc Molnár's tragi-comedy *Liliom* (1909).

94 Theo Zasche: *'Beim Wurstel' im Prater* ('Punch and Judy in the Prater'). Sepia, 18.7 x 18.5 cm. Historisches Museum der Stadt Wien.
Punch and Judy shows drew considerable audiences. 'In no other theatre do people's faces betray such eagerness, such rapt attention, their eyes such amazement, such insatiable longing...'

'Venice in Vienna', which occupied the site of the erstwhile Imperial garden and where, in 1897, the *Riesenrad* (Giant Wheel) was put up. Mock Venetian palaces lined the artificial canals along which members of high society – including on occasion arch-dukes – rowed their pleasure boats and engaged in polite conversation.

The Prater, however, was not simply a playground for the rich, since the so-called Wurstelprater provided a wide range of cheap amusements and, for good measure, a beautiful landscape of trees and meadows. Here, too, were taverns where the entertainment was provided by folk-singers, usually dressed up as 'laundry-maids' or 'cabbies'. In tones varying from the winsome to the harsh they sang songs which, better than any other medium, were able to convey the idiosyncrasies and humour peculiar to the capital. Themselves quintessentially Vien-

nese, they were regarded as children of nature, untutored singers with hearts of gold, who strove to express their philosophy of life in down-to-earth, no-nonsense language. One of their number, a 'cabbie' and much-loved folk-singer by the name of Bratfisch, was actually taken on by Crown Prince Rudolph as his personal coachman.

Petzold describes an evening of folk-song in the course of which his own play, *Heim-kehr eines Zuchthäuslers* ('The Return of a Convict'), was performed. 'It was Saturday night, and there wasn't a seat left in the place. For the most part they were the better kind of working men with their girls, but there were also minor officials and crafts-men and their families.' Whenever he could manage it, Petzold took his mother to hear the folk-singers, especially on All Saints' Day when all good Viennese went to pay their respects to the dead. Indeed, death and

95 Hans Larwin: *Beim Heurigen in Neustift* ('In a Heuriger Tavern at Neustift'). 1908, oil on canvas, 120.5 x 150.5 cm. Historisches Museum der Stadt Wien. The new-vintage wine, or Heuriger, was served in taverns in and around Vienna. It was quite usual for guests to take their own food, and thus save the expense of eating out. Entertainment was provided by musicians playing the fiddle, guitar and clarinet.

the joys of the life to come recur frequently in the folk-songs of the Viennese. 'So bear me to Grinzing/To the cemetery where/ For ever and ever I can sleep off me beer...' Thus Josef Hornig, a popular figure of his day. Death was not ignored or regarded as particularly frightening. With an underlying flippancy that transcended the realities of this life, the Viennese would speculate on the hereafter in a mood of bibulous euphoria: 'Go sell all me duds, I'm off to Heaven...'

Before the First World War folk musicians began to abandon the tavern in favour of the upper-class drawing-room. In 1911 the composer Eduard Kremser wrote: 'The reason may well be that the little man, beset by every-day cares, no longer possesses the means to relax and enjoy himself at Heurigers or in the company of folk-singers.' It was a time when the fortunes of the small business man had taken a sharp turn for the worse.

Dancing was a pastime that also loomed large in Vienna. However the tango, so popular in the other capital cities of Europe, had failed to oust the waltz, still in the ascendant after a reign of more than a century. Every year the aristocracy, or such as had entry to the court, attended the exclusive *Ball bei Hof,* or grand court ball. Somewhat less exclusive was the *Hofball* (court ball), to which three thousand people were invited. These grand occasions were organized with clockwork precision in a setting of costly Gobelin tapestries and amidst cascades of tropical flowers. The orchestra was conducted by Eduard Strauss, the Master of the Imperial Music. Much-coveted mementoes, smuggled out by the guests to their less fortunate fellows, were sweetmeats specially made for the occasion and adorned with the emperor's likeness.

The year 1890 saw the birth of the Hofball's municipal counterpart, the *Ball der Stadt Wien,* which took place in the town hall. It was a glamorous affair put on by the *haute bourgeoisie,* and one for which Johann Strauss composed a special waltz (op. 438) and Carl Ziehrer a piece entitled *Wiener Bürger* ('The Viennese Citizen'). The in-

96 Josef Engelhart: *Gesellschaft im Sophiensaal* ('A Social Occasion in the Sophiensaal'). 1903, oil on canvas, 100.5 x 65.5 cm. Historisches Museum der Stadt Wien. This establishment provided summer entertainment in the form of a vast swimming-pool which, in winter, was converted into a ballroom. The Sophiensaal was often the scene of balls given, in particular, by the upper middle classes. Though the swimming-pool was closed in 1909, the ballroom still survives.

Venedig in Wien.

97 F. Witt: *Venedig in Wien*
('Venice in Vienna'). C. 1895,
water-colour on pencil,
23.8 x 32.6 cm. Design for a postcard. Historisches Museum der
Stadt Wien.
'Venice in Vienna' in the Prater
was a favourite place of entertainment for the upper classes.

98 Wilhelm Gause: *Der Hofball*
('The Court Ball'). 1906, water-
colour, 49.8 x 69.3 cm. Histori-
sches Museum der Stadt Wien.
The court ball was one of the few
grand receptions to be given by
Francis Joseph. Here the emperor
is shown talking to a group of
ladies of high birth, among them
Countess Harrach, Countess
Baworowska, Marie Princess
Liechtenstein-Apponyi and
Countess Marie Kinsky.

99 Felician Freiherr von Myrbach: *'Süsses Mädel' und Soldat
beim Heurigen* ('"Grisette" and
Soldier at a Heuriger'). 1896,
water-colour, 30.2 x 44 cm.
Historisches Museum der Stadt
Wien.
'Men pluck love as they would a
wild rose.' Thus Ludwig Speidel
in 1895, reviewing Arthur
Schnitzler's play *Playing with
Love* in the *Neue Freie Presse*. The
fate of such girls, who went out in
search of pleasure and to 'see a bit
of life', was a favourite theme
among writers and artists.

100 Josef Engelhart: *Ein Ball
auf der Hängstatt* ('A Dance in the
Drying-Grounds'). 1896, oil on
canvas, 100.5 x 150.5 cm. Historisches Museum der Stadt Wien.
Ever since the Biedermeier period
and notably since the revolution
of 1848, the laundry-maid had
been regarded as the epitome of
Viennese humour, *joie de vivre*
and badinage. Here the girls are
dancing to the music of a hurdy-
gurdy – a scene much favoured in
the *feuilletons* of that period.

101 Wilhelm Gause: *Der
Wäschermädlball* ('The Laundry-
Maids' Ball'). 1893, oil on board,
45 x 63 cm. Historisches Museum
der Stadt Wien.
The cabbies' and laundry-maids'
balls were soon aped by the gen-
try, who enjoyed dressing up as
'children of nature'.

102 Café Dobner. C. 1905, photograph. Historisches Museum der Stadt Wien.
The Café Dobner, close by the Theater an der Wien, was a favourite meeting-place for artists. The actor Alexander Girardi is one of the group in the middle of the billiard-room.

103 Wilhelm Gause: *Am Graben* ('In the Graben'). 1888, grisaille, 32.6 x 49.7 cm. Historisches Museum der Stadt Wien.
In the Graben, for a long time a fashionable meeting-place, the Café Schrangl provided additional accommodation in a tent-like annex. The artist has been at pains to fill his picture with typically Viennese features: here a cabby waters his horse and a dog vendor looks for custom; there a laundrymaid delivers the washing, while a shoe-shine boy mingles with the crowd.

104 Felician Freiherr von Myr-bach: *Tarockpartie in der 'Schwemm'* ('Game of Taroc in the "pub"'). 1892, pen-and-ink, 23 x 24.5 cm. Design for illustration to *Wienerstadt – Lebensbilder aus der Gegenwart*, Vienna, 1895. Historisches Museum der Stadt Wien.

'The inn is a powerful, if not *the* most powerful factor in the life of your Viennese. The entrance to this refuge and place of pilgrimage for the hungry – and, still more, for the thirsty – leads through the "atrium", more vulgarly known as the "Schwemme" [pub], an El Dorado favoured by janitors and small shopkeepers, by apprentices and the foot-loose, by coachmen and street-sweepers...' *(Wienerstadt.)*

tellectual *élite* held their own dances, appropriately named '*élite* balls', while less conventionally-minded members of society staged what were known as tramps' balls, at which rags and tatters were *de rigueur*. The proceeds went to those for whom rags were not fancy dress but a matter of grim reality.

Another speciality, the laundry-maids' ball – like that of the cabbies – was regarded as the epitome of things Viennese. Thanks to Josef Sperl, a skilled mason by trade, who chose to follow the occupations of violinist and band-leader, what had once been a tradespeople's ball became one of the city's attractions. In the eyes of society the laundry-maid typified the unspoiled Viennese girl noted for her humour, *joie de vivre* and gift for repartee. In reality, however, she belonged to one of the many declining trades which were no longer able to compete with the large concerns then beginning to flourish in the city.

People from the various nations of the Monarchy, many of them in national dress, flocked to the Prater for the 'five-kreuzer hops', there to dance *ländlers*, polkas, and the *czárdás*. They are described by Felix Salten as follows: 'All these people have one thing in common – they are aliens in this huge metropolis where, swallowed up by their places of toil, they are being bleached, crushed and ground out of existence.' They came to the ball, he says, longing to hear a few words of their mother tongue. In Favoriten, where Czechs were particularly thick on the ground, they actually founded their own small pleasure park in 1885. Still known today as the Bohemian Prater, it exudes an ambience that is all its own.

A specifically Viennese institution which, since the Paris Exhibition of 1878, had found imitators all over Europe, was the coffee-house. It was a meeting-place and playground for various classes, in particular artists, who used it, not only for relaxation, but also for serious debate. The types of coffee-house varied considerably: they ranged from the elegant and richly decorated

105 Theo Zasche: *Karikatur auf die Mode* ('Fashion Caricatured'). *C.* 1900, water-colour on pencil, 43.6 x 30.2 cm. Historisches Museum der Stadt Wien. Fashionable dress was often caricatured by painters. In 1898 the Secessionist journal, *Ver Sacrum,* threw down the gauntlet. 'What is the reason', it demanded, 'for the absence of character and diversity in dress? The very same as accounts for all that is retrogressive in the realm of art, namely, mindless inertia, habitual and unconditional submission to the tyranny of fashion.'

106 Title-page of the monthly magazine, *Wiener Mode.* 1890, print. Historisches Museum der Stadt Wien.
Kolo Moser was for a time a contributor to *Wiener Mode,* a women's magazine that first appeared in 1888. In 1898 the magazine initiated a discussion of the new, loose, unwaisted dress, a form of attire which, however, found little favour outside artistic circles.

107 Theo Zasche: *Fin-de-siècle* interior design in caricature. *C.* 1905, pen and ink, 31.3 x 13.1 cm. Historisches Museum der Stadt Wien.
The influence of Adolf Loos, Josef Hoffmann and Kolo Moser, to mention only a few, is strongly in evidence in the interior design of the turn of the century. The furniture was well proportioned, with sensible uncluttered lines and sparse geometric decoration. This style, characterized by 'new objectivity', was by no means universally accepted.

108 Hilda Jesser: *Weihnachts-einkäufe auf dem Christkindlmarkt* ('Christmas Shopping in the Christkindlmarkt'). 1914–15, coloured woodcut, 29.6 x 20 cm. After *Mode Wien*, No. 12. Historisches Museum der Stadt Wien.
From the mid-nineteenth century until the 1930s, a Christmas market was held in the square known as Am Hof. The Wiener Werkstätte's fashion designer used the occasion to present her collection of winter clothes.

109 Hilda Jesser: *'Gnädige' mit Kindermädchen* ('Lady with Nursemaid'). 1914–15, coloured woodcut, 29.6 x 20 cm. After *Mode Wien*, No. 12. Historisches Museum der Stadt Wien.
Girls from the country, who took service with families in Vienna, usually wore their national costume. Thus in the capital Moravian dress was tantamount to a 'nanny's' uniform and also served to underline the difference between mistress and maid.

110 Afternoon dress. Late nineteenth century, jade-green silk, embroidered with axinites. Fashion Collections, Historisches Museum der Stadt Wien.

111 Wedding gown. *C.* 1902, cream-coloured satin, gauze, trimmed with *passementerie*. Fashion Collections, Historisches Museum der Stadt Wien.

112 Bicycling in Vienna. C. 1900, postcard by Charles Scolik. Historisches Museum der Stadt Wien.
Towards the end of the 1890s bicycling came into fashion both as a sport and as a sociable pastime. Moreover it enabled women to use their limbs without constraint. Rosa Mayreder went so far as to declare that bicycling had done more for female emancipation than all the women's movements put together.

113 Handing in rubber tyres at the Town Hall in aid of the war effort. 1916, photograph by Moriz Nähr. Historisches Museum der Stadt Wien.

After 1915 the Central Powers experienced a severe shortage of raw materials as a result of the Allied blockade. Attempts were made to alleviate the situation with the help of the public.

114 Meals for children. C. 1918, photograph. Historisches Museum der Stadt Wien.

Towards the end of the war food became so scarce that many children starved. Even in more well-to-do households the menu might be restricted to seed-potatoes, polenta and a meat substitute consisting of powdered birch-bark and mushrooms.

115 Women selling red carnations outside Vienna Town Hall. 1919, photograph. Historisches Museum der Stadt Wien. The government had abolished the system of voting by curiae and introduced universal and equal suffrage for men and women alike. In May 1919 the Social Democrats obtained a majority on the Vienna Municipal Council.

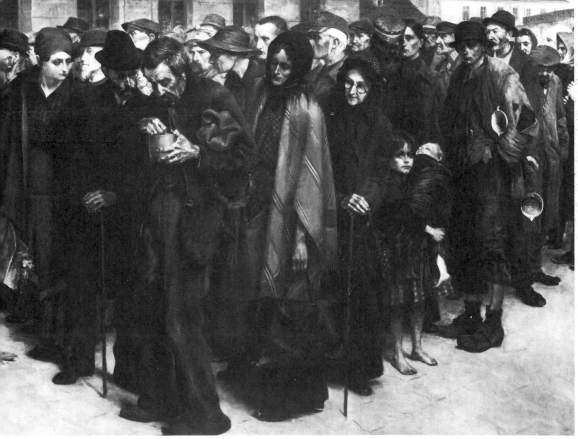

116 Josef Engelhart: *Arme vor einer Volksküche angestellt* ('Poor People queuing outside a Soup Kitchen'). 1918, oil on canvas, 148 x 191 cm. Historisches Museum der Stadt Wien. In his autobiography Engelhart tells of the painter Ludwig Rösch who had fled abroad to avoid war service. On his return to the capital he was to drag a would-be suicide out of the Danube Canal. 'He had numerous experiences of the kind', Engelhart writes, 'for during those miserable months of 1919 and 1920 there were many who wished to bring their lives to an end.' (Josef Engelhart, *Ein Wiener Maler erzählt...*, Vienna, 1943.)

establishments in the Ringstrasse, frequented by the aristocracy and the *haute bourgeoisie,* to the cosy and intimate *Tschecherln* that did business in the outer districts.

The coming of the war

In the period before the First World War the gulf between the classes was a very tangible one, providing a rich source of themes for the writers and artists of the day. The novellas and plays of Arthur Schnitzler, in particular, reveal with exceptional clarity the motive forces behind the complex and sensitive workings of *fin-de-siècle* society. In his *Anatol,* a sequence of dialogues written between 1886 and 1892, the female characters belong to backgrounds which correspond to the social structure obtaining in Vienna at the turn of the century. In the episode 'Christmas Shopping', the dialogue shows how different the outlook is of the two protagonists, working-class girl and upper-class lady. The seamstress, the *süsses Mädel,* makes do as best she can without any hope of bettering herself, yet her lust for life and desire for love remain undiminished. The lady, on the other hand, when discussing love, must confess that 'she lacks the courage for it'; ultimately her lack of courage deprives her, not only of love, but also of fulfilment in life. The compartmentalization of the classes, and their isolation one from the other, precluded all opportunity for mutual understanding. In Schnitzler's play *Vermächtnis* ('Legacy') (1898) the clash between the upper and lower middle-class worlds leads to tragedy and death. The principal characters are concerned not so much with human happiness as with social distinctions.

After the declaration of war in 1914 such niceties lost much of their significance. As the conflict dragged on, putting paid to hopes of an early victory, women increasingly took the place of men in industry. But well before the armistice it became clear that the country's economy was heading for disaster. The collapse, when it came, swept away the then ruling class, already demoralized, and politically unmanned by the crumbling of the House of Habsburg. On 12 November 1918 the proclamation of the Republic of German Austria by the provisional national assembly spelled the end of the Monarchy.

The social upheaval was compounded by inflation and the appalling conditions prevailing after the defeat. Both housing and food were in short supply and social services barely existent. The vast army of unemployed was further swollen by returning ex-servicemen, many impaired in body and mind by their experiences at the front.

Thus a new republic arose out of the ashes of the old Monarchy, its foundations built upon the ruins of the old social structure.

BIBLIOGRAPHY

Adler, Viktor, *Aus seinen Reden und Schriften.* Selected by Anton Tesarek, Vienna, 1947.

Banik-Schweitzer, Renate, and Meissl, Gerhard, *Industriestadt Wien.* Forschungen und Beiträge zur Wiener Stadtgeschichte, Vol. 11, Vienna, 1983.

Bobek, Hans, and Lichtenberger, Elisabeth, *Wien, bauliche Gestalt und Entwicklung seit der Mitte des 19. Jahrhunderts,* 2nd ed., Vienna, 1978.

Braun, Lily, *Die Frauenfrage. Ihre geschichtliche Entwicklung und ihre wirtschaftliche Seite,* Berlin–Bonn, 1979 (1st ed. of 1901 reprinted).

Breicha, Otto, Fritsch, Gerhard, *Finale und Auftakt, - Wien 1898–1914,* Salzburg, 1964.

Chiavacci, Vinzenz, *Wiener Typen,* Stuttgart, 1894.

Chiavacci, Vinzenz, *Aus Alt- und Neu-Wien, Skizzen aus dem Wiener Volksleben,* Vienna, 1910.

Feldbauer, Peter, *Stadtwachstum und Wohnungsnot, Determinanten unzureichender Wohnungsversorgung in Wien 1848 bis 1914.* Sozial- und Wirtschaftshistorische Studien, Vol. 9, Munich, 1977.

Fritsche, Viktor von, *Bilder aus dem österreichischen Hof- und Gesellschaftsleben,* Vienna, 1914.

Grübl, Raimund, *Die Gemeinde-Verwaltung der k.k. Reichshaupt- und Residenzstadt Wien in den Jahren 1889–1893,* Vienna, 1895.

Kläger, Emil, *Durch die Wiener Quartiere des Elends und Verbrechens,* Vienna, 1908.

Lichtenberger, Elisabeth, *Wirtschaftsfunktion und Sozialstruktur der Wiener Ringstrasse.* Die Wiener Ringstrasse – Bild einer Epoche, Vol. VI, Vienna–Cologne–Graz, 1970.

Lichtenberger, Elisabeth, *Die Wiener Altstadt, von der mittelalterlichen Bürgerstadt zur City,* Vienna, 1977.

Mahler-Werfel, Alma, *Mein Leben,* Hamburg, 1960.

Petzold, Alfons, *Das rauhe Leben,* Graz–Vienna–Cologne, rev. ed. 1979.

Popp, Adelheid, *Jugend einer Arbeiterin,* Berlin–Bonn–Bad Godesberg, rev. ed. 1977.

Rauchberg, Heinrich, *Die Bevölkerung Österreichs auf Grund der Ergebnisse der Volkszählung vom 31. December 1890,* Vienna, 1895.

Salten, Felix, *Wiener Adel,* Berlin–Leipzig, 1905.

Salten, Felix, *Wurstelprater.* Vienna–Munich–Zurich, rev. ed. 1973.

Schlögl, Friedrich, 'Wiener Volksleben', in *Die österreichisch-ungarische Monarchie in Wort und Bild,* Vienna, 1886, pp. 91–122.

Schnitzler, Arthur, *Jugend in Wien,* Ed. Therese Nickl and Heinrich Schnitzler, Vienna–Munich–Zurich, 1981.

Schorske, Carl E., Fin-de-Siècle *Vienna. Politics and Culture,* London, 1980.

Vasili, Paul, *Die Wiener Gesellschaft,* Leipzig, 1885.

Wien und die Wiener, Ungeschminkte Schilderungen eines fahrenden Gesellen, Berlin, 1892.

Wienerstadt, Lebensbilder aus der Gegenwart. Prague–Vienna–Leipzig, 1895.

Winter, Max, *Das schwarze Wienerherz.* Ed. Helmut Strutzmann, Vienna, 1982.

Witzmann, Reingard, *Wiener Typen, Historische Alltagsfotos aus dem 19. Jahrhundert.* Die bibliophilen Taschenbücher No. 339, Dortmund, 1982.

Zweig, Stefan, *Die Welt von Gestern. Erinnerungen eines Europäers,* Stockholm, 1942.

Statistische Jahrbücher der Stadt Wien 1883–1914 (Verlag des Wiener Magistrats).

Alltag in Wien seit 1848. Katalog zur Sonderausstellung des Österreichischen Gesellschafts- und Wirtschaftsmuseums, Vienna, 1979.

Das Wiener Kaffeehaus. Von den Anfängen bis zur Zwischenkriegszeit. Katalog zur 66. Sonderausstellung des Historischen Museums der Stadt Wien, Vienna, 1980.

Kaiser Franz Joseph von Österreich oder Der Verfall eines Prinzips. Katalog zur 64. Sonderausstellung des Historischen Museums der Stadt Wien in der Hermesvilla, Vienna, 1981.

Anatols Jahre, Beispiele aus der Zeit vor der Jahrhundertwende. Katalog zur 71. Sonderausstellung des Historischen Museums der Stadt Wien in der Hermesvilla, Vienna, 1982.

Alfons Petzold 1882–1923. Katalog zur 197. Wechselausstellung der Wiener Stadt- und Landesbibliothek, Vienna, 1982–3.

IV   VIENNA AND THE BIRTH OF PSYCHOANALYSIS

Harald Leupold-Löwenthal

Not the least striking feature of what Egon Friedell has described as 'the topography of the Viennese mentality'[1] was the elaboration of new scientific principles for the description of mental processes and, more particularly, of a method for their observation, namely psychoanalysis, as it was called by its creator, Sigmund Freud. It is also characteristic of that topography and that mentality that Freud's first use of the term psychoanalysis should have occurred in a French journal, the *Revue Neurologique*, in 1896,[2] thus preceding by several weeks its appearance in his article 'Weitere Bemerkungen über die Abwehr-Neuropsychosen' ('Further Remarks on the Neuro-Psychoses of Defence') in the *Neurologisches Zentralblatt*.[3] Here Freud, referring to his and Breuer's joint work, writes: 'There, too, some information is to be found about the laborious but completely reliable method of psychoanalysis used by me in making these investigations – investigations which also constitute a therapeutic procedure.'[4]

The specific nature of Vienna's scientific and cultural life at the turn of the century has been discussed so often that we shall not enlarge upon it here. However, the context in which psychoanalysis was born and evolved during the same period must be considered in some detail if we are to acquaint ourselves more closely with the origins of that science. In 1924 Freud himself maintained that psychoanalysis 'may be said to have been born with the twentieth century... But... it did not drop from the skies

ready-made. It had its starting point in older ideas, which it developed further; it sprang from earlier suggestions, which it elaborated.'[5] Thus, while we must obviously take account of the various factors – scientific, cultural and, notably, social – which were then exerting an influence on Freud and the early psychoanalysts, we should also bear in mind that the former, as W.H.

117   Sigmund Freud (1856–1939). 1891, photograph. Sigmund Freud-Gesellschaft, Vienna.
In 1893 Sigmund Freud, in collaboration with Josef Breuer, a specialist in internal diseases, published a work on hysterical phenomena. All his subsequent work was devoted to the investigation of mental illnesses for which there was no organic diagnosis.

PHOTOGRAPHIE des CHAMPS ÉLYSÉES

Mr. le Dr. Freud. Souvenir d'la chelpetrai

country, consisting not merely of one national group of German speakers, but of a conglomeration of the many peoples and nations that went to make up the Habsburg Empire.

In 1910 Freud expressed the wish that Zurich rather than Vienna be made the centre of psychoanalysis.[6] Stripped of its predominantly politico-scientific connotations, that wish, as also his remarks about Vienna in *Geschichte der psychoanalytischen Bewegung* ('The History of the Psychoanalytical Movement'), have often been used as an argument that the birth of psychoanalysis round about 1900 in this particular city was a contingency wholly dependent on the course taken by Freud's own life. Indeed the latter contested Janet's assertion that it was 'Vienna's atmosphere of sensuality and immorality' which had determined the emergence there of psychoanalysis, as, so to speak, a theoretical projection of those circumstances. While repudiating the above, however, Freud wrote: 'Yet Vienna has made every effort to disavow all share in the birth of psycho-analysis. In no other city is the hostile indifference of learned and cultivated circles so plainly apparent to the analyst.' This remark is often cited, in patent disregard of what Freud actually said, as evidence that Vienna had played little or no part in the birth of psychoanalysis.

True, his attitude to the city was distinctly ambivalent, as was that of the majority of its leading scientists, artists and intellectuals. Much of the capital's way of life was foreign, if not repellent to him: '... I had been back here hardly three days,' he wrote on 22 September 1896 to his friend Fliess in Berlin, 'when the whole depressing atmosphere of Vienna descended upon me again. It is a misery to live here, and it is no atmosphere in which hope of completing anything difficult can survive.'[7] Forty years later Freud, by now eighty-three, escaped from Vienna with little or no time to spare after his National Socialist persecutors had bowed to massive international pressure and permitted him to emigrate to England. 'The feeling of triumph,' he wrote on 6 June 1938 in a letter to Max Eitingen, 'of being liberated, is too strongly mixed with sorrow, for in spite

118 Jean Martin Charcot. Photograph. Sigmund Freud-Gesellschaft, Vienna. Charcot, professor at the Salpêtrière in Paris, a hospital for nervous diseases, is known particularly for his work on hysteria, hypnotism and systemic disorders of the spine. His writings were of fundamental importance to Freud's own work.

Auden has it, '*created* a whole climate of opinion'. For there can be no doubt that Freud's work is intimately linked with the changes that have taken place in the world since the turn of the century.

The events of 1866 did not deprive Vienna of its importance. Situated as it was on the border of an exclusively German-speaking national zone, Vienna nevertheless remained what it always had been – the capital of a group of non-German territories. In other words, Austria's position was essentially 'peripheral rather than central', as the Polish count says in Joseph Roth's *Kapuzinergruft*. And it was undoubtedly thanks to that position that Vienna eventually succeeded in becoming, not only the hub of a supranational system, but also a peripheral centre capable of playing more than a purely political and administrative role. In essence Vienna was always swayed by the same emotions that swayed the country at large – a of everything I still greatly loved the prison from which I have been released.'[8]

In 1911 Karl Scheffler voiced the opinion that a man's relationship with Berlin could 'assume many forms, but never that of love'.[9] Vienna, on the other hand, was a city a man could not respect but which, despite 'the whole depressing atmosphere' of the place, he was nevertheless bound to love. For Vienna was, as it still is, chiefly characterized by a collective defence mechanism in which reality is subordinated to fantasy. This *Lieber Augustin* syndrome – still a matter of unconcealed pride to the Viennese today – seemed to Freud utterly alien and outlandish. It was a mentality very prevalent among his early followers and pupils and one with which he felt impelled to take issue. Moreover, the techniques of psychoanalytic treatment and observation, uncovering as they did unconscious associations and defensive attitudes which suppressed or distorted reality, were undoubtedly so foreign to the Viennese as to provide sufficient reason for the repudiation, not only of psychoanalysis itself, but also of its supporters.

As a city in which a demoralized autocracy was seeking to patch up, rather than rule, a multinational empire, Vienna was destined to become, in its own particular way, a melting-pot of peoples, races and classes.

The reign of liberalism in Austria had been comparatively short-lived, despite the fact that the government and the *haute bourgeoisie* saw eye to eye, at least as regards the undesirability of nationalist tendencies. As an important and, in particular, effective political factor, the movement soon succumbed to a combined assault by the forces of nationalism, clericalism and conservatism. In the long run this was to have far graver consequences than those brought on by the great financial crash of 9 May 1873, which occurred at about the same time, ruining, amongst others, the middle-class supporters of liberalism.

Formed in 1902, the Psychological Wednesday Club held weekly meetings in Freud's waiting-room at No. 19 Berggasse to discuss psychoanalysis. Most of its members were Jewish intellectuals with a medical, philosophical or literary background, and all were to some extent opposed to what we now call the Establishment. The latter was then divided into two quite distinct strata, the upper being represented by the court and the aristocracy, the lower consisting largely of Jewish members of the *haute bourgeoisie* who inhabited mansions on the Ringstrasse. The increasingly prosperous lower middle classes, on the other hand, though still not fully enfranchised, were now engaged in a struggle for power in which they had recourse to new methods and new slogans. But of all the weapons in their armoury, anti-Semitism was the most effective and important. At the same time a united working class backed by Social Democracy had become a significant political factor in Austria-Hungary. The logical consequence of Pan-German and Christian Social racialist anti-Semitism was that appalling catastrophe, enacted between 1933 and 1945, 'the final solution of the Jewish Question'. Yet the path of so-called assimilation had been barred to the liberal Jewish bourgeoisie ever since the disgrace of the French army captain, Dreyfus, when a new form of anti-Semitism, this time in the shape of political and not, as before, unmotivated intolerance, had become a terrifying reality.

The attitude adopted towards this problem by the members of the Viennese psychoanalytical circle varied considerably. Freud had always resisted assimilation, remaining consciously a Jew, though not in the religious sense. Others such as Alfred Adler, Otto Rank and Viktor Tausk sought assimilation through conversion, while Theodor Reik joined the university's Zionist society.

To the lower middle classes in Vienna, anything unknown, new or alien was deeply suspect and abhorrent. In Dr Karl Lueger, the city's mayor, they found a perfect image upon which to project, in ideal form, their own particular traits and the narrowness of an outlook whose philistinism had survived all the vicissitudes of Josephinism, the Enlightment and liberalism.

In the words of Hermann Bahr, 'your Viennese always craves an example. To find it, he goes to the theatre, which does not copy, but rather is aped by, life.' Not for nothing has Vienna always been a city of theatre-goers who, however, are generally better able to appreciate the player than the play. 'Penny plain, but with coloured Bengal lights; make-believe, but with a sound core of wholesome reality.'[10]

Freud and his circle were largely unconcerned with the political disputes of the day or with the virulent rivalry between the various nationalities. The latter's autonomy or whether the Monarchy should be dual or triple were to them questions of infinitely less importance than infantile sexuality, the origin of neuroses or the theory of instincts.

A remarkable feature of Vienna at the turn of the century, described by Max Graf as 'a time of sheer virtuosity, effervescent wit and imaginative dilettantism',[11] was the vast gulf that separated the various coteries and classes, despite their physical propinquity. Those who belonged to the 'lower stratum', that is to say, the more successful scientists and the business, banking and industrial *élite*, sought to become assimilated with, and gain a footing in, the 'upper stratum', a process described by Hanns Sachs as follows: 'The manner of life of the privileged class provided the bourgeoisie with an example which they sought to imitate down to the most insignificant particular. (In this the wealthier Jews took the lead, once having overcome the obstacle of their faith.) The result might be anything from vulgar snobbery to excessive aestheticism.' Common to all classes, however, was a characteristic defined by Hofmannsthal as *das Gleitende* and interpreted by Carl E. Schorske as 'a slipping away from life'.[12] In Robert Musil's *Mann ohne Eigenschaften* ('The Man without Qualities') this attitude reappears as an ingredient of the *Gefühlskultur*, a culture governed by emotion rather than reason. One of Musil's characters, an influential publicist, invents the term 'Austrian year' without, however, being able to define it with any precision. 'Recurring again and again, in ever new contexts and combinations, it undergoes dreamlike changes and generates enormous enthusiasm... given wings, perhaps, by a certain vagueness and allegorical quality which tend to deflect one's thoughts from reality to a greater degree even than usual... For vagueness possesses the power to uplift and enlarge.'

The aesthetic *Gefühlskultur* affected by the less socially ambitious circles, however, was totally alien to Freud and the Viennese psychoanalysts. This, their Jewish origins and their disinclination to adapt themselves to the manners and customs of the powerful, all combined to cast them in the role of rank outsiders.

Of the city's intellectual life, Hanns Sachs writes in the same context: 'It is a remarkable fact that in Vienna, which boasted a large and vigorous mercantile middle class, there should have been no intelligentsia to speak of. The vast majority had few if any intellectual interests... the better class of people... preferred artistic pursuits to more exacting intellectual activities. And yet despite, or perhaps even because of, this background of mental indolence – it being often in the nature of things to produce their opposite – there would sometimes shine forth, from this or that individual or small group of individuals, a brilliance of intellect and a love of science such as had scarcely ever been known before... The consciousness of being exceptions to the rule induced these lone wolves to redouble their efforts, and they pursued their goal with an enthusiasm generated from within, an enthusiasm seldom encountered in the strictly hierarchical scientific establishment of Germany.'[13]

Sachs, who joined the Viennese Psychoanalytical Association in 1910, describes in this passage not only 'Freud, master and friend', but also the outlook of a circle of men who still felt themselves to be part of a movement rather than members of a scientific society.

The same conviction emerges from Fritz Wittel's comment on a discussion held on 6 April 1910, when Freud proposed to make Zurich the seat of the International Psycho-analytical Society. He writes: 'Until then we had been just about the opposite of a society and it was a pity that we should become one now.' Tausk is reported as objecting that 'no soil was better suited to the propagation of Freud's doctrine than that of Vienna, for the very reason, perhaps, that it was unhealthy soil. It would be a mistake to regard psychoanalysis merely from the standpoint of medicine, for to do so would be to falsify the picture as understood by us.' Hitschmann even went so far as to express the opinion that 'the people of Zurich, seen as a race, are quite different from us Viennese'.

Schorske has suggested that, at the turn of the century in Vienna, the 'new culture makers' defined themselves as constituting a kind of collective oedipal revolution. But they were rebelling, not so much against their fathers, as against the authority of a paternal culture which was also their heritage.[14]

'Between 1900 and 1910', Otto Friedländer writes,

Vienna was one of the intellectual centres of the world, and was totally unaware of the fact. Here two or three thousand men spoke words and formulated ideas that would convulse the world of the next generation. As ever Vienna remained unaware. Here there lived a small group of men, writers, politicians, lecturers, journalists, artists, officials, lawyers and doctors, all of them moved by the problems of the day, and devising and shaping the future. For all support, those men had a handful, not hordes, of disciples. In blissful apathy, the slumbering town vegetated, never once dreaming what great things were being thought and achieved in its midst... Intellectually, Vienna was at once the most lively and the most unaware city in the world.[15]

By 1900, eight years after the publication of Freud's *Interpretation of Dreams*, no more than 600 copies had been sold.

The position in which the psychoanalysts found themselves at this time in no way resembled that of other innovative move-

DIE

TRAUMDEUTUNG

VON

PROF. DR. SIGM. FREUD.

———

»FLECTERE SI NEQUEO SUPEROS, ACHERONTA MOVEBO«

DRITTE VERMEHRTE AUFLAGE.

LEIPZIG UND WIEN.
FRANZ DEUTICKE.
1911.

120 Sigmund Freud, *Die Traumdeutung* ('The Interpretation of Dreams'). Title-page, 3rd enlarged edition, Leipzig and Vienna, 1900.
'In the pages that follow I shall bring forward proof that there is a psychological technique which makes it possible to interpret dreams, and that, if that procedure is employed, every dream reveals itself as a psychical structure which has a meaning and which can be inserted at an assignable point in the mental activities of waking life.' (Freud, *The Interpretation of Dreams*, Harmondsworth, 1976.)

ments such as, for instance, the Secession; for despite all symptoms of storm and stress, the latter still maintained close links with tradition. Freud and his group, on the other hand, while undoubtedly regarding themselves as the exponents of very advanced and original ideas, had no such tradition either to invoke or to rebel against. Moreover, they remained more or less unaware of the mood that was then permeating all walks of life in Vienna. It was a complex mood in which permanent feelings of foreboding were blended with suppressed anxiety and disquiet – almost, one is tempted to say, with a sense of impending doom. To many people the *fin de siècle* was synonymous with the beginning of the end. Yet there is nothing to show that such feelings were shared by the analysts who, standing as they were on the threshold of tremendous achievements, had no reason, intellectual or otherwise, to prognosticate an 'end'.

For that reason their relationship with contemporary literature, with the poets and writers of *Jung-Wien*, such as Hofmannsthal, Schnitzler, Beer-Hofmann, von Andrian and Bahr, was distinctly cool. Although Freud regarded Schnitzler as his *doppelgänger* because the latter, by intuition and subtle self-analysis, knew everything that Freud had laboriously discovered by studying others, these two Jewish doctors exemplify the differences between their two chosen professions – medicine and literature respectively. While

Freud found Schnitzler's preoccupations with the polarity of love and death uncannily familiar, his own theory of Thanatos and Eros in *Jenseits des Lustprinzips* ('Beyond the Pleasure Principle') led him to draw a totally different and much less noncommittal conclusion from what both men could see to be life as actually lived and sensed rather than recorded – a peculiar blend, that is, of pleasure and death, lightheartedness and pessimism, anxiety and resignation, luxuriance and sobriety. In their vulgar form, all these manifested themselves, as they still do, in the *pompes funèbres* beloved of the Viennese, as well as in the sweet-sour flirtation with doom which recurs even today in the *Heuriger* songs. Schnitzler always felt himself to be a spectator of the perpetually changing scene

121 Stairway at No. 19 Berggasse, Vienna 9.
Sigmund Freud lived in this house where from 1891 until 1938 he also had his famous consulting-room until compelled to leave Austria after the *Anschluss* of 1938.

122 Max Pollak: *Sigmund Freud am Schreibtisch* ('Sigmund Freud Seated at his Writing-Table'). 1914, 47.5 x 46.5 cm. Sigmund Freud-Gesellschaft, Vienna.

about him – a sympathetic spectator whose deep insights enabled him to produce a coherent story from the fortunes of his characters. His object, however, was not to change their lot, but merely to describe it.

To Freud and his disciples, on the other hand, such an attitude was inconsistent with a rational and scientific outlook. Indeed, their aims were those described by Hermann Bahr in 1891. 'The new psychology', he wrote, 'will search out the basic elements of psychology, its rudiments concealed in the darkness of the mind before they have emerged into the broad light of day..., the chaotically confused emotional process which, in the form of a simple conclusion, will in due course propel them over the threshold of consciousness.'[16]

By the turn of the century Vienna saw the emergence of numerous scientific and artistic trends and the consequent formation of groups which cannot be regarded merely as a local and specifically Viennese expression of movements and tendencies elsewhere in Europe. In their own eyes, these groups were young and modern by comparison with the old, traditional forms and modes of thought. While at first glance the Vienna school of psychoanalysis would seem to belong to their number, it was in fact neither a movement of renewal, nor the heir to an earlier tradition, to be developed or discarded as the case might be. Rather, it was something entirely new, such as had never been experienced or thought of before. Nor is this invalidated by the fact that certain psychoanalytical propositions and theories can be traced back to an earlier source.

Equally important was another factor of which Freud wrote in 1925: 'Nor is it, perhaps, entirely a matter of chance that the first advocate of psychoanalysis was a Jew. To profess belief in this new theory called for a certain degree of readiness to accept the situation of solitary opposition – a situation with which no one is more familiar than the Jew.'[17]

But it was not simply their greater ability to endure an outsider's lot that induced so many Jewish doctors, scholars and intellectuals to join Freud's circle in Vienna. The preponderance of Jews among innovative and pioneering scientists, writers and musicians may in part be attributed to the tendency of their non-Jewish colleagues to cling too closely to tradition, to what has stood the test of time, to familiar forms and styles – in short, to everything that is familiar and comforting because not frighteningly new. Needless to say, the first bold step into the unknown was usually taken by those among the intellectually active who were burdened little, if at all, by such considerations.

A catalyst for the new psychology, Sigmund Freud could boast a quality possessed by few others and which has nothing to do with a man's place of origin, be it town, province or country. It was a quality described by Stefan Zweig in an ovation delivered beside Freud's bier in London on 26 September 1939.

Because of him, both we and our times have again learned the exemplary lesson that nowhere on earth is there a more magnificent form of courage than the free, independent courage of a man of intellect. Never must it be forgotten that it was his courage which enabled him to acquire the knowledge which others failed to acquire because they did not dare to do so, let alone expound and profess it. He, however, did dare and kept on daring and, heedless of all opposition, continued, until the last day of his life, to press forward alone into untrodden territory. What an example he has set us by his intellectual gallantry in the war eternally waged by mankind in pursuit of knowledge![18]

BIBLIOGRAPHY

1 Friedell, Egon, *Kulturgeschichte der Neuzeit*, London, 1947, p. 512.

2 Freud, Sigmund, *Heredity and the Aetiology of the Neuroses*, Complete Psychological Works, Standard Edition, Hogarth Press, 1962, Vol. III, p. 144.

3 Freud, Sigmund, *Further Remarks on the Neuro-Psychoses of Defence*, ibid., Vol. II, p. 162.

4 Breuer and Freud, *Studies on Hysteria*, ibid., Vol. II.

5 Freud, Sigmund, *A Short Account of Psycho-Analysis*, ibid., Vol. XIX, p. 191.

6 Freud, Sigmund, *On the History of the Psycho-Analytical Movement, ibid.*

7 Freud, Sigmund, *The Origins of Psycho-Analysis*, Basic Books, Inc., New York, 1954, Letter 96, p. 204.

8 Freud, Sigmund, *Letters of Sigmund Freud*, Hogarth Press, London, 1961, pp. 441–2.

9 Scheffler, Karl, *Berlin, ein Stadtschicksal*, Berlin, 1911.

10 Handl, W., and Bab, J., *Wien und Berlin*, Berlin, 1918.

11 Graf, Max, *Aus der inneren Werkstatt des Musikers*, Stuttgart, 1911, p. 249.

12 Schorske, Carl E., Fin-de-Siècle *Vienna. Politics and Culture*, London, 1979, New York, 1980, p. 19.

13 Sachs, Hanns, *Freud, Meister und Freund*, London, 1950, p. 33.

14 Schorske, Carl E., *op. cit.*

15 Friedländer, Otto, *Letzter Glanz der Märchenstadt*, cited from F. Hennings, *Solange er lebt*, Vienna, 1968, p. 88.

16 Bahr, Hermann, *Zur Überwindung des Naturalismus*, Stuttgart, 1968, p. 57.

17 Freud, Sigmund, *The Resistances to Psycho-Analysis, ibid.*, Vol. XIX, p. 222.

18 Zweig, Stefan, 'Worte am Grabe Sigmund Freuds, gesprochen am 26. September 1939, im Krematorium London, Erbe und Zukunft', in *Zeitschrift für Literatur, Musik, Geschichte und Philosophie*, 2 (1947), pp. 101–2.

V THE VISUAL ARTS IN VIENNA FROM 1890 TO 1920

Hans Bisanz

The Ringstrasse

In late December 1857, Francis Joseph gave the people of Vienna a Christmas present in the form of a decree permitting the demolition and redevelopment of the defence works and glacis which had hitherto divided the inner city from the suburbs. The Christmas present he chose for himself, however, was nothing less than the Ringstrasse. The concept of this magnificent boulevard as a *Gesamtkunstwerk*, or 'total work of art', embraced all durable forms of visual art, down to craft manufacture and landscape gardening. Basically grandiose in character, the style of its public buildings was echoed by that of the adjacent domestic and office premises which went up at the same time.

The revival of historicism found expression in the architecture, monuments and allegorical wall-paintings of the Ringstrasse buildings, in which a wealth of eclectic borrowings made manifest to the observer the continuity between his own present and the great epochs of the past, at the same time instilling into him a sense of the undiminished greatness and importance of the Imperial house and of the Monarchy.

So slowly did work go ahead on the Ringstrasse scheme that the underlying idea eventually became outmoded, for in the meantime this vast monument to the concept of state had repeatedly been called in question by economic crises and the unstable political situation, both at home and abroad. This meant that, by the 1890s, whatever was put up as part of the scheme was already an anachronism. The monuments of the late phase are mostly devoted to artists rather than to the military who, significantly enough, had been given priority during the early stages of the programme. The monuments to Beethoven (by Kaspar Zumbusch), Mozart (by Viktor Tilgner) and Grillparzer (by Karl Kundmann) were not completed until 1880, 1896 and 1899 respectively. Makart, on the other hand, the most important artist of the Ringstrasse period, was similarly honoured only four years after his death in 1884 when a memorial, designed by Tilgner, was put up in the Stadtpark, adjoining the Ring.

Over the decades, nearly all the great styles of the past – neo-Gothic, neo-Renaissance and neo-Baroque – had been revived by the architects and artists of the Ringstrasse, most of whom had, by the 1890s, moved on to Rococo forms. As examples we might cite Tilgner's sculpture and Eduard Veith's Volkstheater paintings, or again, the work done in the Kunsthistorisches Museum between 1890 and 1892 by the Klimt brothers, Gustav and Ernst, in collaboration with Franz von Matsch. (The same important team had already been responsible for the ceiling paintings of the lateral staircases in the Burgtheater.) The work of Gustav Klimt, in particular, betrays the influence of Frederick Leighton and Lawrence Alma-Tadema, artists whose cool classicism is mingled with the sensuality of

Salon art. Certain characteristics of the Secessionist, *fin-de-siècle* style are in evidence in various decorative features, such as Eduard Lebiedsky's mosaic frieze above the main doors of the Parliament building (1900) and Karl Kundmann's Athene fountain (1902) which precedes it.

The artists directly employed on the Ringstrasse buildings had, for their main task, the allegorical illustration of whatever scheme was in hand – examples being the *Kreislauf des Lebens* ('Life Cycle'), by Hans Canon for the Natural History Museum and *Triumph der Gerechtigkeit* ('The Triumph of Justice') by August Eisenmenger for the Law Courts. As the Ringstrasse concept began to fade, however, another group of artists came to the fore, who were concerned, not with figurative allegorical work of an official kind, but rather with painting such as landscape, townscape and the interior. Being uncommitted to the principle of the 'total work of

123 Viktor Tilgner: *Mozart Monument* (1896).
A monument exemplifying the rococo sculpture of the late Ringstrasse phase, it undoubtedly contributed to the depreciation of Mozart's music which was then all too common.

124 Ernst Klimt: *Spanien und Niederlande* ('Spain and the Netherlands'). 1890–1, plaster ground, 230 x 230 cm and 230 x 80 cm.
After the illustration in the portfolio *Zwickelbilder im Stiegenhause des k.k. Kunsthistorischen Hof-Museums zu Wien*, 1893.)
The explanatory text by Albert Ilg reads: 'A page dressed in the fashion of Philip IV's day is a deliberate invocation of Murillo and Velasquez. He holds a table-cloth embroidered in *punto España*. The costume worn by the lady in the spandrel resembles that of the women of rank portrayed by Anthony van Dyck.'

SPANIEN UND NIEDERLANDE.

VON ERNST KLIMT.

125 Theodor von Hörmann: *Im Wald von Fontainebleau* ('In the Forest of Fontainebleau'). C. 1890, oil on wood, 26 x 35 cm.
Historisches Museum der Stadt Wien.
Having completed his studies at the Vienna Academy, Hörmann went to Paris in 1886 to resume them under the decorative artist Raphael Collin. He then rounded off his education with trips to Brittany, Barbizon and Italy.

art' and its concomitant historicism, they were more receptive to the artistic developments of their own day. An interest in French *plein-air* painting brought them into touch with Impressionists, whose vibrant dissolution of outlines they interpreted for the most part in a poetic, individualistic manner.

Thus Jakob Emil Schindler and Tina Blau-Lang might be described as representatives of a specifically Viennese 'affective Impressionism', while other members of the group, such as Eugen Jettel and Hugo Darnaut, tended more towards the austere, scientific Impressionism of French provenance. Carl Schuch and Theodor von Hörmann on the other hand – both of them particularly successful painters at that time – owed their knowledge of that school to their student days in Paris.

Pioneers of the Secession

Young writers and critics, who repudiated the art of the Ringstrasse, found this autonomous, immediate style very much more to their liking. In 1895 Hugo von Hofmannsthal, discussing Hörmann's memorial exhibition, wrote: 'Just now, perhaps, there is nothing in Vienna that is so rewarding to look at and reflect upon…'[1] Two years earlier he had expressed his delight at finding a kindred spirit in Richard Muther, the author of *Geschichte der Malerei* ('History of Painting'): 'If I am not mistaken', he writes, 'Mr Richard Muther is Keeper of the Royal Print Room in Munich. He will forgive me for saying, and I say it with pleasure, that one would never suspect as much… Here, in this frank and lively book, we all at once discover everything by which our sense of form and colour has hitherto been stimulated… Thus, all derivative painting, everything that has succumbed to that fearful scourge of nineteenth-century art – eclecticism –… is elbowed aside… and out of the medley there arises, refreshingly and significantly, only that which is true and original… our own genuine art.'[2]

126 Susanne Granitsch: *Selbstbildnis* ('Self-Portrait'). 1899, oil on canvas, 120.5 x 72.5 cm. Historisches Museum der Stadt Wien.

Theodor von Hörmann was to receive special acclaim from the Vienna Secessionists who looked upon him as the champion of their movement. In 1897 they chose for their honorary president another advocate of autonomous, 'genuine' art, namely Rudolf von Alt whom they admired for his tireless spirit of experimentation and his courage in retaining a certain sketchiness in his drawings and water-colours. His *Blumenstilleben mit der Tochter Luise im Hintergrund* ('Still-Life with Flowers; in the Background Luise Alt') (1895) creates an impression of liveliness and immediacy, while still bearing almost imperceptible traces of the Ringstrasse style, of that lushness so dear to Makart in whose studio he had worked some ten years earlier.

Alt's basic approach is characterized by an artistic consistency which refuses to compromise. Unlike his more complaisant

127 Rudolf von Alt: *Blumenstilleben mit Louise Alt im Hintergrund* ('Still Life with Flowers; in the background Louise Alt'). 1895, water-colour (gouache), 56.5 x 38.5 cm. Historisches Museum der Stadt Wien.
The approach chosen by the then eighty-three-year-old artist combines a naturalistic rendering with a showy floral opulence which betrays the residual influence of the representational art of the Ringstrasse.

128 Franz Alt: *Brunnen im Hof der österreichisch-ungarischen Bank* ('Fountain in the Courtyard of the Austro-Hungarian Bank'). 1891, water-colour, 22.2 x 15.5 cm. Historisches Museum der Stadt Wien.
The bank, designed by Heinrich von Ferstel, was built between 1855 and 1860, while the fountain, by Anton Dominik Fernkorn, dates from 1861. Franz Alt spent the years 1876 to 1881 in France where he came into contact with Impressionism.

brother Franz, a painter still in thrall to Biedermeier idyllicism, he had difficulty in finding patrons. Writing from Venice to his wife in 1864, he told her: 'That Franz should in some ways have been more fortunate than I does, I believe, sadden you unduly... yet his nature is quite different, as was his introduction to the world... What else can I do but devote all my energies to my work and put my trust in that?'[3]

In the more private sphere of autonomous art there were also some gifted women, among them Tina Blau-Lang and Olga Wisinger-Florian, both pupils of Schindler, as well as Susanna Granitsch whose *Selbstbildnis an der Staffelei* ('Self-Portrait on Easel') (1899) is convincing by reason of its lively technique and sureness of delineation.

What the Secessionists admired in these artists, who had detached themselves from the art of the Ringstrasse, was that, unlike the ideal painters of the historicist school, they depicted reality in terms of their personal experience. It soon transpired, however, that the leading members of the Vienna Secession were in their turn engaged in constructing not only a 'total work of art' but also an ideal world, albeit in a new context, and using a new formal idiom. That the Secession was directly linked to the Ringstrasse is evident from the reappearance in new guise of many of its characteristics. As an example we might cite the paintings done by Gustav Klimt in the Burgtheater and the Kunsthistorisches Museum, or again, the publication *Allegorien*, the first instalment of which appeared in 1882. This initial series took the form of pattern-books, compiled in the spirit of historicism, for use in schools, workshops and offices, thus ensuring the popularization, as well as the widest possible dissemination, of a multitude of allegorical motifs.

In the second series, *Allegorien, Neue Folge*, published between 1895 and 1900, the earlier propagandist and didactic aims were largely abandoned; indeed, now that the Ringstrasse concept was beginning to fade, the series showed a distinct tendency to abandon the official in favour of the personal. In the foreword the publisher, Martin Gerlach, writes: 'For our first theme I chose one redolent of life and gaiety, namely "wine, love, music, dance and song", which will be followed by the figuratively inexhaustible theme of the arts and sciences and the joyous cycle of the seasons, together with the light-hearted sports associated with them.' Radiating pagan *joie de vivre*, this new prospectus, within whose purview the 'arts and sciences' become, in Nietzsche's sense of the term, a 'joyous science', could hardly be expected to serve any other than a purely artistic purpose. The change of function is implicit in the subject-matter which, no longer concerned with the Establishment, has shifted to a far more personal plane. For though the allegories were still largely drawn from ancient mythology, they now embodied the stages of man and his states of mind.

This closer association between the mythological and the personal may be attributed not least to the demands previously put forward by men such as Nietzsche. As early as 1872, in the *Geburt der Tragödie* ('Birth of Tragedy'), the latter had already spoken of 'man who, eternally hungry and deprived of myths, digs and burrows in search of his roots, even though he must dig for them in remotest antiquity.' In 1861 a considerable stir was created by *Das Matriarchat*, a work in which the Swiss scholar, Johann Jakob Bachofen, set out the results of his investigations in the field of legal history.

Allegorien, Neue Folge contains several folios, notably those by Max Švabinský and Kolo Moser, in which the mythological rendering of human states of mind clearly reveals a development tending towards the psychoanalysis of Sigmund Freud, particularly as expounded in the *Traumdeutung* ('Interpretation of Dreams') (1900). Psychoanalysis itself was subsequently to invoke precedents in the visual arts, notably in the work of Max Klinger, whose graphic cycles anticipated the study and formulation of the unconscious.

A contribution by Gustav Klimt to *Allegorien*, also belongs in this context, namely his oil-painting *Liebe* ('Love') (1895). Love as a fundamental human predicament is translated by Klimt into a

129 Gustav Klimt: *Tragödie* ('Tragedy'). 1897, black chalk, pencil, heightened with gold wash, 41.9 x 30.8 cm. Folio 66 in the portfolio *Allegorien*, N. S., Verlag Gerlach & Schenk, Vienna, 1895–1900. Historisches Museum der Stadt Wien.
Discernible in this early work by Gustav Klimt is the influence of the English Pre-Raphaelites and the Dutch and Belgian Symbolists, whose ideal painting caused him to turn away from the materiality of 'earthly things'.

130 Gustav Klimt: *Junius* (the goddess Juno as an allegory of the month of June). 1896, black rubbed chalk, pencil, wash, heightened with white and gold, 41.5 x 31 cm. Historisches Museum der Stadt Wien.

dreamlike world in which occult powers hover like a vision above the two lovers. The pair are presented, now as real persons in modern dress, now as 'background figures', timeless, immutable forces of destiny. The disquieting presence of the latter is foreshadowed in the chorus-like allegorical groups depicted by Klimt in his university paintings and Beethoven frieze.

Johannes Dobai draws attention to the 'somewhat melancholy tone' of Klimt's *Love* which, he says: 'is in many ways comparable to the mood of one of Arthur Schnitzler's stories'.[4] His comparison is supported by Hofmannsthal's comment on *Anatol*. 'Schnitzler', he writes, 'takes less pleasure in the light shed by love, in the brilliance of its direct rays, than in their prismatic reflection at the periphery... the shadowy forms behind them.'[5]

The relationship of the momentary to the eternal is also found elsewhere in *Allegorien*, as, for example, in Heinrich Lefler's *Der Ball* ('The Ball'). Here an elegant 'drawing-room' occasion merges into a dreamlike 'dance of life' without an end or a beginning.

In examples such as these, the influence of western Symbolism is elucidated in a specific manner. Psychological questions ought not, it was held, to be left open; rather – and this without detracting from their mystery – solutions should be found for them. This rational approach, as distinct from 'decadence' and 'satanism', may be regarded as the particular achievement of Viennese art and literature just before the turn of the century, an achievement that was to receive its scientific imprimatur in Freud's *Interpretation of Dreams*.

The problems then posed and the way

131 Heinrich Lefler: *Tanz* ('Dancing'). Folio 42, *Allegorien*, N. S., Verlag Gerlach & Schenk, Vienna, 1895–1900.
When compared with Klimt's allegorical compositions, this triptych by Lefler seems almost mundane. Yet under Beardsley's influence what appears to be a mere 'drawing-room' occasion becomes a 'dance of life' of universal significance.

they were expressed were largely derived from western Europe. Klimt's *Love* betrays the influence of the Belgian, Fernand Khnopff, and Lefler's *The Ball* betrays that of the English artist, Aubrey Beardsley. That the West should have exerted so much influence postulates a grave loss of confidence, not only in progress, but also in naturalistic literature. For, with the coming of Symbolism, considerable powers of imagination were released, thus calling in question the old shibboleths.

'Art now wants to get away from naturalism and look for something new. What that may be, no one knows; the urge is confused and unsatisfied... Only to get away, to get away at all costs from the clear light of reality into the dark, the unknown and the hidden.'[6] Hermann Bahr's critical assessment, made in 1894, gives proof of Austrian interest in Symbolism – and anticipates the Austrian response.

That interest, expressed by the new generation, met with little but incomprehension. In 1893 Hofmannsthal, complaining about the selection procedure at the Künstlerhaus, wrote: 'During the past fifteen years, about as much light has been shed by great European art on the Viennese scene as may filter into a dark room through a crack in the door,'[7] and in a review of the International Art Exhibition of 1894 he deplored, amongst other things, the absence of that great 'stylist', Burne-Jones.[8]

Thus Hofmannsthal championed the cause, not only Hörmann but also of Burne-Jones, the first being representative of avant-garde realistic art, the second, of the idealist art practised in England by the Pre-Raphaelites, in Holland by Jan Toorop and in Belgium by Fernand Khnopff. The latter trend was taken up in Vienna by artists whose style was based on the allegorical art of the Ringstrasse and who were later to form part of the Secession. Of these, a notable example is Gustav Klimt who was

132 Gustav Klimt: *Liebe* ('Love'). 1895, oil on canvas, 60 x 44 cm. Folio 46 in the portfolio *Allegorien*, N. S., Verlag Gerlach & Schenk, Vienna, 1895–1900. Historisches Museum der Stadt Wien.
The subject, to which Klimt returned again and again, is here treated allegorically in a manner which lifts it out of the realm of the personal.

influenced first by Makart and then by Ferdinand Laufberger, a typical Ringstrasse artist, under whom he studied.

From the very beginning, then, the Viennese Secession was split into two groups, 'naturalists' and 'stylists', with numerous shades of opinion in between. Stimulating though it may have been at the outset, that polarity harboured the seeds of the conflict which eventually came to a head in 1905.

The Secession

The Secession, led by Klimt, was founded by some of the younger Künstlerhaus members, in revolt against the tutelage of their elders. The Künstlerhaus – still in existence today – had been founded in 1861, the heyday of the Ringstrasse project with which, much to its benefit, it was closely associated, as it also was with the influential Academy of Fine Arts where many of its members taught.

This endless consorting with the Establishment was not to the taste of the younger generation whose artistic interests, as has been shown in the case of *Allegorien,* tended increasingly towards the private world of the individual. They not only felt the selection procedure to be unfair, but differed radically from their elders on the subject of the exhibitions themselves, which they considered to be both pretentious and grossly overstocked. For what the Secessionists demanded was quality rather than quantity.

When, in 1896, Hermann Bahr criticized the Künstlerhaus, with its cluttered wall, for being 'simply a covered market, a bazaar where vendors can display their wares',[9] he was expressing the longing felt by the younger generation for an art in which politics and commerce played no part. Indeed, the Secession's rules called for 'exhibitions untainted by commerce', and for the dissemination of Austrian art abroad; recourse was also to be had to the 'most important artistic achievements of other countries... with a view to stimulating production at home and making the Austrian public aware of artistic developments generally.'

By way of reaction to the tutelage of the past, the rules also made provision for democratic procedures within the association: 'The selection committee shall consist of all those full members present in Vienna, together with such corresponding members as may be staying there throughout the period in which the selection committee is in session.' Full membership was confined to artists of Austrian nationality; foreign artists who had made 'an outstanding contribution to art' were elected corresponding members.[10]

There can be little doubt that the association's rules were, to a great extent, thrashed out in the course of coffee-house discussions. The (still extant) Café Sperl in the Gumpendorferstrasse had, since the 1890s, served as a venue for two coteries who eventually amalgamated to form the Secession, one being the Siebener-Club, the other the Hagengesellschaft named after the landlord of the inn at which the company used to eat. These social occasions were used by the young men to air their dissatisfaction with the Künstlerhaus in caricatures and cartoons. After 1895 members of the Siebener-Club (including Kolo Moser, Josef Hoffmann, Joseph-Maria Olbrich and Max Kurzweil) used to draw 'postcards' for each other's delectation. These postcards represent their first experiments in the new language of ornamental forms evolved by Viennese Art Nouveau.

Mention has already been made of Secessionist contributions to *Allegorien.* Other published works by members of that group consisted in illustrations for a booklet to be presented to ladies on the occasion of the Vienna Municipal Ball of 1897. Particularly striking is Kolo Moser's illustration of Schubert's song *Irrlicht* ('Will o' the Wisp'), showing an exceptionally ecstatic, maenad-like female figure in which both ornament and general outline describe the sinuous, linear movement of Art Nouveau. And here it is pertinent to recall that famous 'expressive' dancers such as Ruth St Denis and Loïe Fuller (of whom Kolo Moser made drawings) were performing in Vienna at this particular time. Indeed, what Hofmannsthal wrote about the former in 1906 might

133 Kolo Moser: *Gesang. Liebe. Musik. Tanz.* ('Song, Love, Music, Dance'.) Folio 28, *Allegorien und Embleme,* N. S.
The many volumes of this publication, the first of which appeared in 1882, included contributions from Viennese as well as Munich artists.

MVSIK   TANZ   GESANG & LIEBE

Chant. Amour. Musique. Danse.   Gesang. Liebe. Musik. Tanz.   Song. Love. Music. Dance.

equally be said of the dancer in our illustration. Her dancing, he observes, 'is almost lascivious and yet it is chaste. It is wholly abandoned to the senses and yet indicative of higher things. It is untamed, yet subject to eternal laws.'[11]

On 25 May 1897 nineteen of the younger members of the Künstlerhaus, who seven weeks earlier had banded together to further their own interests within that organization, decided to secede from it once and for all. Klimt was elected president of the Secession, and Rudolf von Alt, a youthful octogenarian, its honorary president.

For the Secession's first exhibition, held from March to June 1898 in the Horticultural Society's Floral Halls, Gustav Klimt designed a poster showing Theseus, under the aegis of Pallas Athene, locked in struggle with the Minotaur. When, however, the poster was actually placed on show, Theseus' taut belligerent pose and heroic nakedness had been much impaired by the censor's insistence that the existing fig-leaf be reinforced with something more substantial. The traditional antique figures chosen by Klimt were here fulfilling a new function. Athene, already patroness of the Munich Secession, stands guard with spear and shield over the youthful association. As protagonist of what is new and enlightened, Klimt's Theseus (bathed in light) lunges at the Minotaur (black against a dark background) symbolizing obscurantism. It is not surprising that Theseus' movement should be from right to left, since to the European, who reads and writes in the opposite direction, 'left' is synonymous with 'backward' and 'obscurantist'.

In addition to the new role allotted to the characters of antiquity as champions of the Secession against the Künstlerhaus and its supporters, the poster also reveals the new formal idiom of Viennese Art Nouveau. In contrast to the voluminous, markedly three-dimensional art characteristic of the Ringstrasse period, the figure of Theseus, for all its dynamism, appears light and transparent. Not only are the contour and inner detail of the nude ornamentally stylized, but the figure itself is disposed parallel to the picture, thus enhancing the latter's

two-dimensional character. The same applies to Athene who is shown in strict profile, while her shield, a grinning Gorgon's head, underlines the polemic content of the poster. In an oil-painting done in the same year (1898), Klimt again portrays Pallas Athene, this time frontally and with a Gorgon's head which, even more outrageously, sticks out its tongue at the enemy.

The Secession's first exhibition was visited by the emperor to whom, in Rudolf Bacher's drawing, Rudolf von Alt is about to be presented. The drawing is a true-to-life, 'naturalistic' document with little or none of the stylization which predominated, naturally enough, in applied graphics – in, for example, the Secession's journal or exhibition posters such as that described above.

On 21 June 1897 the Secession brought out a periodical entitled *Ver Sacrum* ('Sacred Spring') which survived until 1903, and must be counted as one of the most important of its kind in Europe. It followed in the

136 Rudolf Bacher: *Eröffnung der 1. Ausstellung der Wiener Secession* ('The Opening of the Vienna Secession's First Exhibition'). 1898, pencil, 34.5 x 45.6 cm. Historisches Museum der Stadt Wien.
From left to right: the emperor's aide-de-camp, Francis Joseph I, Gustav Klimt (president of the Secession), Rudolf von Alt (honorary president), Josef Engelhart, Otto Friedrich, Carl Moll, Adolf Hoelzel, Hans Tichy, Kolo Moser, Joseph Maria Olbrich and Rudolf Jettmar.

footsteps of its German predecessors, *Pan* (1895) and *Jugend* (1896) whose aims it embraced. Like *Pan*, it was intended to appeal to the bibliophile but also, like *Jugend*, to the man in the street. However, its principal purpose was to keep the public informed, in word and picture, of the aims of the Secession, its exhibitions and its attitude to the art of the day as well as to questions involving art and politics. *Ver Sacrum* was the only periodical of its kind to be directly produced by the members of a progressive artists' association.

Little attention has hitherto been devoted to the journal's militancy[12] which found expression in vehement protests, not only against the official promotion of 'Ringstrasse art', but also against the arbitrary award of commissions, regardless of competition results. Another of its manifestations was the avowed intention to gain a new position of strength from which to negotiate with the authorities.

The pictorial section contained, not only illustrations of works of art and of exhibition furnishings, but also numerous examples of the new 'art of the book'. Picture and text, it was felt, must no longer be distinct but must interact. The integration of the two was wholly consistent with the concepts of the 'total work of art' which, both in *Ver Sacrum* and at the Secessionists' exhibitions, was to find expression in this interaction of the various branches of the art concerned.

In an article entitled *Buchschmuck* ('The Decoration of Books'), the German publicist Wilhelm Schölermann takes issue with the earlier, detached mode of illustration. '...I am more than grateful', he writes, 'to any artist who can make me conscious of the obscure feelings which, when I am reading, emerge from the depths of my subconscious mind... Illustration of this kind is absolutely justified... It constitutes, as it were, not only an ornament, an embellishment, but

137 Josef Maria Auchentaller: Border with a poem in *Ver Sacrum*, Vol. 1, No. 7, 1898.
Ver Sacrum, the journal of the Vienna Secession, remained in publication until 1903. Even at this early date attempts were being made to achieve a closer relation between picture and text – in this case between border and poem. As Wilhelm Schölermann remarked in the ninth number, the book designer should be to the poet what 'the harp accompaniment is to the song'.

138 Josef Hoffmann: Cover design for *Ver Sacrum*, Year 2, No. 7, 1899.
The Secession's determination that art should thrive and flourish is symbolized in this architecturally compact foliate design.

VER SACRUM.

Wieder draussen im weiten All
Wird es Frühling.
Mit dem blassen Gold
Der Primeln schmückt sich die Flur;
Der Weissdorn leuchtet,
Es leuchtet die rosige Pfirsichblüte —
Und im ergrünenden Wald
Singt die Drossel.

Aber in stillen,
Geheimnisvoll umzirkten Zaubergärten
Blüht die Kunst.
Dort, in ewigem Sonnenlicht,
Schattenlos überwipfelt,
Hauchen den schweren Duft,
Leuchten in durchsichtiger Irispracht
Weitkelchige Liliaceen und Tulipanen.
Falter, breitflüglig,
Stahlblau und flammenroth,
Umschweben sie,
Und auf des Rasens Smaragd,
Lastenden Silbergefieders,
Schreiten weisse Pfauen. —

Traumhaft,
In zarter, schimmernder Gliederhoheit,
Die Häupter umkränzt mit Blumensternen,
Wandelt ein Menschenpaar.
Sanft aneinander geschmiegt,
Wandelt es auf verschlungener Pfade Windungen
Höher, immer höher hinan —
Bis zum achat'nen Säulenhalbrund,
Das in den Azur des Himmels ragt.
Rubine blitzen, Saphire und Opale
An den gold'nen Capitälen
Und an den goldenen Sockeln.
Auf hundertstufiger,
Weit ausgebuchteter Onyxterrasse
Thront die Sphinx.
Mit marmor'ner Brust,
Doch den geschmeidigen Löwenleib
In jeder Faser glutdurchzittert,
Thront sie,
Grossäugig ins Unendliche blickend,
Über dem Räthselabgrund der Schönheit.

FERDINAND v. SAAR.

also and at the same time a profoundly appropriate allegory in line and colour... The book illustrator is to the writer what the harp accompaniment is to the song.'[13]

It was a field in which *Ver Sacrum* was soon to outstrip its western exemplars. Belgian, Dutch, German and, above all, English influences – William Morris had founded the Kelmscott Press in 1891 – were quickly assimilated and their various tendencies intensified. Josef Maria Auchentaller's floral borders in the Art Nouveau style are much more closely related to the text than the earlier examples by Otto Eckmann in *Pan*. Having familiarized themselves with the abstract ornamentation of the Belgian, Henry van de Velde, Wilhelm List and Ernst Stöhr experi-

mented, each in his own way, with illustrative linear compositions.

At the turn of the century Viennese art tended increasingly to clarify and geometrize the floral forms of Art Nouveau. Thus, in some of his work for *Ver Sacrum*, Moser has recourse to regular square or rectangular forms, which also recur in his and Josef Hoffmann's designs for the Wiener Werkstätte, and exemplify the typically Viennese *Quadratl* style. These workshops were to prove particularly receptive to the influence of Charles Mackintosh and the Glasgow School, as also to that of Dutch book designers.[14]

Ver Sacrum appeared once a month in 1898 and 1899 and thereafter twice a month until it ceased publication in 1903. The final

the connection between Kolo Moser's contribution and the 'expressive dancing' of that time.

141 Kolo Moser: *Liebe* ('Love'). Detail from circular picture, 1895, pen-and-ink, diam. *c.* 30 cm. Historisches Museum der Stadt Wien.

issue contains the admission that, 'by its very nature, the journal could never have enjoyed a large circulation'. No mention is made, however, of the early hopes that it might reach wide sections of the population; indeed, from the very start, such hopes were doomed to disappointment for, as a finely produced 'collector's item', it could not be other than expensive.

The Wiener Werkstätte

The gulf dividing the ideal from the real is even more apparent in the history of the Wiener Werkstätte, whose origins may be traced back to the utopian socialism of John Ruskin and William Morris. Having been founded in 1903 by, amongst others, Josef Hoffmann and Kolo Moser, the Wiener Werkstätte may be regarded as a 'branch house' of the Secession. A perusal of *Ver Sacrum* reveals that both pursued a parallel course in which a predilection for floral forms gradually gave way to geometrical ones. Moreover, the same artists were not infrequently active in both, as the examples of Hoffmann and Moser go to show. For, true to the spirit of the 'total work of art', some of the Secessionists sought to extend their activities to several different branches of art, all of which – as they had learned from the English Arts and Crafts Movement – were of equal value.

Indeed, English influence is particularly noticeable in the period prior to, and contemporaneous with, the existence of the Wiener Werkstätte. As early as 1864, when historicism was in its heyday, the South Kensington Museum in London had served as a model for the Austrian Museum of Art and Industry (now of Applied Art). Following Arthur von Scala's appointment as director in 1897, the dialogue with England, as also with the U.S.A., was intensified. The affiliated School of Arts and Crafts was founded three years after the completion of the museum. By 1899, when Hoffmann, Moser, Alfred Roller and Arthur Strasser joined the teaching staff under the new director, Felician von Myrbach, the historicist generation had largely been superseded.

An example of the early assimilation of English and Scottish influences is the armchair attributed to Joseph Maria Olbrich which, generously proportioned though it is, creates an impression of transparency. The inclusion of pieces from Britain in the Secession's eighth exhibition (1900) intensified the trend towards the geometric and the vertical – elements which, in the work of Kolo Moser and Joseph Hoffmann (particularly in the latter's craftwork) were gradually to oust the sinuous forms of Art Nouveau.

From the beginning, the School of Arts and Crafts was intimately linked with the Wiener Werkstätte, the agent responsible for translating into reality the new concept of the craft product as an essential compo-

nent of an aesthetic world that embraced every aspect of life. In the *Agenda of the Wiener Werkstätte*, drawn up by Moser and Hoffmann and published in 1905,[15] we read:

The hand of the craftsman has been replaced by the machine, the craftsman himself by the business man. To swim against the tide would be madness. Nevertheless, we founded our Werkstätte with the intention of providing, here on our own soil and amid the cheerful din of the workshop, a centre of calm where any devotee of Ruskin and William Morris would be welcome.

Moreover, the democratization of materials is to be achieved by recourse, not only to 'a multitude of semi-precious stones...', thus 'saving the cost of diamonds', but also to 'copper which, in artistic terms, is to us no less valuable than precious metals'. On the other hand, and by way of contrast to industrial book production, use is to be made of 'the best boards', 'the best paper' and 'splendid leather'. The element of contradiction already inherent in the *Agenda* was to dog the Wiener Werkstätte – not to mention *Ver Sacrum* – until the very end, in 1932. Their products, directed at the many, were nevertheless so costly as to be beyond the pockets of all but a few. Thus at the turn of the century the artist craftsmen, and indeed, most other artists, were working almost solely for the benefit of the upper class, the progressive cultural *élite* of the elegant Hietzing and Hohe Warte districts.

Craft manufacture was seen, not as an occasional source of individual pieces, but rather as part of a whole which, ideally,

142 Josef Hoffmann (made by J. J. Kohn): Arm-chair ('sitting machine'). C. 1905, beech, stained mahogany, plywood boards, brass frame, 110 x 62 x 83 cm. H. (of seat) 26 cm. Private collection. Hoffmann made his mark chiefly as an interior designer. He also designed furniture and craft articles.

143 Joseph Maria Olbrich (ascription): *Armlehnensessel* ('Arm-chair'). 1898, solid maple, upholstered in cloth, 109 x 58 cm, 5 x 52 cm. Private collection. The chair (made by Josef Niedermoser) comes from the Vienna apartment of the actress Maria Wölzl. Here we have an early example of the influence exerted by British designers following Arthur von Scalas's appointment as director of the Austrian Museum of Art and Industry in 1897. (Christian Witt-Dörring.)

144 Kolo Moser (made by Portois & Fix, Vienna): Büffet, 'Der reiche Fischzug' ('Sideboard, "Rich Haul of Fish"'). 1900, maple, mahogany and cherry-wood, brass mountings, legs mounted in brass, 180 x 167 x 69 cm. Österreichisches Museum für angewandte Kunst, Vienna. In *Acht Jahre Secession* (Vienna, 1906, p. 207), Hevesi wrote: 'The sideboard, of which the carcase is enlivened by oblique planes in vertical intarsia panels on a blackish ground, bears Moser's celebrated trout motif, reciprocally disposed in his favourite manner so that light and dark set the scene for the above-mentioned processes.'

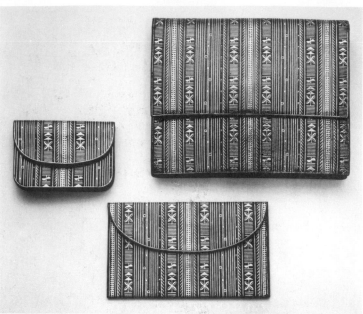

145 Kolo Moser (made by E. Ba-
kalowitz): Glass jug, Vienna,
1899–1900, H. 15.5 cm. Private
collection.

146 Josef Hoffmann, handbag,
purse and card-case. 1911, black
grain leather embossed in gold;
card-case: 8 x 13 cm. Österreichisches Museum für angewandte Kunst, Vienna.
After Kolo Moser, Josef Hoffmann was the Wiener Werk-
stätte's chief proponent of
geometrization and simplification.

147 Josef Hoffmann: Tea service.
Wiener Werkstätte, 1905.
Brass with wood handles, H. (of
samovar) 24 cm. Private collection.

148 Gustav Klimt: sketch design
for 'Philosophy'. 1900, black
chalk and pencil on squared paper,
89.6 x 63.2 cm. Historisches Museum der Stadt Wien.
'Philosophy' was the first of
Klimt's university paintings to be
rejected by the faculty members,
many of whom, caring little or
nothing for art, had been outraged
by what they regarded as the
disproportionate significance accorded to 'World Enigma', the
powerful figure on the right, as
compared with that of
'Knowledge' (bottom right).

would embrace every branch of art. It was
an ideal more easily realized on a comparatively small scale, as for example in
private houses, apartments, offices and exhibition rooms, for the larger – and more official – the scale, the greater the difficulties
became. Only two examples of large-scale
'total works of art' still survive as witnesses
to Viennese Art Nouveau, namely Josef
Hoffmann's Palais Stoclet in Brussels
(1905–11), fitted out by members of the
Wiener Werkstätte, and Otto Wagner's
Steinhof church (1904–8) with windows by
Kolo Moser and sculpture by Othmar
Schimkowitz.

Gustav Klimt

A great but uncompleted project was that
of Klimt's university paintings which,
moreover, vanished during the Second
World War. These Faculty pictures, designed for a public building in the
Ringstrasse, gave rise to a struggle between
Klimt and the powers that be. For seven
years he was subjected to a martyrdom comparable only to that of the Swiss artist Ferdinand Hodler and the Norwegian Edvard
Munch, both of whom similarly clashed
with the authorities.

In his designs for the Faculty pictures,
Philosophy and *Medicine,* Klimt gave expression, in the form of large, upward-drifting
groups of figures, to the primary questions
of mankind. In *Jurisprudence,* on the other
hand, which stands in line of succession to
the Beethoven frieze, the figures are more
economically disposed. The caption to
Philosophy in the catalogue of the seventh
Secession exhibition reads: 'Left-hand
group of figures: Genesis, Fruitful Existence, Evanescence. Right: The Globe of
the World, the Riddle of the World. Below
there rises up a luminous figure, Knowledge.' *Ver Sacrum* explains the design for
'Medicine' in the following terms: 'Between
becoming and evanescence life runs its
course, and it is life itself that... creates the
ills for which Aesculapius's daughter
Hygieia has, with her miraculous powers,
discovered the palliatives and remedies.'[16]

Attacks in the press, in particular a con-
certed campaign by presumptuous pro-
fessors whose indignation, moral or otherwise, had been aroused by the scheme, finally led to its abandonment.

The Beethoven frieze, a monumental
work by Klimt, has been preserved, though
not originally intended to survive. It was
painted for the Secession's fourteenth exhibition as one of the association's contributions to the setting of the statue of
Beethoven by Max Klinger. In this boldly
conceived frieze, Klimt sets out to depict a
symphony of life in which man's sufferings,
miseries and longings find redemption in
art. Embodiments of good and evil en-
counter him on his path to perfection. In the
last panel, a pair of lovers reflect the spirit of
Beethoven's Ninth Symphony, the 'kiss of
the whole world'. Dividing Beethoven's
time from that of Klimt were Schopen-
hauer's and Nietzsche's reflections on the
redemptive powers of art.

Discernible in Klimt's Stoclet frieze, executed not long afterwards, is a thematically
less elaborate version of the monumental
concept which found expression in the Beet-

149 Gustav Klimt: *Bildnis Emilie Flöge* ('Portrait of Emilie Flöge'). 1902, oil on canvas, 181 x 84 cm. Historisches Museum der Stadt Wien.
Emilie Flöge was the owner of an exclusive dress shop in the Mariahilfer Strasse, the interior fittings of which were designed by Josef Hoffmann. This portrait of Klimt's life-long love is the earliest example of that artist's ornamental style.

150 Gustav Klimt: *Beethovenfries, 'Die feindlichen Gewalten'* ('Beethoven frieze, "The Hostile Powers"'). 1902, casein paint, 214 x 636 cm.
The frieze was painted in the left aisle of the hall of the Secession building on the occasion of the fourteenth exhibition there. Its theme is Beethoven's Ninth Symphony, as also the redeeming power of art generally. In the portion shown here are allegories of the hostile powers that oppose the redemption of mankind.

hoven frieze. In the allegories of the Powers of Good ('The Strong, Well-armed Man', 'Pity', 'Poetry', and 'The Kiss'), Klimt penetrates into the religious dimension, thus transcending the decorative which, in the allegories of suffering and the Hostile Powers ('Gorgons', 'Sickness', 'Madness', 'Death'), itself becomes a means of expression. 'In the female figures of the "Hostile Powers"', Marian Bizanz-Prakken writes, 'Klimt made full use of his decorative and stylistic virtuosity in giving expression to what is at one and the same time evil and yet seductive.'[17]

It was, indeed, these same 'Hostile Powers' which drew down upon their author the special virulence of the conservative press. Hermann Bahr collected a number of such pronouncements from which he formed an anthology entitled *Gegen Klimt (Anti-Klimt)*. One extract reads: '...Suitable as these paintings might be for a den of vice, the scene of pagan orgies, they are utterly inappropriate in [exhibition] rooms to which the artists have been bold enough to invite respectable matrons and young girls.' The same critic goes on to speak of 'the infamous way in which the noble human frame is caricatured.'[18]

Ludwig Hevesi, on the other hand, a well-intentioned critic and chronicler of the Secession, wrote:

> The left-hand aisle contains a delightful frieze painting by Gustav Klimt, so replete with his bold, autocratic personality that we have to restrain ourselves from calling it his best work. If, like all the rest of the exhibition, it is doomed to destruction when that event is over, a masterwork will have been sent up in smoke upon Beethoven's altar.[19]

Egon Schiele also intervened in an effort to save the frieze which was eventually removed from the wall. In 1973 the paintings were acquired by the state and are at present being restored.

In 1903 Klimt spent some time in Ravenna where he made a study of the mosaics, a study which, in his so-called 'golden style' (a phase that ended about 1910), led him to place in-

creasing emphasis on decorative monumentality. One of the most important works of this period is the icon-like oil-painting, *Der Kuss* ('The Kiss'), in which the loving couple of the Stoclet and Beethoven friezes embrace one another on a flower-strewn knoll, their bodies towering towards a starry sky.

The mosaic panel executed by the Wiener Werkstätte in the dining-room of the Palais Stoclet in Brussels (1905–9) also belongs to the period of Klimt's 'golden style'. Here a love poem is rendered in the language of ornament. A lone figure of a girl ('Expectation') confronts an embracing couple ('Fulfilment'). In a golden thicket of scrollwork, the human figures, whose activities have been translated into the universal, acquire a monumental calm.

151 Gustav Klimt: *Kopfstudie für den Beethovenfries* ('Study of head for the Beethoven frieze'). *C.* 1902, black chalk, 43.5 x 32 cm. Historisches Museum der Stadt Wien.

152 Gustav Klimt: *Der Kuss* ('The Kiss'). 1907–8, oil on canvas, 180 x 180 cm. Österreichische Galerie, Vienna.
The picture is one of the most important works done in Klimt's 'golden style' and reflects the hieratic severity of the mosaics at Ravenna which the artist visited in 1903. Here the theme of love is raised to the plane of the sacred and cosmic.

153   Alfred Roller: Poster for the Secession's fourteenth (Beethoven) exhibition. 1902, coloured lithograph, 95.5 x 63 cm. Historisches Museum der Stadt Wien.
The focal point of this important exhibition was Max Klinger's statue of Beethoven, though the influence of Klimt's frieze was to prove more enduring.

154   Max Kurzweil: Poster for the Secession's seventeenth exhibition. 1903, coloured lithograph, 95.5 x 31.5 cm. Historisches Museum der Stadt Wien.

155   Friedrich König: Poster for the twenty-first exhibition. 1904, coloured lithograph, 95.5 x 63 cm. Historisches Museum der Stadt Wien.

156   Adolf Boehm: *Landschaft* ('Landscape'). 1901, oil on canvas, 100 x 84 cm. Historisches Museum der Stadt Wien.
As in the case of Kandinsky, Kupka and Hoelzel, our example demonstrates the susceptibility of the ornamental idiom of *fin de siècle* art to autonomous experiments in which form, having evolved its own laws, can be condensed into a new kind of landscape.

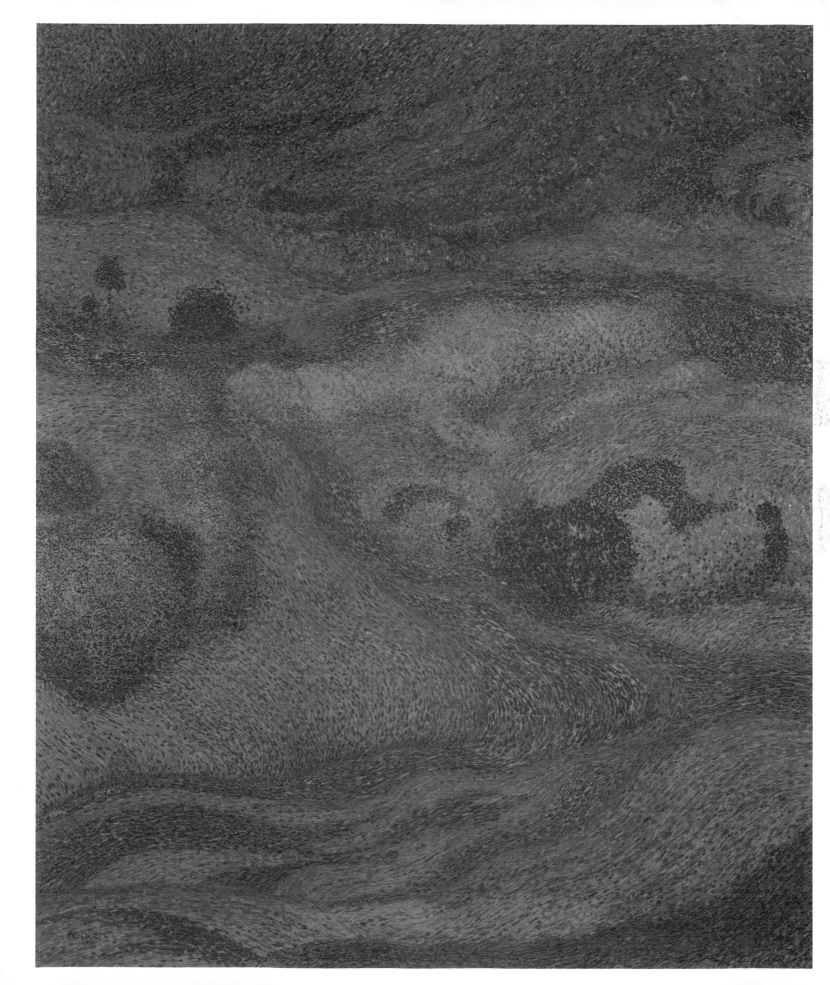

Of this work Max Eisler wrote that 'seen in the context of Klimt's œuvre, it implies a loss of monumental freedom and size, a retreat to the material limitations of craftwork, but also and at the same time, it implies for Viennese craftwork an unprecedented sublimation and refinement.'[20] The somewhat resigned tone of Eisler's opening words is wholly attuned to the situation in which Klimt found himself after the rejection of his designs by the university.

Stylists and naturalists

In 1905 that artist, together with other 'stylists' such as Auchentaller, Boehm, Hoffmann, Moser and Roller, resigned from the Secession on the grounds that they could no longer be associated with the more realistic 'naturalists' who refused to commit themselves to the 'total work of art'. Known as the Klimt Group, they held their exhibitions in 1908 and 1909, in the Kunstschau, a temporary pavilion built by Josef Hoff-

mann on the site later occupied by the Konzerthaus. It was there, and not in the Secession building, that *The Kiss* was exhibited in 1908.

In the same year a pageant was held in honour of the sixtieth anniversary of Francis Joseph's accession to the throne. The architectural features were designed by Joseph Urban, and the costumes (for historical and folklore tableaux) by Heinrich Lefler, Berthold Löffler, Remigius Geyling and Oskar Kokoschka. Thanks to the Kunstschau and the aforementioned pageant, 1908 represents a high-water mark in the decorative phase of late Art Nouveau, as exemplified in the work of the Vienna Pottery, founded in 1905, and the drawings of C.O. Czeschka and of Berthold Löffler. The influence of these and other like-minded artists was to persist until the outbreak of war in 1914.

The waning of historicism, and the consequent lowering of barriers between the various branches of art, detracted from the role of the monumental sculptor who, round about the turn of the century, found

157 Ferdinand Andri: *Butterbäuerin* ('Butter-Maker'). 1901, coloured lithograph, 15.7 x 16.2 cm. Historisches Museum der Stadt Wien.

158 Max Kurzweil: *Der Polster* ('The Cushion'). 1903, coloured woodcut, 28.6 x 25.9 cm. Historisches Museum der Stadt Wien.
'The Cushion' can, perhaps, be described as the most popular work of this notable Art Nouveau artist.

159 Max Kurzweil: *Dame in gelbem Kleid* ('Lady in Yellow Dress'). 1899, oil on canvas, 171.5 x 171.5 cm. Historisches Museum der Stadt Wien. Kurzweil was a founder member of the Secession, and this picture appeared in the association's fourth exhibition. A typical early example of Viennese Art Nouveau, it still betrays the influence of the 'floral period'.

136

160 Josef Hoffmann (?): Door panel. *C.* 1905, wood, mother of pearl, intarsia. Historisches Museum der Stadt Wien.

161 Michael Powolny: *Zwei Putten, 'Frühling' und 'Sommer'* ('Two Putti, "Spring" and "Summer"'). 1908, faience, H. 37.5 cm. Österreichisches Museum für angewandte Kunst, Vienna (contemporary photograph). Berthold Löffler and Michael Powolny were the leading lights of the Wiener Keramik (Vienna Pottery), founded in 1905. The fruits of their collaboration – and there are many of them – reveal the progress of Viennese Art Nouveau from the ethereally delicate to the robustly jocund.

162 Josef Hoffmann: Goblet. 1920–5, Wiener Werkstätte, H. 31.5 cm. Historisches Museum der Stadt Wien.

163 Ladies' Shoes. C. 1914,
Wiener Werkstätte, colour printed
rep. Fashion Collections,
Historisches Museum der Stadt
Wien.

164 Goblet. 1919, Wiener
Werkstätte, white glass, painted,
H. 20.8 cm. Historisches Museum
der Stadt Wien.

165 Carl Otto Czeschka:
Ex libris Emma Bacher, 1909.
During the first decade of the
twentieth century, the delicate
female figures of Viennese Art
Nouveau increasingly gave way to
cheerful putti like those by
Powolny in Plate 161, or again to
the previously unsung charms of
maidens whose Amazonian
qualities derive from Diana rather
than Aphrodite.

himself compelled to forfeit to the craftsman many of the assignments that would otherwise have come his way. Moreover, the dematerialization and two-dimensionality then being advocated by 'stylist' architects, painters and graphic artists ran wholly counter to the essentially three-dimensional nature of the sculptor's art.

In consequence of this trend, sculptors dwindled in number. Among the founding members of the Secession there were only two such artists, who were later joined by one other, Richard Luksch. Other sculptors, though by no means inimical to Art Nouveau, chose to remain in the Künstlerhaus, amongst them Carl Wollek, the subtle delicacy of whose design for the Mozart fountain (1905) earned him the commission, in preference to his Secessionist competitor, Luksch.

Some of the Secessionist painters and graphic artists, for instance Josef Engelhart and Ferdinand Andri, were also practising sculptors, though of the 'naturalist' rather than the 'stylist' persuasion. From the dual nature of their activities it may be supposed that the concept of the 'total work of art' was not altogether foreign to them. But adhering as they did to materiality, they saw little to interest them in the two-dimensional art of their stylist *confrères*.

Though the Secession still retained a fair quota of talented artists, its quality was undoubtedly impaired, not only by the defection of the Klimt group, but also by the consequent severing of its links with the Wiener Werkstätte and the School of Arts and Crafts. Together with these institutions, the Klimt group continued to display, in the Kunstschau exhibitions of 1908 and 1909, the kind of art that was designed to appeal almost exclusively to the upper classes. Before long, however, some of the younger members – for instance Oskar Kokoschka and Egon Schiele – began to look for new modes of expression.

166 Berthold Löffler: Poster for *Die Fledermaus* ('The Bat'), a theatre and cabaret. 1907, lithograph, 63 x 43.5 cm. Historisches Museum der Stadt Wien.
In September 1907 a theatre and cabaret by the name of *Die Fledermaus* was opened in the Kärntnerstrasse. The fittings, designed by Josef Hoffmann, were made by the Wiener Werkstätte. Among those who wrote plays for the theatre were Peter Altenberg, Hermann Bahr, Franz Blei and Hanns Heinz Ewers.

167 Anton Klieber: *Uhr* ('Clock'). C. 1910, faience, H. 28 cm. Österreichisches Museum für angewandte Kunst, Vienna.
An example of the consolidation and clarification of both ornament and basic shape. Geometrization in pottery – here somewhat understated – was accompanied by a growing trend towards the uncompromising use of black and white.

168 Carl Otto Czeschka: *Die Nibelungen*. 1909. Text by Franz Keim. Verlag Gerlach & Wiedling, Vienna–Leipzig. After the series *Gerlach's Jugendbücherei*, Vol. 22. The influence of these courtly and decorative, yet highly expressive, illustrations has been manifold and long-lasting, being still discernible in Fritz Lang's film of the same name.

169 Wilhelm Bernatzik: *Eingang zum Paradies* ('Entrance to Paradise'). 1903–4, oil on canvas, centre panel: 147 x 150 cm, side panels: 147 x 38 cm. Private collection, Munich.
This triptych appeared in the Secession's twentieth exhibition. It is a notable example of the important role played by religion in the art of that time.

140

9

38

170 Berthold Löffler: Postcard for the Adria Exhibition. 1913. During the latter phase of Viennese Art Nouveau, when putti were coming increasingly into vogue within the movement, mythological allusions tended to be treated in a light-hearted manner. Here a water-sprite is asserting its right to an element customarily assigned in mythology to women.

171 Carl Wollek: *Grabmal für die 1911 in Wien verstorbene Adrienne Neumann* ('Memorial to Adrienne Neumann, who died in Vienna in 1911'). 1912, bronze sarcophagus, 244 x 130 x 144 cm, H. (of figure) 172 cm. Historisches Museum der Stadt Wien.
The Neumann memorial, designed by one of Vienna's most important Art Nouveau sculptors, betrays the influence of Italian Renaissance models.

142

172 Carl Wollek: *Mozartbrunnen* ('Mozart Fountain'). 1905, Vienna, 4th District.
Like other sculptors, who saw in the Secession's espousal of the two-dimensional in art a threat to those who worked in three dimensions, Wollek remained faithful to the Künstlerhaus. However, in his subtle modelling of figures, in which the influence of Rodin and Minne is plainly revealed, he has much in common with the Secessionists.

173 Franz Barwig (the Elder):
Sitzender Bär ('Seated Bear').
C. 1905, wood, H. 60 cm.
Historisches Museum der Stadt
Wien.

175   Ferdinand Andri: *Erzengel Michael* ('The Archangel Michael'). 1905.
Like Josef Engelhart Andri was first and foremost a painter and graphic artist. His angel, executed for Josef Plečnik's Zacherl House (cf. Pl. 221) built between 1903 and 1905, occupies a prominent position on the façade. Its formal rigour harmonizes convincingly with the austerity of the architecture.

174   Josef Engelhart (sculptor), Josef Plečnik (architect): *Karl Borromäus-Brunnen* ('Karl Borromäus Fountain'). 1909, Vienna, 3rd District.
Above the figures of putti, a scene from the life of the saint depicts the Plague in Milan.

176 Carl Moll: *Winter* (Hohe Warte, Vienna). 1903, coloured woodcut, 42.6 x 43 cm. Historisches Museum der Stadt Wien.
This woodcut appeared in the *Jahresmappe der Gesellschaft für vervielfältigende Kunst.* The villas put up by Josef Hoffmann on the Hohe Warte must be numbered among his most important early architectural works.

177 Wilhelm Bernatzik: *Sommernacht* ('Summer Night'). 1899, coloured lithograph, 24.7 x 40.3 cm. Historisches Museum der Stadt Wien.
This folio appeared as a supplement to the first number of the journal *Ver Sacrum.*

178 Maximilian Lenz: *Herbst* ('Autumn'). 1898, coloured lithograph, 20.1 x 19.6 cm. Historisches Museum der Stadt Wien.

147

The Hagenbund

Mention has already been made of the important part played in the Secession's antecedents by a group of artists known as the Hagengesellschaft. Most of its members left the Künstlerhaus at the same time as the Secessionists, from whom they were in turn to part company three years later with the founding of the Künstlerbund Hagen, better known as the Hagenbund, a society which, from modest beginnings, was to acquire ever greater authority. Among its founders, special mention should be made of the painter and graphic artist Heinrich Lefler and his brother-in-law, the architect Joseph Urban. Like the Secession, the Hagenbund had at first intended to remain within the Künstlerhaus as a 'state within a state' but, in the event, had left that institution in November 1900, nine months after its own inception.

Accordingly, the first two Hagenbund exhibitions were mounted in the Künstlerhaus, while the third was held in the Miethke Gallery. From January 1902 the society exhibited in a market-hall in the Zedlitzgasse, adapted to their requirements by Joseph Urban.[21] Above the entrance to the (no longer extant) building, Wilhelm Hejda's polychrome relief, *Pallas Athene als Beschützerin der Künste* ('Pallas Athene as Patroness of the Arts'), vividly recalls the early days of the Secession. Indeed, at this stage the Hagenbund displayed distinct stylistic tendencies. But whereas the Secession had drawn its regular customers mainly from upper-class districts, the new-comers, faced with an already saturated market, endeavoured from the outset to appeal to those sections of the public who, though of less exclusive provenance, were now likewise beginning to take an interest in Art Nouveau. In particular the Hagenbund addressed itself to the younger generation, notably in the field of illustration. Thus during those early years the seeds were already being sown of what would later be extreme avant-garde views.

One outward manifestation of the difference between the Secession and the Hagenbund is the presentation of early Hagenbund catalogues, whose covers, though similarly decorated with ornamental motifs, are a good deal less lavish than those of the association. The influence of folk art is clearly discernible in the society's approach to book decoration, especially in the illustrations to the celebrated series, *Gerlach's Jugendbücherei*, the joint work of the founder members, Lefler and Urban (of

179 Hans Ranzoni: Poster for the Fifth Hagenbund Exhibition, Vienna. 1902, coloured lithograph, 52 x 36.5 cm.
Despite affinities in the decorative formal idiom, the fairy-tale wood, the magical realm of Hagenbund art, displays fewer mythological overtones than does the symbolism of the Secessionists.

148

whom the first drew the figures, the second the architectural features and decorative borders), as well as Fahringer. The element of folklore and fairy-tale in these illustrations is reflected in the design of the society's exhibition catalogues and posters. As an example we might cite Hans Ranzoni's 'Fairy Wood', announcing the fifth exhibition in 1902.

Even before the founding of the Hagenbund, Lefler and Urban had adopted and elaborated English models as, for instance, in the illustrations to *Rolands Knappen* ('Roland's Pages') by Musäus (about 1897)

or, again, in the allegorical 'Playing Cards', which reveals the influence of Beardsley's work in its more scurrilous aspects. Indeed the society's decorative sensibility tended, not so much towards the mythological and religious, as towards narrative, caricature and humour.

Another painter and illustrator of considerable repute was Oskar Laske, whose narrative invention even then invited comparison with Pieter Brueghel the Elder.[22] For his motifs, Laske turned not only to literature, but also and with increasing frequency to the realistic if unusual folklore of the Orient and of the Monarchy's more distant provinces.

Popular humour and caricature were also employed by this group as a political weapon. When, for example, the Municipality in 1912 refused to renew their lease of the hall in the Zedlitzgasse, Otto Barth designed a catalogue whose cover left no room for doubt as to the quandary in which this had placed the Hagenbund. For the next seven or eight years the now homeless society had perforce to hold its exhibitions elsewhere, for the most part in the Secession building. In 1920, however, it was able to return to the original premises where it remained until its dissolution in 1938.

To the avant-garde upper-class *élite,* the decorative tendencies of the Secession, the Kunstschau and the Wiener Werkstätte stood for emancipation from the official world of the Ringstrasse. At the same time those tendencies were conducive to the establishment of new cultural conventions which became comprehensible to the eye in the context of the 'total work of art' and, on a higher plane, in the construction of a mythologically determined conceptual world. The liberating elements of this trend were taken over and elaborated by the Hagenbund, although the new impulse which led artists to concentrate on the untrammelled individuality of man was eventually to come from Expressionism.

At the same time the Secession's Impressionist Exhibition (1903), which also included works by Toulouse-Lautrec and van Gogh, their Hodler and Munch exhibition (1904), and the van Gogh exhibition in the

180 Otto Barth: Cover for a Hagenbund exhibition catalogue. 1912.
The felling of the tree of art is an allusion to the plight of the association in 1912, after the Vienna Municipality had refused to renew the lease of the Zedlitzhalle, where they held their exhibitions.

Miethke Gallery (1906), provided similar impulses, the influence of which is clearly discernible in the works of Richard Gerstl, Oskar Kokoschka and Egon Schiele.

Richard Gerstl

Being older than the other two Austrian artists, Gerstl is more likely to have seen some of these exhibitions. We shall discuss him first since, in formal terms, his highly idiosyncratic work developed very rapidly and placed him ahead of his time. He studied at the Academy, first under the Ringstrasse painter, Christian Griepenkerl and, later, under Heinrich Lefler, after which he completed his training with the Hungarian artist Holosy in Nagy-Banya. His entire output was confined to the two years preceding his death in 1908.

At the outset he employed a mosaic-like technique which still betrays the influence of pointillism and Art Nouveau. But his progress towards dynamic violence was to induce a clean break with all forms of systematization. In defiance of the decorative principles which still governed the artistic climate of his day, Gerstl cast aside the trappings of external beauty and plunged headlong into dissonance. Divorced from ornament, he pursued an independent course towards abstraction, characterized, on the one hand, by a disruption of form far exceeding the subtle Impressionist dissolution of contours and, on the other, by the vehemence of the now almost autonomous brush-strokes.

A loner, Gerstl never joined an association. His personal intercourse was confined – as is also apparent from his portrait studies – to Alexander von Zemlinsky and the group of musicians around Arnold Schoenberg. What is new in this artist is expressed in his technique as such, upon which neither traditional reasoning nor a consideration of his choice of subjects – portraits and landscapes – can shed any further light. His fundamental outlook is comprehensible only in terms of his personal handwriting or, as Werner Hofmann puts it:

Peculiar to this form of Expressionism is the fact that it tends neither to metaphysics nor to social criticism. Loneliness and despair, conflicts and tormented attitudes – these will be sought for in vain… Gerstl's creative impulse probably sprang from his questioning of the world and the permanence of things – doubts which the act of painting seems to be desperately combating. It was from that desperation that he drew the strength to approach the world positively, through the medium of colour.[23]

Oskar Kokoschka

Gerstl's friend, Schoenberg, to whom he gave lessons on painting, was acquainted with the architect Adolf Loos, and he in turn with Karl Kraus, Peter Altenberg and Oskar Kokoschka. It was at the Kunstschau in 1908 that Loos first became aware of Kokoschka's talent and his original and vigorous mode of expression. He encouraged the young artist, who had been trained in the School of Arts and Crafts, to leave the decorative ambience of the Wiener Werkstätte for which he had been designing fans and postcards. In addition Kokoschka had been responsible for some of the traditional and historical costumes worn on the occasion of the imperial jubilee for which he had also produced a poster (in the event rejected). At first sight, it may seem surprising that Loos, as an architect and ardent advocate of structural clarity, should have expressed admiration for Kokoschka whose chief characteristic – at first mainly as a poet – was his dynamic intensification of forms. Common to both men, however, was the rejection of ornament and the affirmation of functionalism in the arts and crafts. Loos was convinced that, for the architect as for the painter, functionalism implied an awareness of human problems. 'Imagine', he demands of painters, 'the moment of birth and death, the screams of an injured son, a mother's death-rattle, the last thoughts of a dying daughter – and then imagine all this going on in one of Olbrich's bedrooms!'[24]

181 Richard Gerstl: *Die Schwestern* ('The Sisters'). 1904–5, oil on canvas, 175 x 150 cm. Österreichische Galerie, Vienna. According to the sisters Karoline and Pauline Fey, Gerstl painted the picture for inclusion in his portfolio when seeking admission to Heinrich Lefler's master class at the Academy of Fine Arts.

That such themes should be liberated from formal decorative convention was a demand more readily met by Kokoschka than was the requirement that they be disassociated from mythology. It was with words – in his poetic work *Die träumenden Knaben* ('The Dreaming Boys') – that he first began to destroy the aethereal world of Art Nouveau, though vestiges of that world are still apparent in his illustrations, despite the greater harshness and angularity of the forms. By contrast, the illustrations (1909) to his play *Mörder, Hoffnung der Frauen* ('Murderer, Hope of Women'), match the violence of the text, for what were originally ornamental forms here acquire a new function, being welded into a whole by a vigorous and dynamic use of line.

More remote influences, now barely discernible, are the ancient mythological texts which, along with the Viennese Art Nouveau tradition, led him to study, in particular, Johann Jakob Bachofen's *Matriarchat*. Thus, the struggle between the sexes in *Murderer, Hope of Women* reflects the struggle between the male, solar principle and the female, lunar forces. Seen from this viewpoint, the problems surrounding love and death acquired a new significance. It was to Robert Briffault, a disciple of Bachofen's, that he owed 'the Greek interpretation of the "stuff as dreams are made on", Eros and Thanatos'.[25] Fascinated by the danger of the female lunar aspect, which also reabsorbs life, he produced works in which Eros is eclipsed by Thanatos, among them *Stilleben mit Hammel und Hyazinthe* ('Still Life with Wether and Hyacinth') (1909), a symbol of 'soundless disintegration'.[26]

What is new about Kokoschka's mythology, as compared with Klimt's Beethoven frieze and university paintings, is an even closer identification with vital and often personal human problems. At the same time it is a mythology whose immediate expression is no longer committed to the supremacy of beauty but which, now freed from convention, also lays bare all the forces of hatred and destruction.

The autobiographical element in the illustrations to his play *Der gefesselte Kolumbus* ('Columbus in Chains') (1912–13) is of

182   Richard Gerstl: *Selbstbildnis mit Palette* ('Self-Portrait with Palette'). *C.* 1907, oil on canvas, 186.5 x 58.5 cm. Historisches Museum der Stadt Wien.
Although untrained, Richard Gerstl was an exceptionally talented painter whose work was well in advance of its time. It was not until several decades had gone by that his pictures were rediscovered and at last given their due.

183   Richard Gerstl: *Liechtenstein-palais im 9. Wiener Gemeinde-bezirk* ('Liechtenstein Palace in the 9th District'). *C.* 1907, oil on canvas, 55.5 x 69 cm. Historisches Museum der Stadt Wien.
View from the artist's studio.

the lunatic girl OK

184 Oskar Kokoschka: *The Lunatic Girl. C. 1909*, pencil and water-colour, 41 x 31 cm. Historisches Museum der Stadt Wien.
This may possibly be a portrait of the dancer Bessie Bruce, who was a friend of Adolf Loos, the architect.

185 Oskar Kokoschka: *Die Träumenden Knaben, Das Mädchen Li und ich* ('The Dreaming Boys, The Girl Li and Myself'). 1908, coloured lithograph, 24 x 29 cm. One of the eight illustrations to the poem 'The Dreaming Boys' published by the Wiener Werkstätte. In the text Kokoschka employs a disjointed, if expressive and incantatory language, while in the illustrations his powers of imagination have created an all-embracing dream world, an image of the exotic extending far beyond the compass of European folklore.

ich greife in den see und
tauche in deinen haaren/
wie ein versonnener bin
ich in der liebe alles wesens/
und wieder fiel ich nieder
und träumte/
zu viel hitze überkam mich
in der nacht/ da in den wäl-
dern die paarende schlange
ihre haut streicht unter dem
heißen stein und der wasser-
hirsch reibt sein gehörn
an den zimmtstauden/ als
ich den moschus des tieres
roch in allen niedrigen
sträuchern/
es ist fremd um mich/ je-
mand sollte antworten/
alles läuft nach seinen ei-
genen fährten/ und die
singenden mücken über-
zittern die schreie/
wer denkt grinsende götter-
gesichter und fragt den sing-
sang der zauberer und alt-
männer/ wenn sie die boot-
fahrer begleiten/ welche
frauen holen/
und ich war ein kriechend
ding/ als ich die tiere suchte
und mich zu ihnen hielt/
kleiner/ was wolltest du
hinter den alten/ als du die
gottzauberer aufsuchtest/
und ich war ein taumelnder/
als ich mein fleisch er-
kannte/
und ein allesliebender/ als
ich mit einem mädchen
sprach/

dieses buch wurde geschrie-
ben und gezeichnet von
Oskar Kokoschka/ verlegt
von der wiener werkstätte/
gedruckt in den offizinen
Berger und Chwala/ 1908

186 Oskar Kokoschka: *Plakatentwurf zum Kaiser-Jubiläums-Huldigungsfestzug* ('Design for a poster for the Imperial Jubilee'). Vienna 1908, tempera on board, 134 x 92 cm. Historisches Museum der Stadt Wien. Kokoschka was one of the many artists who designed posters for the Imperial Jubilee. The one reproduced here was probably exhibited in the Kunstschau's poster room.

187 Oskar Kokoschka: *Skizzen zur Winzergruppe* ('Sketches for a Group of Vintagers'). 1908, pencil, ink, water- und body colours, 31.8 x 45 cm, much annotated. These are sketches for costumes to be worn by some of those taking part in a procession on the occasion of the Imperial Jubilee.

188 Oskar Kokoschka: *Stilleben mit Hammel und Hyazinthe* ('Still Life with Wether and Hyacinth'). 1909, oil on canvas, 87 x 114 cm. Österreichische Galerie, Vienna. Dr Oskar Reichel, the Viennese collector, had invited Kokoschka to the Feast of the Passover, in preparation for which a lamb had been slaughtered. The ritual provided the inspiration for this allegory on man's impermanence.

particular significance, since the all-powerful Moon Woman of the text has been given the features of Alma Mahler. The stormy love affair between Gustav Mahler's widow and the artist is immortalized in his monumental oil-painting, *Die Windsbraut* ('Bride of the Wind') (1914). While the intensity of the lived experience is conveyed by the dynamic brushwork, there is a cosmic quality about the treatment of the figures which recalls Klimt's *The Kiss,* painted six years earlier.

Egon Schiele

Like Kokoschka (four years his senior), Egon Schiele was at first much influenced, not only by the tradition of Viennese Art Nouveau, but also by the work of Hodler, van Gogh and the Belgian sculptor George Minne. Unlike Kokoschka, however, he at once set about demythologizing the conceptual world. What chiefly concerned him were love, life and death. However, these problems, central to man's existence, were presented out of context with an immediacy and candour which, notably in his erotic pictures, were taken to the point of provocativeness and exhibitionism. No doubt it was the polarity between life and death that, in the same year (1911), led Schiele to produce works which reveal a vital intensification of forms, for example, his *Selbstbildnis* ('Self-Portrait'), and others in which (not without reminiscences of Klimt) sleep and trance-like states lead away from life.

Free experimentation during the years 1913 and 1914 brought Schiele very close to Cubism, yet at the same time, unlike Kokoschka (let alone Gerstl), his work still retains to some extent what were the predominantly graphic principles of Art Nouveau, whose sinuous lines thus recur, if in a different context (1911–12, 1917–18). An avant-garde feature of his art, and one that transcends experimentation, is the humanist commitment to which the works are subordinated. Under the influence of Nietzsche, Rimbaud and Whitman, he champions, in letters and poems, the cause

of individual freedom as opposed to official collectivism, while love and friendship, freely entered into, are the only ties he is prepared to countenance. In a letter to Arthur Roessler, a critic, writer and friend, he impugns all those who, as he believes, obstruct the free development of the individual, 'perpetual uniform-wearers..., officials, teachers..., parsons, conformists, nationalists, patriots'.[27] The desired goal, 'to be oneself', he equated with life; conformists, the uniformed enforcers of bourgeois convention and dogmas, with non-life.

Thanks to Roessler's good offices, Schiele also did work for Franz Pfemfert, editor of the Berlin periodical *Die Aktion* which, by reason of its critical attitude in social matters and its uncompromising stand against militarism and war, was far more radical than Herwarth Walden's *Der Sturm* to which Kokoschka contributed.

That an artist, venturing into new realms of freedom, is liable to suffer is underlined in Schiele's poster 'Self-Portrait as St Sebastian'. It recalls the passage from *Thus Spake Zarathustra* in which Nietzsche writes: 'Yet he who, by his act of creation, has achieved self-mastery finds himself confronted by the Pharisees. For what they hate most is the creative man, he who shatters the tablets and the old values. That man they call a criminal.'

The trauma of the First World War lent topicality to the Expressionist theme of man's universality. The horror of those years led many artists to make an intensive record of their experiences. Thus the narrative invention of Oskar Laske in his portfolio 'Faust Impressions' (1919) culminates in a Walpurgisnacht, or witches' sabbath, that bears the unmistakable imprint of the war. In his work, *Der brennende Mensch* ('The Burning Man') (1922), Anton Hanak relates Schiele's subject-matter to concrete events, and portrays the intensity of life which, 'burning from within', is exposed to the threat of destruction from without.

While *Die Spieler* ('The Gamblers') by Robert Pajer-Gartegen, a member of the Hagenbund (1920), still displays Expressionist features, such as the stark contrast between black and white, and the tense at-

189 Oskar Kokoschka: *Die Windsbraut* ('The Bride of the Wind'). 1914, oil on canvas, 181 x 220 cm. Kunstmuseum, Basle.
Kokoschka and Alma Mahler are shown in a storm-tossed boat driven by the elements. The picture may be interpreted as a memorial to their love and, at the same time, to its ending.

158

190 Egon Schiele: *Selbstbildnis*
('Self-Portrait'). 1911, oil on canvas, 27.5 x 34 cm. Historisches
Museum der Stadt Wien.
This markedly expressionist example of the apotheosis of a man
tempered by suffering and constantly under threat calls to mind
the solemnity of a medieval icon.

191 Egon Schiele: *Rückenakt*
('Girl's Back'). 1911, body colours
on pencil, 48.2 x 32.2 cm.
Historisches Museum der Stadt
Wien.

192 Egon Schiele: *Arthur Roessler.* 1914, pencil, 48.6 x 31 cm. Historisches Museum der Stadt Wien.
One of the preliminary drawings for the engraving that appeared later in the year. Schiele, who had already painted portraits in oils, had been befriended by Roessler, a helpful and understanding man, in 1910.

193 Egon Schiele: *Frau mit rotem Rock* ('Woman Wearing a Red Skirt'). *C.* 1909, pencil and body colour, 44.9 x 31.6 cm. Historisches Museum der Stadt Wien.

194 Egon Schiele: *Selbstbildnis als heiliger Sebastian* ('Self-Portrait as St Sebastian'). 1914–15, pen-and-ink, body colours, 67 x 50 cm. Poster design. Historisches Museum der Stadt Wien.
The theme of the artist who exposes himself to hostile criticism recalls the passage in *Thus Spake Zarathustra* where Nietzsche says: 'Yet he who, by his act of creation, has achieved self-mastery, finds himself confronted by the Pharisees…'

195 Egon Schiele: *Tod und Mädchen* ('Death and the Maiden'). 1915, oil on canvas, 150 x 180 cm. Österreichische Galerie, Vienna.

196 Egon Schiele: *Mutter mit zwei Kindern* ('Mother and Two Children'). 1917, oil on canvas, 150 x 158.7 cm. Österreichische Galerie, Vienna.

197 Egon Schiele: *Vier Bäume* ('Four Trees'). 1917, oil on canvas, 110.5 x 141 cm. Österreichische Galerie, Vienna.
A dominant theme in Schiele's painting is loneliness, the sense of being forsaken. Here it finds unequivocal expression in the four trees, symbolizing the human predicament.

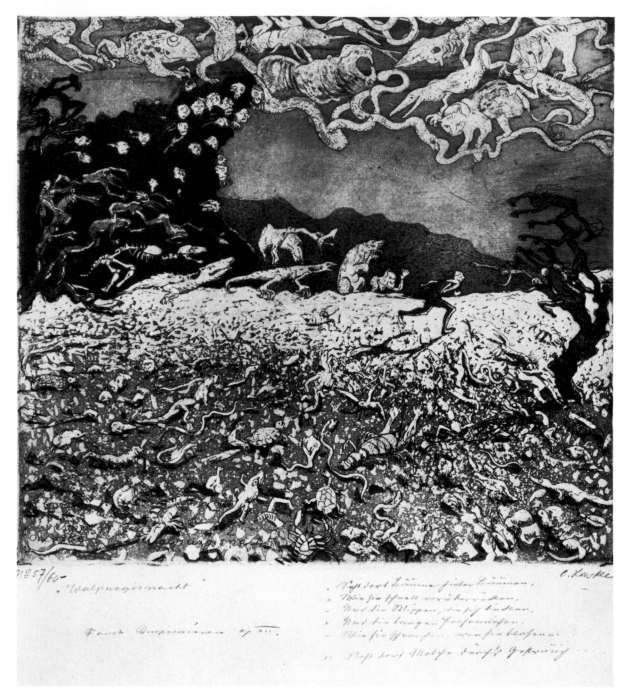

198 Oskar Laske: *Walpurgisnacht*
('Walpurgis Night'). 1919, etching,
plate: 29.3 x 32 cm; folio:
42.2 x 54.4 cm. Historisches
Museum der Stadt Wien.
The sense of chaos engendered by
the First World War is reflected in
Laske's portfolio *Faust Impressions*
(Verlag Neuer Graphik, Vienna,
Op. XII).

199 Max Oppenheimer: *Bildnis
Egon Schiele* ('Portrait of Egon
Schiele'). *C.* 1907, oil on canvas,
47 x 45 cm. Historisches Museum
der Stadt Wien.

titudes of the gamblers themselves, the work already foreshadows the *Neue Sachlichkeit* (new objectivity) of the inter-war period with its geometricity and two-dimensionality of forms. It was a movement in which the Hagenbund, whose adherence to Social Democracy dated from the end of the First World War, was to play a major role until its dissolution.

There can be no denying that, from the early years of the twentieth century, Austria also harboured artistic trends which glori-fied war and deplored the emergence of democratic freedoms, thus preparing the ground for the disaster of 1938. They are not discussed in this essay; rather, it intends to show that in the field of the fine arts, no less than in those of literature and science, the country produced a succession of extremely talented and enlightened men capable of contributing to the further emancipation of humanity.

NOTES

1 Hugo von Hofmannsthal, *Gesammelte Werke, Reden und Aufsätze* I, Frankfurt am Main, 1979, p. 560.

2 Ibid., pp. 519 ff.

3 Cited from catalogue *Werke von Jakob, Rudolf und Franz Alt*, Historisches Museum der Stadt Wien, 1976, pp. 5 ff.

4 Johannes Dobai, 'Zu Gustav Klimts Gemälde "Der Kuss"', in *Mitteilungen der Österreichischen Galerie*, Vienna, 1968, p. 100.

5 Hofmannsthal, p. 161.

6 Hermann Bahr, *Zur Überwindung des Naturalismus*, Stuttgart–Berlin–Cologne–Mainz, 1968, p. 111.

7 Hofmannsthal, p. 525.

8 Ibid., p. 532.

9 Hermann Bahr, *Secession*, Vienna, 1900, p. 2.

10 *Ver Sacrum*, I (1898), fasc. 1.

11 Hofmannsthal, p. 500.

12 Excerpts from James Shedel, *Art and Society – The New Art Movement in Vienna 1897–1914*, Palo Alto, c. 1981; Hans Bisanz, 'Ver Sacrum – kunstpolitische und künstlerische Ziele' in *Katalog VS*, Historisches Museum der Stadt Wien, 1983.

13 *Ver Sacrum*, I (1898), fasc. 9.

14 Marian Bisanz-Prakken, 'Das Quadrat in der Flächenkunst der Wiener Secession', in *Alte und moderne Kunst 1982*, nos. 180–1, pp. 37 ff.

15 Catalogue *Die Wiener Werkstätte*, Österreichisches Museum für angewandte Kunst, 1967, p. 21.

16 *Ver Sacrum*, IV (1901), fasc. 9.

17 Marian Bisanz-Prakken, *Gustav Klimt – Der Beethovenfries*, Munich, 1980, p. 71.

18 Cited from ibid., p. 208.

19 Ludwig Hevesi, *Acht Jahre Secession*, Vienna, 1906, p. 392.

20 Cited from Otto Breicha (ed.), *Gustav Klimt – Die goldene Pforte*, Salzburg, 1978, p. 131.

21 Robert Waissenberger, 'Der Hagenbund 1900–1938' in *Mitteilungen der Österreichischen Galerie*, Vienna, 1972, pp. 64 f.

22 Cf. catalogue *Der Hagenbund*, Historisches Museum der Stadt Wien, 1975, p. 12.

23 Werner Hofmann, *Moderne Malerei in Österreich*, Vienna, 1965, p. 110.

24 Adolf Loos, *Sämtliche Schriften*, I, Vienna-Munich, 1962, p. 240.

25 Oskar Kokoschka, *Mein Leben*, Munich, 1971, p. 62.

26 Werner Hofmann, in *Katalog Experiment Weltuntergang*, Hamburger Kunsthalle, 1981, pp. 66, 71.

27 Cited from catalogue *Egon Schiele – Zeichnungen und Aquarelle*, Historisches Museum der Stadt Wien, 1981, pp. 19 ff.

VI   ARCHITECTURE IN VIENNA, 1890–1920

Renata Kassal-Mikula

By the early 1890s, the old inner core of Vienna had been encircled by a ring of splendid monumental buildings. All the arts had contributed to the beautification, renovation and aggrandizement of the Imperial capital. For the planning and building operations which had followed the decision to enlarge the city in 1857 had, within a few decades, brought into existence the Votive Church, the Opera, the Parliament building, the town hall, the university, the Burgtheater and the Hofmuseum, not to mention mansions and apartment blocks. The Ringstrasse, a 'total work of art' on a grandiose scale, owed its existence to the wave of optimism that typified the *Gründerzeit* but which, towards the end of the century, had already begun to subside. By then the great architects of the Ringstrasse, Eduard van der Nüll, August von Sicardsburg, Theophil Hansen, Heinrich von Ferstel, Friedrich von Schmidt, Gottfried Semper and Karl von Hasenauer had concluded their work. All were historicists of one kind or another, and it was they who gave a specifically Viennese flavour to the *Gründerzeit* style – a style notable, in particular, for its unique combination of architecture, painting, sculpture and the applied arts. Their buildings echoed official intentions by creating an environment in which lavish display was elevated to a principle. Towards the turn of the century doubts began to be cast on values which sanctioned the adoption of styles of earlier epochs, and this more particularly in architecture, the vehicle *par excellence* for political pretensions. However, neither the rejection of past achievements nor the emergence of a new architectural idiom manifested itself in the form of a vast ensemble such as the Ringstrasse, but rather in individual works, randomly distributed throughout the city.

The process of re-evaluation was accelerated in 1890 when Vienna was enlarged for the second time by the incorporation of outer suburbs situated outside the Lines. Although some of the Ringstrasse projects had still to be completed, attention was now diverted to tasks that called for a speedy solution. Among the schemes envisaged were a building programme for each zone, an efficient communications system, and the regulation of the Danube Canal and the River Wien.

In 1892–3, this new phase was ushered in by a competition for a 'general redevelopment plan' covering the entire urban area, and by the institution of the Vienna Transport Commission. Monumental architecture was now to play second fiddle to structural engineering. Yet the positive impact made by the *Stadtbahn* (city railway) and the regulation of the Wien and the Danube Canal on the urban scene may be attributed to the happy decision not to entrust those tasks to technicians alone, but also to enlist the help of artists.

Plans for a metropolitan railway had been in existence from the time of the city's first enlargement in 1857. Their implementation was delayed by the insistence of the military that connections be built to all the major rail-heads – a demand that paid scant regard to the requirements of the population at large.

When work began in 1893, the general layout, comprising the Outer Suburban, Gürtel, Wien Valley and Danube Canal lines, had already been determined. Otto Wagner was called in to advise on the aesthetic aspects of the scheme.

Otto Wagner

It was the first major public undertaking with which the architect, now in his fifties, had been entrusted.[1] Trained at the Vienna Academy under van der Nüll and Sicardsburg, and afterwards in Berlin, his earlier jobs had largely been confined to apartment houses. Wagner's avant-garde project for the offices of the Provincial Bank, built in 1882, won him considerably less acclaim than did his historicist buildings of 1879 and 1881, the first commemorating the Imperial silver wedding, the second the arrival of Crown Prince Rudolph's fiancée, Stephanie of Belgium. Nevertheless, Wagner did not participate in any of the larger Ringstrasse projects, nor, during the 1880s, did he succeed in winning the international competitions for the cathedral and Reichstag building in Berlin, or the stock exchange in Amsterdam. He therefore worked largely for his own account, building not only apartment blocks, but also a town palace and a summer residence. It was in the course of such private ventures that he evolved most of the artistic principles which were to revolutionize Viennese architecture during the 1890s.

Public recognition finally came in 1894, when he replaced Hasenauer as professor and head of the Academy's Special School of Architecture. Though this afforded greater scope for his artistic activities, both practical and theoretical, his influence was confined to circles that were receptive to what was new. The turning-point in his career was marked by the appearance in 1895 of his text book *Modern Architecture,* a manual for the new era. The views it put forward may be summed up in the maxim that modern life is the only point of departure for the creative artist. In terms of function and form this signified a revival of the principles propounded by Gottfried Semper, whom Wagner greatly admired. Indeed the device *artis sola domina necessitas,* which graced Wagner's designs (1892–3) for the General Redevelopment Plan, was to become his guiding principle where art was concerned.

So as to speed up work on the city railway project, Wagner set up a large drawing office in which he installed some seventy collaborators. That office was to become one of the most important hearths of the new Viennese architecture, for it brought together a group of talented architects – men such as Olbrich (whom Wagner appointed chief draughtsman and manager), Hoffmann, Plečnik, Max Fabiani and Leopold Bauer – each capable of contributing his own creative ideas. Wagner and his team designed some thirty stations for the city railway, as well as bridges and viaducts, thus fulfilling the intention that the transport system should be artistically pleasing and that its stations should constitute new focal points for the community.

Each line acquired its own individual character, governed as it was by topo-

202 Otto Wagner: Gumpendorferstrasse Station, Vienna City Railway, Gürtel line. 1893–1898, photograph from Otto Wagner, *Einige Skizzen, Projekte und ausgeführte Bauwerke,* Vol. 2, Vienna, 1897.
This building is typical of the stations erected by Wagner on those sections of line which ran above ground. There are stations on either side of the track.

203 Otto Wagner: Bridge over the Wienzeile on the Vienna City Railway, Gürtel line. 1893, photograph. Historisches Museum der Stadt Wien.
The bridge links the Gürtel and Wien Valley lines. Wagner gave it a striking silhouette by means of tall pylons which act as focal points for the whole area.

graphical differences. Every detail, in particular the station buildings, displayed a hitherto unparalleled simplicity and practicality of design. New materials, new proportions, the exposure of girders and other structural elements, the emphasis on flat wall surfaces interrupted, now by horizontal bands, now by unframed windows – all these served as a means towards the elimination of historicism. In executing the project Wagner resorted, not only to the formal principles of the early nineteenth century, to classicism and Biedermeier, but also to contemporary trends in West European art.

A notable example of this attempt to achieve a synthesis of art and technology is the bridge over the Wienzeile. Here, the abutments to the prefabricated iron members assume the form of imposing pylons which provide visual points of reference in a large open space. The monumental treatment of this link between the Gürtel and Wien Valley lines was occasioned by the proposal to build a Wien Boulevard, a grand thoroughfare in the construction of which Wagner hoped to participate.

In 1898 he put up two stations on opposite sides of the Karlsplatz. Instead of the conventional mode of construction, he used a steel skeleton, while the walls were hung with marble slabs rather than faced with stucco. Because the two pavilions occupied sites in one of Vienna's most important squares, special attention was paid to their design which comprises a central superstructure and rich ornamentation. The new Secessionist style, now fully fledged, thus gained a footing in the heart of the city.

Another station on the Wien Valley line, the Court Pavilion, built in 1897–8, must be accounted the most unusual of all the city railway buildings. Situated in Hietzing, not far from the imperial residence of Schönbrunn, it was intended for the sole use of the emperor and his court, though why such a need should ever have been envisaged is difficult to see. In fact, the only time the emperor ever set foot in the station was in 1901, when on his way to open another section of line. The functional character of the city railway, so rigorously accentuated elsewhere, is here masked by Imperial trap-

204 Otto Wagner: Karlsplatz Station, Vienna City Railway, Wien Valley line. 1898, photograph. Historisches Museum der Stadt Wien.
The two stations on opposite sides of the square are early examples of skeleton construction. Designed by Olbrich, one of Wagner's main collaborators on this project, they display the sinuous forms of Secessionist Art Nouveau.

205 Otto Wagner: Court pavilion, Hietzing, Vienna City Railway, Wien Valley line. 1897–8, photograph. Historisches Museum der Stadt Wien.
The station, lavishly appointed by Wagner, was built solely for the benefit of the emperor and the court, though it was seldom if ever used by them.

206 Otto Wagner: Design for the central building (Hall of Honour) of the new Academy of Fine Arts. 1898, pencil, pen-and-ink, coloured wash, body colour white, heightened with gold, 104.1 x 70.7 cm. Historisches Museum der Stadt Wien.
This being the year (1898) of the Imperial Jubilee, Wagner hoped, vainly as it happened, to obtain the assignment by submitting opulent designs for a monumental building.

207 Otto Wagner: Competition design for the Postal Savings Bank. 1903, pen-and-ink, coloured wash, 85.7 x 41.6 cm. Historisches Museum der Stadt Wien.
The Postal Savings Bank is the only building designed by Wagner in the Ringstrasse area. His close attention to the functional aspects pointed the way to modern architectural practice.

·MITTELBAV·DER·GESAMMTANLAGE·

PROJECT·FVR·DEN·NEVBAV·
DER·KAIS·KÖNIGL·AKADEMIE·
DER·BILDENDEN·KVNSTE

A·D·MDCCCIC   OTTO·WAGNER·

WETTBEWERB·FVR·DEN·BAV·
DES·K·K·POSTSPARKASSEN=
AMTES·FAÇADENDETAIL 1/50

·K·K·POSTSPA

pings; the central structure, for example, has been given a Baroque dome, while the *porte-cochère* of glass and iron is richly ornamented. Inside, however, the new Secession style predominates, especially in the furnishings. So inspired did this solution appear that, in 1899, it was discussed at length in the Secession's journal, *Ver Sacrum*.

Wagner's work on the city railway placed him in the forefront of the new architecture. Indeed, such was the multiplicity of technical and artistic requirements that his efforts were of necessity channelled along modern lines. The city railway, like the contemporary Nussdorf Dam – whence the Danube Canal was regulated – exemplifies Wagner's ability to lend artistic refinement to the work of the engineer, and to achieve a unity of form and function that was well ahead of its time. The exposure of structural detail and the new method of wall cladding were to remain essential features of the modern style.

Despite these exemplary solutions to the tasks he had been set, Wagner was unable to find appropriate work in the public sector. Once again his own master, he had recourse to that great stand-by of the nineteenth-century Viennese architect, the apartment block, to which he proceeded to give a new image. In 1898–9 he put up two such blocks, No. 38 and No. 40, Linke Wienzeile. Opulent in appearance, and taller than the old suburban houses among which they stood, they were originally intended to grace the Wien Boulevard which, in the event, was never brought to completion. In earlier apartment houses, the first floor, occupied by the proprietor, had always been accentuated, but in Wagner's design all but the ground storey are of equal height, while on the street side the treatment of the unframed windows is similar throughout. The decoration also departs from the usual formula in that in No. 38 it is concentrated on the upper part of the façade, whereas in No. 40 it is evenly distributed. The floral ornamentation applied to both buildings is in the early Secession style deriving from West European Art Nouveau.

Not only the two apartment houses but also the earlier buildings in the Karlsplatz

testify to Wagner's espousal of that style. He joined the Secession in 1899, two years after its foundation, a step which seconded the association's efforts to bring about a change in artistic taste and to establish links with the international avant-garde. Thus Klimt, as spokesman for the painters, was joined by Wagner as chief representative of the new architecture.

The latter continued to seek the major assignments that had so far eluded him, as may be seen from the designs, prepared in the 1890s, for a Plaster Cast Museum, the new Academy of Fine Arts, the Kapuziner-

208 Otto Wagner: Apartment house, No. 38 Linke Wienzeile. 1898, photograph. Historisches Museum der Stadt Wien.
The two adjoining apartment blocks, Nos 38 and 40, were of a new and up-to-date type in that all the storeys were of equal height. The decorative elements, no longer historicist, are in the Secessionist style.

209 Otto Wagner: Banking Hall
of the Postal Savings Bank.
1904–6, photograph. Historisches
Museum der Stadt Wien.
The large glass-roofed hall forms
the centre of the building and is
easily accessible from the street.
Wagner designed all the fittings,
including the warm air-heating
vents.

210 Otto Wagner: Design for the
Kaiser-Franz-Joseph-Stadt-
museum. 1909, pencil, pen-and-
ink, 48.5 x 67 cm. Historisches
Museum der Stadt Wien.
For more than a decade after the
turn of the century Wagner was
engaged in preparing designs for a
City Museum. These efforts came
to nothing, for influential opponents objected to the erection of
so modern a building in the
Karlsplatz.

177

kirche and the Imperial Mausoleum at the Hofburg.

When Wagner won the competition for the Postal Savings Bank in 1903, he was able at last to put up a building in the neighbourhood of the Ringstrasse. Situated between the Danube Canal and the Stadtpark, this area was the last to be developed under the urban enlargement plan of 1857. In accordance with Wagner's concept, the new layout was to take the form of a regular grid, a scheme which involved the demolition of the old Francis Joseph Barracks. This did not, however, signal the end of the military's long stay in the city centre, for a new War Ministry was subsequently erected on the same site.

In the Postal Savings Bank, Wagner was able to realize on a grand scale his own conception of a functional building. The clearly structured ground plan, with its centrally situated, glass-roofed banking hall and rational system of stairways and corridors, was matched by a no less clearly articulated elevation. Though he had to depart in some respects from his competition sketch, Wagner adhered rigorously to his principles of modern design. Besides reinforced concrete and marble cladding, he made use of aluminium, both as a decorative and as a constructional material.

The marriage of structural and formal elements in pursuit of the task at hand was so perfectly effected as to constitute a prototype of the new architecture, a form which had now attained international status. For Vienna had not only drawn level with similar developments elsewhere in Europe, but had herself become a model.

A similar effect was sought by Wagner in his design for the Steinhof Church, to be built in conjunction with a pavilion-style mental hospital of which it would form the centre. This was one of the municipal schemes devised, not without an eye to political gain, by Karl Lueger, mayor of Vienna, to whose Christian-Social convictions the inclusion of an ecclesiastical element would also bear witness. Despite Wagner's long association with the scheme, culminating in the construction of the church (1904–7), he was not entrusted with

any other buildings in the complex. Every aspect of his design for the church was dictated by its function as a place of worship for the sick, or rather for the staff and the less obstreperous patients. Thus a first-aid room was provided in the basement while, in the interior, the absence of piers enabled every member of the congregation to have an uninterrupted view of the ceremony. The church, a centralized building on a Greek cross plan, was visible from a considerable distance away and, thanks to its simple, cubic forms, produced a striking effect. As in the Postal Savings Bank, the cladding consisted of marble slabs secured with bolts. Each detail of the scheme – the windows by Kolo Moser, Carl Ederer's altarpiece and Othmar Schimkowitz's plastic decoration – testifies to the formal genius of Art Nouveau. After the international acclaim accorded to these two buildings, the Postal Savings Bank and the Steinhof Church, there seemed every likelihood that modern architecture, with Otto Wagner as its leading proponent, would proceed from strength to strength. But this was not to be, for a conservative reaction had set in which, amongst other things, put paid to his scheme for the Kaiser Franz Joseph Museum.

The building, a municipal museum adumbrated by Lueger and his city council, was to occupy a site at the narrow eastern end of the Karlsplatz. By 1902, the closing date for the competition, Wagner had already submitted two preliminary designs. There ensued interminable delays, during which the merits of the various projects were hotly debated. However, conservatism eventually won the day when Wagner's latest design of 1909 was rejected in favour of Friedrich Schachner's essay in neo-Baroque. Nor did Wagner's plans for another site, this time on the Schmelz, find acceptance.

With his failure to obtain the commission for the municipal museum, Wagner lost his last chance of erecting a monumental building in Vienna. Equally unsuccessful were attempts to secure approval for his ideas on the redevelopment ot the Karlsplatz, in association with his scheme for the museum. Since the turn of the century he, as well as other architects, had been applying

211 Otto Wagner: *Kirche am Steinhof* ('Steinhof Church'). 1904, pen-and-ink, coloured wash, 47 x 56 cm. Historisches Museum der Stadt Wien.
The Church of St Leopold was situated at the centre of the complex formed by the Lower Austrian Mental Institute. Built between 1904 and 1907, it is the Secession's most important work in the field of ecclesiastical architecture. Modern building methods (steel construction and walls faced with slabs) combine with artistic furnishings to form a unique *Gesamtkunstwerk* ('total work of art').

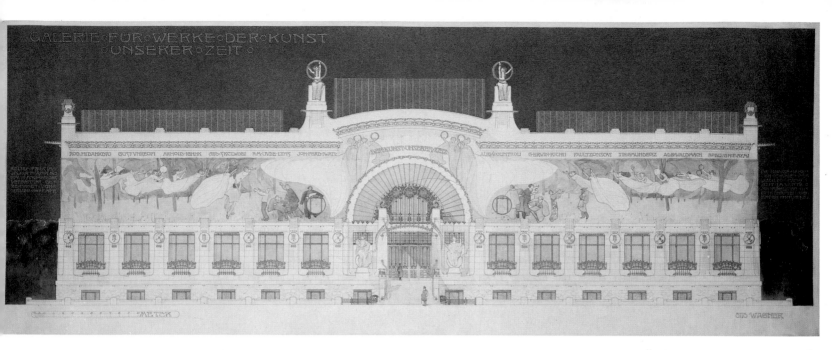

GALERIE·FÜR·WERKE·DER·KUNST
·UNSERER·ZEIT·

DIE·KULTUR·DENKMAL·VOR·DEM·KAISER·FRANZ·JOSEF·STADTMVSEVM·

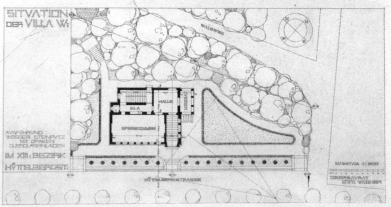

SITVATION
DER·VILLA·W·

216 Otto Wagner: Lupus
Hospital. 1908–13, photograph
from Leopold Bauer, 'Otto
Wagner', *Der Architekt,*
Vol. XXII, 1919, Pl. 11.
Wagner was much concerned that
architecture should contribute to
improvements in hygiene. The
commission for the hospital
enabled him to put his ideas into
practice.

217 Otto Wagner: Theoretical
design for the 22nd District.
1910–11, pencil, pen-and-ink,
61 x 82 cm. Historisches Museum
der Stadt Wien.
Wagner was greatly concerned
with the problems posed by town-
planning. In order to cope with
the constant expansion of the city,
he proposed that each new district
should have its own particular
centre.

218 Egon Schiele: *Otto Wagner.*
1910, pencil, water-colour, body
colour white, 52.5 x 26 cm.
Historisches Museum der Stadt
Wien.
It was through a circle of friends
at the Café Heinrichshof that
Wagner first came to know the
young painter Egon Schiele. This
study for an oil-painting was
found amongst Wagner's effects.

Wagner's followers

Much the same may be said of a younger architect, Joseph Maria Olbrich[2] who, for several years, worked closely with Wagner on the city railway. The creative talents he then displayed led the Secession (of which he was a founder member) to entrust him with the design of its exhibition hall near the Naschmarkt. In the space of six months, from April to November 1898, a building went up which was wholly in keeping with the legend that graced its entrance: 'To the age its art – to art its freedom'. The design, based on a sketch by Klimt, was unprecedented in the history of Viennese architecture.

In order that the building might adequately fulfil its function, Olbrich dispensed with permanent partitions. Instead, the roof was carried by six piers, between which movable room-dividers could be introduced. It was an ideal solution which fully answered the need for flexibility of layout, and greatly facilitated the development of a new aesthetics in the presentation of works of art. Indeed, it was that presentation which lent such novelty to the group's exhibitions and contrasted so strongly with the uninspired clutter on the walls of the Künstlerhaus. In his elevations, Olbrich restricted himself to simple, cubic forms with predominantly flat wall surfaces. Decoration was concentrated on the main door and the dome, the latter a confection of laurel leaves in gilded metal, known to one and all as the 'golden cabbage'.

The impulses to which Olbrich gave such original form in this building came, as so often in the case of the Secession, from the West. Like Hoffmann, Olbrich complemented the sinuosity and flamboyance of the Viennese style with more rigorous elements. So far as Vienna was concerned, the Secession building not only crowned but marked the end of what had been an exceedingly promising career. For in 1899, after Wagner had failed to secure him a professorship at the School of Arts and Crafts, Olbrich moved to Darmstadt in response to an invitation from the Grand Duke Ernest Ludwig of Hesse. Here, on the Mathilden-

höhe, he was to find ample scope for his architectural talents. Wagner was to make one further attempt to secure him a teaching post from which he could make a living; its failure meant that Olbrich's ability was permanently lost to his native city.

219 Joseph Maria Olbrich: Secession. 1898, photograph. Historisches Museum der Stadt Wien.
The exhibition building of the Secession (founded in 1897) is a consistent architectural statement, in an urban context, of the association's aims. It was to remain the most important example of Olbrich's work in Vienna, since he left the capital for Darmstadt soon aferwards.

220 Gustav Klimt: *Entwurf für das Gebäude der Wiener Secession* ('Design for the Secession building'). *C.* 1897, black chalk, coloured wash, 11.3 x 17.7 cm. Historisches Museum der Stadt Wien.
Klimt was the first president of the Secession and, as his sketch shows, was not without influence on the design of its premises.

221 Josef Plečnik: Zacherl House. 1903–5, photograph. Gerhard Trumler, Vienna.
The Zacherl House is one of the most striking shop and apartment blocks to have been built in the Inner City after the turn of the century. Like Wagner, Plečnik used cladding for his façades – in this case granite slabs – to produce an unusual visual effect.

A similar fate was to overtake Josef Plečnik[3] who, like Olbrich, had worked with Wagner. Though recommended by the latter and selected to succeed him at the Academy in late 1911, he was eventually rejected by that influential element which opposed any perpetuation of Wagner's régime. The professorship went instead to Leopold Bauer, a more malleable pupil of Wagner's, while Plečnik left Vienna in 1914 to practise in Prague and Laibach (now Ljubljana). Nevertheless, his most important work was produced in the Austrian capital where he was lucky enough to find a client who was prepared to give him a free hand. This was the manufacturer, J. E. Zacherl, for whom, between 1903 and 1905, he built a large shop and apartment block near St Stephen's Cathedral. The use of the latest techniques in iron construction was not the only novel feature of the building, known as the Zacherl House. For the cladding, consisting of granite slabs held in place by vertical sections, represented an entirely new departure in the treatment of façades. Also new was the rhythmical articulation of the walls by these supporting members which, carried up through several storeys, terminated below the roof, not in ornamental elements, but in carved atlantes. The focal point of the building, a huge bronze figure of the Archangel Michael by Ferdinand Andri, is a

later addition dating from 1909. For his second major work in Vienna, the parish church of the Holy Ghost on the Schmelz, Plečnik again had recourse to the latest techniques, this time in concrete construction.

Another young architect whose outstanding gifts Wagner had been quick to recognize was Max Fabiani.[4] In 1894 he became a member of Wagner's city railway team with which he remained for two crucial years. It was a time of intellectual ferment, and one of mutual benefit to both men who were in general agreement as to every aspect, whether theoretical or practical, of the modern architectural idiom then in process of manufacture. Like Wagner, Fabiani was a highly versatile artist who, in the course of his long life, was to find employment at many levels, but more especially as a town planner, in cities throughout what had once been the Monarchy. As was the case with Wagner and Loos, certain aspects of his architecture were too far in advance of his time to appeal to contemporary taste. Two of his early works, dating from the turn of the century and already anticipating Loos's Michaeler

House, embodied a new concept of functionalism. The first was a shop put up between 1898 and 1900 in the Ungarngasse (3rd District) for the furniture company Portois & Fix, of which both the interior and the exterior betrayed a formal severity as yet unattained by Wagner himself. The façade, divided into three bays and comprising window surrounds clad with green slabs, was entirely free of the florid decoration then in vogue. The second building, that of the Artaria publishing house in the Kohlmarkt, was completed in 1901. The simplicity of its design, which pointed the way to future developments, found little favour in Vienna where ornamentality still reigned supreme.

The difficulties encountered by Olbrich and Plečnik, as representatives of the new architecture, in finding, in Vienna, work commensurate with their abilities, typifies the quandary facing the Wagner school[5] as a whole. After 1918 only a few of the Academy's more promising students were able to hold their own in the capital. Some, like Hermann Aichinger and Franz Gessner, found employment in municipal housing schemes, while Leopold Bauer, Emil Hoppe, Marcel Kammerer and Otto Schönthal continued in private practice. Many of Wagner's pupils went home – that is to say, back to the Succession states – after the end of the First World War. Between 1894 and 1912, Wagner had nurtured a wealth of talent that would have been capable of great things in the coming decades, had not the advent of the war led to the suspension of all major undertakings.

Wagner had ensured that his pupils' projects should be brought out in carefully produced publications, while many also featured in the journal *Der Architekt*. They covered a wide range of themes, including simple country houses, papal palaces, monumental châteaux and ideal urban projects. These designs reflect not only Wagner's own style, but also the particular commissions upon which he happened to be working at the time. From Josef Hannich's project for an extension to the Hofburg, published in the *Ehrenjahr Otto Wagners* in 1912, it is evident that, notwithstanding the

222 Josef Plečnik: *Grabmalentwurf* ('Design for a memorial'). 1905, pen-and-ink, brown wash, 24 x 18 cm. Historisches Museum der Stadt Wien.

223 Leopold Bauer: Sketch from 'Beiträge zu Raumgestaltungen für eine Kunstausstellung in Düsseldorf' (Contributions to the Spatial Design of an Art Exhibition in Düsseldorf) in *Ver Sacrum*, 1902, No. 21.
Bauer was one of the more noteworthy architects of the Otto Wagner school, his chief work being the Austrian National Bank building in Vienna.

224 Max Fabiani: Portois & Fix Building. 1899–1900, Ungargasse 51, 3rd District, Vienna, photograph of 1901. After Marco Pozzetto, *Max Fabiani*, Vienna, 1983, Pl. 37.
This building for a furniture company, designed by Max Fabiani, one of Otto Wagner's pupils, is a typical example of the architecture of the Art Nouveau period. Not only is it functional, but it also makes an aesthetic contribution to the urban scene.

city railway, the Postal Savings Bank and the Steinhof church, monumental schemes still occupied an important place in Wagner's affections. Indeed, whether a commission was traditional, as was usually the case, or functional – a stadium or an airport – the Wagner school displays a certain tendency to megalomania and the use of an inflated formal vocabulary which prefigures later Fascist developments, a case in point being the project for a Hall of Fame on the Leopoldsberg.[6] The proposal, made in 1904, to build an Austrian Valhalla on this historically momentous site was but one of the belated if vain attempts to inject new life into the national concept of empire.

225 Josef Hannich: Design for an extension to the Hofburg. 1912, photograph from *Das Ehrenjahr Otto Wagners,* Vienna 1912, Pl. 46.
Many of the designs produced by Wagner's pupils betray the extent to which their master continued to adhere to the nineteenth-century tradition, for all the modernity of certain of his buildings.

226 Karl Troll and Franz Biberhofer: Design for an Austrian Hall of Fame on the Leopoldsberg. 1904, pencil, pen-and-ink, coloured wash, 65.5 x 90 cm. Historisches Museum der Stadt Wien.
As the Monarchy drew to a close, art was called in to breathe new life into the concept of state, a concept which had long been wasting away. Historically momentous sites were chosen for the purpose, in this case the Leopoldsberg, once the seat of the Babenberg family, and the place from which the troops which raised the siege of Vienna in 1683 started out.

227 Heinrich Lefler and Joseph Urban: Exhibition building for the Hagenbund (Zedlitzhalle). 1902, photograph. Historisches Museum der Stadt Wien.
The Hagenbund, an association founded after the Secession, was similarly devoted to the cause of modern art, but was unable to erect a building of its own. The conversion of an existing market hall was entrusted to Lefler and Urban, whose main field of activity was in craft industry.

228 Max Hegele: Lueger Memorial Church in the Central Cemetery. 1908–10, photograph. Bildarchiv der Österreichischen Nationalbibliothek, Vienna.
The church was commissioned by Karl Lueger as part of his municipal building programme, and it is here that he was buried. The design is based on Wagner's Steinhof church but on a larger scale.

190

The Secession was not the only representative of the new trends in Viennese art. Dedicated to the cause of modern art, the Hagenbund[7] did not, like the Secession, put up a new building for its own use, but instead made do with a converted market-hall. The adaptation, entrusted to Heinrich Lefler and Josef Urban, reveals the craft background of both these artists, even though they employed Secessionist motifs throughout.

The dialogue with the Secession and its main proponent, Otto Wagner, is again in evidence in the church built in the Central Cemetery between 1908 and 1910, at the behest of the mayor, Karl Lueger.[8] For, by opting for a domed, centrally planned building, the architect, Max Hegele, has followed Wagner's celebrated example, the Steinhof Church, without, however, having recourse to modern methods of construction.

Josef Hoffmann

Modern architecture was to attain a new high-water mark in the work of a man who came to notice shortly before the turn of the century. Josef Hoffmann was another pupil and collaborator of Wagner's.[9] His work bears the stamp not only of his master's artistic genius, but also of the rebellious spirit that persisted on the eve of the founding of the Secession. Initially Hoffmann applied himself to the design of furniture, craft manufactures, and interiors. From the outset, however, he endeavoured to strike a balance between the disciplined formal principles of Wagner and the influence of western Art Nouveau.

As a founder member of the Secession, Hoffmann, together with Olbrich, set the style for its early exhibitions. Hoffmann's aim was to present a global spectacle conceived in terms of space, exhibits, appointments and appropriate colour schemes. This concept, which was entirely new to Vienna, found expression in, for instance, the third exhibition of 1899 which revolved around Max Klinger's *Christ on Olympus*. At the fourteenth exhibition in 1902 he reached his peak as an interior designer. On this occasion Klinger's statue of Beethoven formed the centre-piece, while a great allegorical frieze by Klimt graced the upper part of the walls. Sculpture and frieze, combined with Hoffmann's treatment of space,

229 Josef Hoffmann: Left-hand Hall at the Fourteenth Secession Exhibition. 1902, photograph from *Deutsche Kunst und Dekoration*, No. 9, 1902, p. 484. Hoffmann's concept of space in terms of clear forms was ideally suited to the display of Klinger's statue of Beethoven and Klimt's frieze. The artistry of his design for the exhibition won him much acclaim.

191

together constituted a unique 'total work of art'. The clearly defined sequence of smooth and roughly plastered wall surfaces, the alternation of piers and openings and their articulation by rigorously simple forms, gave a new dimension to spatial art. What Hoffmann had elaborated in the ephemeral field of exhibitions, he was subsequently to translate into more permanent form in the domestic sphere. Largely as a result of his successful participation in the International Exposition in Paris (1900), he was able, unlike Wagner, to establish connections with the liberal upper classes, in whom he found a wealthy clientele prepared to accept his modern designs for villas and apartments.

In 1899, Hoffmann, then twenty-nine years old, was awarded a teaching post at the School of Arts and Crafts where he was to remain for the next few decades. It was a position which gave him a free hand in artistic matters. The Klinger exhibition shows how rapid was his development, for by now he had forsaken the sinuous style of the early Secession and was tending towards classicism. The change may be attributed to his intimate contacts with the Glasgow School, especially Charles Rennie Mackintosh and his wife Margaret Macdonald. Indeed, the display of their work at the eighth Secession exhibition in 1900 was to exert a lasting influence on Viennese art.

Britain also provided the inspiration for an artists' colony where the avant-garde might give free rein to their talents. Olbrich, the originator of the scheme, hoped to find a site amidst the verdure of Hietzing or the Hohe Warte. His place was eventually taken by Hoffmann. When Carl Moll and Kolo Moser decided to build their houses on the Hohe Warte, they were joined by two other clients, Victor Spitzer and Hugo Henneberg. Thanks to his involvement in the Secession, Hoffmann was on good terms with this circle, whose common aim was the realization of ideal concepts. The first of the group of villas deliberately designed to form an ensemble were the semi-detached houses built for Moll and Moser in 1900 and 1901, followed by those of Henneberg and Spitzer. Asymmetrical articulation and

timber-framing were features already current in Austrian villa architecture where they were employed to produce a picturesque effect. Here Hoffmann's work betrays the influence of English models, in which the reversion to the medieval craft tradition represented an attempt, on the part of the Arts and Crafts movement, to obviate the dangers of stereotyping and to combat the primacy of the machine. That Hoffmann was pursuing similar aims is evident from his subsequent founding of the Wiener Werkstätte. However, his tendency towards classical axiality, always latent and already apparent in the Henneberg House, was to become ever more pronounced as time went on.

In his interiors, Hoffmann exploits to the full the spatial possibilities inherent in the Secession exhibitions. Characteristic of this work are the subtle lighting effects, the disposition of service and leisure areas, and perspectives affording glimpses of the countryside. The simplicity for which he strove in the Moll-Moser building was always to alternate with more lavish solutions.

Formal austerity is even more strongly in evidence in the 'West End' Sanatorium put

230 Josef Hoffmann: The Moll-Moser House on the Hohe Warte. 1900–1, photograph from *Der Architekt,* Vol. IX, 1903, p. 85. Hoffmann built this house for his fellow artists Carl Moll and Kolo Moser. English influence is apparent in the design.

231 Carl Moll: *Salon des Wohnhauses Moll* ('Drawing-room in the Moll House'). 1903, oil on canvas, 135 x 89 cm. Historisches Museum der Stadt Wien. The two semi-detached houses built in 1900–1 for Moll and Moser were the first in a scheme for an artists' colony on the Hohe Warte devised by Secessionist members and their patrons. This early example of Hoffmann's work shows that he was already a master of interior design.

232 Carl Moll: *Wohnzimmer mit Anna Moll, der Gattin des Malers* ('Living-room with Anna Moll, the Artist's Wife'). *C.* 1910, oil on canvas, 100 x 100 cm. Historisches Museum der Stadt Wien.
An example of an interior furnished in the style of Art Nouveau.

233 Josef Hoffmann: Dining-room of the Purkersdorf Sanatorium. 1904, photograph after Eduard F. Sekler, *Josef Hoffmann – Das architektonische Werk*, Salzburg–Vienna, 1982, Pl. 286. Although the 'West End' sanatorium catered exclusively for private patients, Hoffmann set his face against all forms of embellishment. He concentrated solely on what was functional, even to the extent of leaving the concrete ceiling exposed.

234 Josef Hoffmann: Dining-room in the Palais Stoclet, Brussels, with a frieze of mosaics by Gustav Klimt, 1906–11, photograph after Eduard F. Sekler, *Josef Hoffmann – Das architektonische Werk*, Salzburg-Vienna, 1982, Pl. 111.

235 Josef Hoffmann: Palais Stoclet, Brussels. 1906–11, photograph from *Moderne Bauformen*, Vol. XIII, 1914, p. 3. This outstanding example of modern architecture also represents the peak of the Wiener Werkstätte's achievements in the field of interior design. Nowhere, save in Brussels, did the opportunity present itself – thanks to the generosity of the client concerned – for the full deployment of the artistic principles embodied in that organization, founded by Hoffmann in 1903.

up in Purkersdorf, west of Vienna, in 1904–5. The building, intended for the use of private patients, was designed by Hoffmann down to the very smallest detail. Display is utterly eschewed, even to the extent of leaving exposed the steel and concrete ceiling of the vast dining-room.

The year 1903 saw the foundation by Hoffmann and Fritz Wärndorfer of the Wiener Werkstätte, renowned for their achievements in the field of craft manufacture. It was not in Vienna, however, that the range of skills incorporated in the workshops was to find full deployment, for Hoffmann's masterpiece, the Palais Stoclet, was sited in Brussels. Thanks to the generosity of the client, this monumental villa gave ample scope to Hoffmann's talents as craftsman and architect. The remarkable effect produced by the building is achieved by the versatile use of square blocks, the embossed copper mouldings that accentuate the angles, and the new visual dimension thus acquired by the marble slabs, a form of cladding already employed in Vienna by Otto Wagner. In the dining-room is an outstanding wall mosaic, by Gustav Klimt who, thanks to an ample supply of precious materials, was able to exploit to the full the decorative potential of Art Nouveau.

Meanwhile the Secession had been the scene of dramatic events, for in 1905 Klimt and his circle, including Hoffmann and Wagner, had left the association. In 1908, on the sixtieth anniversary of the emperor's accession, the group mounted an exhibition on the site earmarked for the Konzerthaus (concert hall). For the occasion Hoffmann designed the vestibule, whose cool severity reflects the growing emphasis on classical forms. It was a development in which another disciple of Wagner's, Emil Hoppe, also took part, with his 'Court in Concrete Architecture'. The classical idiom is also apparent in Hoffmann's villa architecture of that period, notable examples being the Villa Ast and the Villa Skywa-Primavesi,

236 Josef Hoffmann: Vestibule of the Kunstschau. 1908, Wiener Werkstätte postcard No. 1, colour print, 14 x 9.1 cm. Historisches Museum der Stadt Wien. Hoffmann was a member of the Klimt Group which had resigned from the Secession in 1905. He was entrusted with the overall architectural design for this important exhibition.

237 Emil Hoppe: 'Courtyard with buildings in concrete' in the Kunstschau. 1908, Wiener Werkstätte postcard No. 4, colour print, 14 x 9.1 cm. Historisches Museum der Stadt Wien. This small courtyard with buildings in concrete by Hoppe, a pupil of Wagner's, draws attention to modern building materials, the functional use of which was recommended by the Viennese *avant-garde*.

238 Otto Schönthal: *Villa Vojczik.* 1902, Linzer Strasse 375, 14th District, Vienna. Photographed in 1984, after the restoration of the building. Historisches Museum der Stadt Wien.

239 Josef Hoffmann: Villa Skywa-Primavesi. 1913–15, photograph after Eduard F. Sekler, *Josef Hoffmann – Das architektonische Werk,* Salzburg–Vienna, 1982, Pl. 367. Hoffmann was fortunate in attracting a succession of clients who commissioned him to build large houses. The Villa Skywa-Primavesi dates from the phase in which Hoffmann began to adopt neo-classical elements.

built between 1913 and 1915. Vertical fluting was to become a constantly recurring feature in the articulation of his façades.

Despite the hazards to which modern art was increasingly exposed and, notwithstanding the difficulty of securing architectural commissions in time of war, Hoffmann could still rely on a wealthy clientele that provided him with employment, and even subscribed to his idea that interior design should embrace all aspects of life. In the post-war years he was therefore able to carry on much as before, while his work on municipal housing schemes and his Werkbund activities earned him further acclaim and opened up new possibilities.

Adolf Loos

As compared with Hoffmann and Wagner, who were deeply involved in Vienna's cultural life through their friendly intercourse with other artists, Adolf Loos[10] worked in isolation. After studying in Dresden he spent three years in the United States and returned to Vienna in 1896. There he became known primarily as a theoretician. In 1898, before he had parted company with the Secession, he wrote a paper for *Ver Sacrum* entitled 'Potemkin's City'. This marked the beginning of his long polemic against the art of the preceding decades, a polemic which soon came to embrace contemporary architects also. His aesthetic principles were derived from two main sources: early nineteenth-century art which, like Wagner, he hailed as a consummate blend of form and function, and Anglo-Saxon domestic architecture, which was to exert a strong influence on his interior design. At this stage he was still of one mind, not only with Wagner and Hoffmann, but also with most other architects of the day. However, his feet were already set on a more radical course which was to compound his isolation.

Initially, Loos devoted himself to the design of interiors for shops and apartments. His interpretation of modern style is apparent in the shop (no longer extant) he designed in 1898 for the men's outfitters,

Goldman and Salatsch. Heedless of everything save what was purely functional, he achieved his effect by the use of superior materials such as cut glass, fine wood and brass. The interior he designed in 1899 for the Café Museum, a meeting-place for writers and artists, was quite unlike that of any other coffee-house in the city, for with its central cashier's desk it was a deliberate throw-back to Viennese Biedermeier. The cool, plushless elegance of the interior aroused considerable indignation and earned the establishment the sobriquet 'Café Nihilism'.

The importance attached by Loos to the domestic sphere, the individual's private environment, is evident from his own living-room, designed in 1903 for his apartment in the Bösendorferstrasse (now the Historisches Museum der Stadt Wien). With its plain brick fire place, inglenook and exposed beams, it creates an atmosphere of intimacy such as he must have encountered in Anglo-Saxon countries. The saying 'an Englishman's home is his castle' had been translated into the Viennese idiom.

His essay, *Ornament and Crime*, published in 1908, stirred up a violent controversy which was revived two years later

240 Adolf Loos: Goldmann & Salatsch, men's outfitters. 1898–1903, photograph. Loos-Archiv der Graphischen Sammlung, Albertina, Vienna.
In this early work, his first commercial commission, Loos's rejection of decorative incidentals is already apparent. The functional appointments achieve their stylish effect through the use of superior materials such as brass, mahogany and cut glass.

241 Adolf Loos: Café Museum. 1899, photograph. Loos-Archiv der Graphischen Sammlung, Albertina, Vienna.
The unemotional modernism of this interior is a deliberate refutation of the Ringstrasse style. In his search for new designs Loos had recourse to the coffee-house tradition as exemplified in the Biedermeier period. To those who misunderstood him the place was known as the 'Café Nihilism'.

242 Adolf Loos: Dining-room and living area in the architect's apartment. 1903, photograph. Historisches Museum der Stadt Wien.
Loos's own apartment in Bösendorferstrasse 3 betrays the extent of the influence exerted upon him by America. It was he who introduced into Viennese architecture certain Anglo-Saxon domestic features such as the open fireplace.

243 Adolf Loos: Michaeler House. 1909–11, photograph. Loos-Archiv der Graphischen Sammlung, Albertina, Vienna.
Loos's Michaeler House gave rise to considerable controversy. In a square of such historical importance, the rigorous simplicity of the exterior was regarded as a provocation. Indeed, ever after the building of this 'eyebrowless' house, the emperor is said to have kept the curtains drawn in the Hofburg.

when he gave practical form to his principles in the Michaelerplatz building (1910). Here a shop, its main entrance surrounded by polished marble, is surmounted by an apartment house with a flat, undecorated façade and unframed 'eyebrowless' windows. This epoch-making building displayed features – rigorous vertical and horizontal articulation, regular fenestration, straight, unbroken roof-line, total absence of ornament – of such originality as to arouse a storm of protest. Feelings were further inflamed by

the choice of site, almost next door to the Hofburg, where the presence of a work of such uncompromising simplicity seemed tantamount to *lèse-majesté*. However, Loos enjoyed the full confidence of his clientele, and thus was able to complete a project which was to effect a revolution in architecture.

Loos's ideas on modern design also found expression in the villa. In the Steiner House, as in his Michaelerplatz building of similar date, he employs simple architectural

244 Adolf Loos: Steiner House. 1910, photograph. Historisches Museum der Stadt Wien. In designing private houses Loos still adhered to the principle of simplicity and unpretentiousness. The external appearance of a building was dictated by the disposition of the rooms within.

methods to achieve an effective solution. Thus, the elevation evolves from within so that the fenestration is dictated by the disposition of the rooms. Another solution that anticipated future developments was the multi-purpose living-room as the focal point of a house.

A new type evolved by Loos is exemplified by the Scheu House (1912), which was given a stepped façade. It was work such as this that earned him the title of founder of modern architecture. Since his overriding concern was to build practical houses suited to human needs, he was inevitably restricted to a clientele prepared to dispense with outward display. The housing estates and tenement blocks built by Loos during the 1920s show that he remained faithful to the principles he thought appropriate to the times. Very few people in Vienna, however, became immediately aware of the full import of his architecture.

Friedrich Ohmann

Friedrich Ohmann,[11] a pupil of Ferstel's and a teacher at the Prague School of Arts and Crafts, steered a course midway between modernity and the *Heimatstil* – a derivative of Austrian Baroque. In 1898 he was called to Vienna to superintend the artistic side of the regulation of the River Wien and, in the following year, was appointed architect of the new wing of the Hofburg.

The first of these two important commissions was similar to that entrusted to Wagner in connection with the construction of the Wien Valley line, a scheme that was to go hand in hand with the regulation of the river. Both were responsible for the appearance of buildings which belonged more to the province of the civil engineer. Thus their work has contributed materially to the townscape of that particular part of Vienna. Since the only part of the Wien to be arched

245 Friedrich Ohmann and Josef Hackhofer: Design for the arching over of the River Wien in the Stadtpark. After 1898, pen-and-ink, coloured wash, crayon, paper glued on canvas, 73 x 122.8 cm. Historisches Museum der Stadt Wien. Ohmann and Hackhofer were responsible for the artistic side of the regulation of the River Wien. At the point where the river emerges into the open they erected a grandiose gateway in which architecture, sculpture, water and vegetation combined to produce an ensemble in the Art Nouveau style.

246 Ludwig Baumann: *Konsularakademie* ('Consular Academy'). 1904, water-colour over ink, 60 x 99.7 cm. Historisches Museum der Stadt Wien. Late historicism increasingly gave way to vernacular Baroque, a development that was welcome to the Establishment because of its patriotic evocation of Austria's greatness.

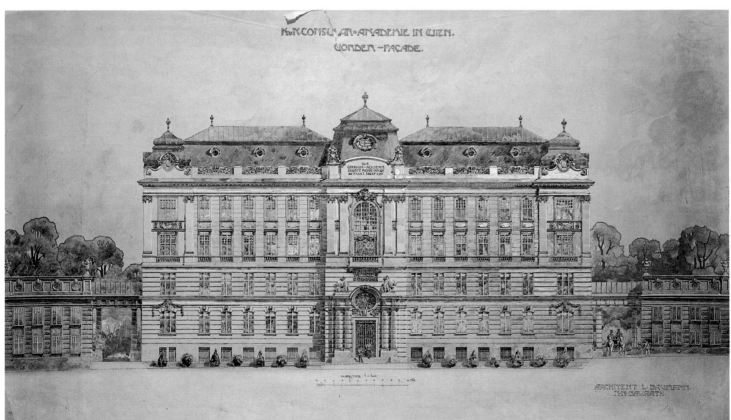

K.u.K. CONSULAR-AKADEMIE IN WIEN.
VORDER-FACADE.

ARCHITEKT L. BAUMANN.
IN NEUBAU.

over was the reach between the Naschmarkt and the Stadtpark, particular importance was attached to the design of the arches at either end. The lower arch, where the Wien debouched into the Stadtpark, was given a splendid setting by Ohmann, consisting of architectural and plastic elements, and a most effective cascade. Though Secessionist forms are everywhere apparent, they are fully integrated with nature,[12] for Ohmann was at pains to combine architecture, sculpture, water and vegetation into a single whole. In this he was acting in accordance with one of the principles of the Secession, of which he was a founder member.

Whereas two further works, the Imperial glass-house in the Burggarten, and the architectural layout of the Empress Elisabeth monument in the Volksgarten, were executed in the Secessionist style, Ohmann's plans for the Hofburg were predominantly historicist. However, he was unable to make any appreciable headway with the latter scheme, from which he resigned in 1907. In 1916, after he had failed, like Wagner, to gain approval for his solution to the problem of the Karlsplatz, Ohmann turned his attention to the square around the Votive Church, for which numerous proposals had already been put forward.[13] Heinrich von Ferstel, the builder of the church, had kept a wary eye on the development of its immediate surroundings. After his death in 1883, however, criticism began to be voiced about the unsatisfactory impression created by this national monument. Once again, Otto Wagner was amongst those who put forward a solution. Ohmann's proposal was that the church should be given a setting that would comprise a Habsburg Museum, Habsburg monuments, including a memorial to the newly deceased Emperor Francis Joseph, and a new university library. The design of the proposed museum and monuments might be regarded as a final flurry of patriotism half-way through the war in the year of the monarch's death.

It was a scheme that incorporated the principles laid down in 1889 by Camillo Sitte in his book on urban architecture[14] which attacks the grid system adopted during the enlargement of the city, and deplores the primacy of the street and the desolate nature of many of the squares. The models advocated by Sitte were the medieval city with its organic development, and the picturesque perspectives of the Baroque square. This architect's reversion to romanticism as opposed to rationalism, notably in the form propounded by Otto Wagner, was to find widespread support.

A discussion of early twentieth-century Viennese architecture that was confined solely to the work of men such as Wagner, Hoffmann, Loos and Olbrich would present an entirely false picture of the actual state of affairs. For modern architecture never came into its own to the extent hoped for by its advocates, being far outstripped in this respect by more traditional styles. While the ideas of the Secession were accessible only to a well-educated élite, the majority of clients tended to employ only those architects who continued to adhere to historicism. In its late form, in the 1890s, the latter underwent a change, when the neo-Renaissance style began to give way to Baroque.[15]

248   Karl König: Palais Herberstein. 1894–7, photograph. Historisches Museum der Stadt Wien.
König is a typical representative of those architects who had recourse to the Baroque. It was to them, and not to the Secession, that recognition, both public and private, was accorded.

Late phase of historicism

While the Secession, through its dialogue with contemporary trends in West European and, particularly, British art, was engaged in establishing international contacts, Austria's own past was being quarried by artists of a different school. Baroque art, long regarded as decadent, was now enjoying a revival, thanks largely to Albert Ilg's pseudonymous *Die Zukunft des Barockstils* ('Future of the Baroque Style'), published in 1880. Other works followed, adding to the stock of knowledge of Austrian Baroque which now began to be reflected in many new buildings. Patriotism contributed not a little to the adoption of a style which, as the nation lurched from crisis to crisis, was all the more welcome to officialdom, in that it represented a symbol of Austria's past greatness.

The same sentiments were doubtless instrumental in the decision to complete, along the lines laid down by Fischer von Erlach, the Michaelerplatz façade of the Hofburg, a building which for 200 years had remained a mere torso. A popular neo-Baroque architect, Karl König,[16] was responsible for the Palais Herberstein, built between 1894 and 1897 close to the Michaeler wing of the Hofburg. It exemplified the appeal made by Baroque monumental pathos to the taste of a client governed by considerations of self-aggrandizement. The rounded angle surmounted by a dome was a time-honoured motif which was already much in evidence in the Viennese townscape.

The repeated difficulties experienced by the Secessionists in achieving their artistic aims – the rejection of Wagner's plans for the municipal museum, Olbrich's departure for Darmstadt and the outcry against Loos's Michaelerplatz building – bear witness to the powerful opposition encountered by the moderns. The dismissive attitude of the public, who invariably raised a furor when confronted with the unfamiliar, was shared by Francis Ferdinand, the heir apparent.[17] During the years leading up to the war, when he became increasingly influential in the sphere of art, Francis Ferdinand was an outspoken advocate of historicism.

An architect after the heir apparent's own heart was Ludwig Baumann.[18] As senior architect to the industrialist, Arthur Krupp, he had been responsible for numerous buildings in Berndorf, including a church whose design was derived from the Karlskirche. Having come to prominence with his designs in Austrian late Baroque for the World Exhibition in Paris (1900) and the Consular Academy in Vienna (1902), he was put in charge of the Hofburg project by Francis Ferdinand in 1908. This was the last attempt to complete the building which constituted the focal point of the Ringstrasse. As far back as 1870, Semper and Hasenauer had designed, for the site between the old Hofburg and the Mews, an 'Imperial forum' which they believed to be an ideal solution, since it would give material form to the Austrian Imperial idea. As the latter began to wane in the 1890s, however, the project also lost momentum, a momentum it never really recovered, despite drastic cuts in the original programme. Nevertheless, the *corps-de-logis* was completed by Baumann in 1916. The Baroque and classical parts of the Hofburg were not pulled down as planned, since their demolition was opposed on conservationist grounds by Francis Ferdinand.

The extent to which the climate had changed may be gauged from the War Ministry competition results of 1907–8, when the designs submitted by Wagner and Loos were rejected in favour of Baumann's neo-Baroque solution. This, the last monumental building in the Ringstrasse, marked the return of 'traditional forces [which] now made their re-entry in modern, bureaucratic form'.[19] On the roof of the long building's central block Baumann placed a triumphalist group as symbol of the military aspirations that were shortly to have such catastrophic consequences.

Exaggerated monumentality as a sign of commercial prowess was a feature of a number of Viennese banks[20] put up after the turn of the century. The shortage of sites in the Inner City usually meant that earlier structures had to be demolished to make

way for new ones, a case in point being the old War Ministry which was replaced between 1913 and 1915 by the Lower Austrian Escompte-Gesellschaft building. Ernst von Gotthilf and Alexander Neumann, architects who specialized in commissions of this kind, represented the classical tendency typical of the period.

249 Ludwig Baumann: War Ministry. 1909–13, photograph. Historisches Museum der Stadt Wien.
Though both Loos and Wagner had competed for the honour of building this, the last monumental structure in the Ringstrasse, the commission was eventually awarded to Baumann, a protégé of the Heir Apparent, Francis Ferdinand, whose strong opinions on the subject of art were not without influence.

250 Ernst von Gotthilf and Alexander Neumann: Lower Austrian Escompte Gesellschaft (Provincial Bank). 1913–15, photograph from *Die bildenden Künste und der Architekt*, Vol. I, 1916–18, Pl. 11.
In the final years of the Monarchy a number of new banks were built in Vienna. Their monumentality, unusually decked out along neoclassical lines, was calculated to inspire confidence in the soundness of these institutions.

251 Water-Tower on the Wienerberg. 1898, photograph. Historisches Museum der Stadt Wien.
A display of opulence was not considered a necessary adjunct to the many industrial buildings and other installations put up in Vienna during the nineteenth century. Here form is subordinated only to function. However, such structures also contributed to the development of modern architecture.

The Konzerthaus (1912–14) in the Lothringerstrasse, also built in the classical style, was the work of Fellner and Helmer, an architectural partnership responsible for numerous theatres, both in Vienna and elsewhere in the Monarchy.

The Ringstrasse project had speeded up the development of new methods and materials. Iron roof trusses became the rule in monumental buildings, though kept strictly out of sight, since the opulent display then still *de rigueur* precluded the exposure of structural members. Otto Wagner was the first to flout this convention, though even he subordinated technology to art.

Industrial and functional architecture

The same cannot be said of the many industrial and functional buildings[21] which sprang up in Vienna. In their case, there could be no question of opulent display, for growing industrialization and the expansion of public works called for the economic application of techniques and materials, the latter consisting chiefly of rough bricks, iron and, later, concrete. Functional building was largely based on British models, since Britain, at that time the leading industrial nation, not only possessed a command of modern technology, but had devised the most efficient means of applying it to various types of building. That such methods could also be used in structures designed for pleasure is shown by the Giant Wheel put up by an English firm in 1896–7, on the occasion of the 'Venice in Vienna' exhibition. English engineers were likewise responsible for the building of the

Simmering Gasworks some twelve months later. The cubical forms typical of this type of architecture recur in the water tower erected on the Wienerberg in 1898.

At the time, there was no suggestion that industrial buildings might possess any artistic merit of their own, but later on their aesthetic qualities came to be appreciated, while the contribution they had made to modern architecture was accorded general recognition.

207

NOTES

1 Heinz Geretsegger and Max Peintner, *Otto Wagner*, Salzburg, 1964 (1st ed.).

2 *Joseph M. Olbrich*, Katalog der Ausstellung in Darmstadt, Vienna–Berlin–Darmstadt, 1967.
Joseph Maria Olbrich, Die Zeichnungen in der Kunstbibliothek Berlin, Kritischer Katalog, Berlin, 1972.

3 Damjan Prelovšek, *Josef Plečnik, Wiener Arbeiten von 1896 bis 1914*, Vienna, 1982.

4 Marco Pozzetto, *Max Fabiani – Ein Architekt der Monarchie*, Vienna, 1983.

5 Marco Pozzetto, *Die Schule Otto Wagners 1894–1912*, Vienna–Munich, 1979.

6 *Die Türken vor Wien. Europa und die Entscheidung an der Donau 1683*, Katalog der 82. Sonderausstellung des Historischen Museums der Stadt Wien, Vienna, 1983, cat. no. 29–61 (Selma Krasa).

7 *Der Hagenbund*, Katalog der 40. Sonderausstellung des Historischen Museums der Stadt Wien, Vienna, 1975.

8 Renate Wagner-Rieger, *Wiens Architektur im 19. Jahrhundert*, Vienna, 1970, pp. 248 ff.

9 Eduard F. Sekler, *Josef Hoffmann, Das Architektonische Werk*, Salzburg–Vienna, 1982.

10 Ludwig Münz and Gustav Künstler, *Der Architekt Adolf Loos*, Vienna–Munich, 1964.
Burkhardt Rukschcio and Roland Schachel, *Adolf Loos, Leben und Werk*, Salzburg–Vienna, 1982.

11 Ferdinand von Feldegg, 'Friedrich Ohmann's Entwürfe und ausgeführte Bauten', special issue of *Der Architekt*, Vienna, 1906.

12 Maria Pötzl-Malikova, *Künstlerische Entwicklung 1890–1918*, pt. 2 of Vol. 9, *Die Plastik der Ringstrasse, Die Wiener Ringstrasse – Bild einer Epoche*, Wiesbaden, 1976, pp. 37 ff.

13 Hans Tietze, 'Friedrich Ohmanns Entwurf für eine Neugestaltung des Votivkirchenplatzes', in *Die bildenden Künste*, Vol. 1, 1916–18, p. 161 *(Der Architekt)*.

14 Camillo Sitte, *Der Städtebau nach seinen künstlerischen Grundsätzen*, 1st ed., Vienna, 1889.

15 Renate Wagner-Rieger, pp. 231 ff.

16 *Bauten und Entwürfe von Carl König*, ed. by his pupils, Vienna, 1910.

17 Elisabeth Springer, *Geschichte und Kulturleben der Wiener Ringstrasse*, Vol. 2 of *Die Wiener Ringstrasse – Bild einer Epoche*, Wiesbaden, 1979.

18 Ludwig Baumann, *Mein Lebenslauf und meine Tätigkeit*, Vienna, 1931.

19 Carl E. Schorske, Fin-de-Siècle *Vienna. Politics and Culture*, New York, 1980, p. 90.

20 Karl Holey, 'Neubauten Wiener Banken', in *Die bildenden Künste*, Vol. 1, 1916–18, p. 1 *(Der Architekt)*.

21 Robert Waissenberger, 'Wiener Nutzbauten des 19. Jahrhunderts als Beispiele zukunftsweisenden Bauens', in *Wiener Schriften*, no. 38, Vienna–Munich, 1977.

VII MUSIC AND OPERA

Kurt Blaukopf

The years around the turn of the century are characterized by the endeavour to establish Austria's independence in the fields of literature and the visual arts. As early as 1894 the Viennese literary journal, *Neue Revue*, was demanding that 'Austrian literature should again be fully emancipated from that of Germany',[1] while *Ver Sacrum*, the official organ of the Association of Austrian Artists, announced that it aimed to 'present Austria as an autonomous artistic factor'.[2]

No such declarations were, to our knowledge, made in the sphere of music in which Austria's identity was so patent as to obviate the need for rhetoric. Nor was it necessary further to reinforce a confidence already bolstered by an established compositional tradition, a high standard of musicianship and, most important of all, massive reserves of musical dilettantism. All but one of Anton Bruckner's nine symphonies had been published by the turn of the century, while the œuvre of Johannes Brahms – a 'naturalized' Viennese – had gained recognition and a faithful following long before the period we are concerned with here. Though his name is still as illustrious as ever, some of his contemporaries have failed to sustain their once glorious reputation, being remembered only as lesser luminaries who nevertheless helped to enrich the musical life of the city, men such as Johann Nepomuk Fuchs, Robert Fuchs, who numbered Gustav Mahler among his pupils, Hermann Grädener and Karl Goldmark.

252 Ludwig Michalek: *Johannes Brahms.* Charcoal drawing, 44 x 30 cm. Historisches Museum der Stadt Wien.
Unlike Anton Bruckner, Brahms was held in high esteem by Eduard Hanslick. His compositions were seen as placing him in the mainstream of the Viennese classical tradition, and were always acclaimed in the capital. The first performance of his Second and Third Symphonies was given by the Vienna Philharmonic under Hans Richter.

Brucknerians and Brahmsians

In the 1890s music, unlike the other arts, was not as yet engaged in the search for an identity. Nor did it, until later, experience an innovative impulse comparable to that of the Secession. Nevertheless, musical circles had become embroiled in a heated controversy over the attitude to be adopted towards Richard Wagner and Bayreuth. One of the functions of the Vienna Academic Wagner Society, founded in 1872 by, amongst others, Karl Goldmark, was to perpetuate this confrontation between the two parties – on the one hand, the protagonists of the 'music of the future' and of Wagner's *Gesamtkunstwerk* ('total work of art'); on the other, the advocates of the autonomy of instrumental music, rooted as this was in the Viennese tradition. Those protagonists who subscribed to Eduard Hanslick's school of aesthetic autonomy looked to Brahms as their champion, while the Wagnerians paid homage to Bruckner. Much of the skirmishing that went on between Brahmsians and Brucknerians now seems to us almost incomprehensible, for we are instinctively aware that the two B's have long since made their peace in the symphonic pantheon where another B, to wit Beethoven, occupies the most prominent place.

The cohort of Brucknerians included, amongst others, Hugo Wolf. Listening to his song cycles today, it is difficult to understand why he should have felt impelled to take issue with the Brahmsians. His musical criticism, however, is more revealing, for his vehement championship of Wagner, Liszt and Bruckner and his avowed distaste for Brahms are of themselves sufficient explanation for his ostracism by the latter's adherents, devoted as they were to the formative principles of absolute music in the Viennese tradition. Some idea of Hugo Wolf's pugnacity may be gained from a letter to Hermann Bahr, dated 21 March 1890: 'Of all the composers alive today', wrote Wolf, 'only two are worthy of discussion, and those two are: Anton Bruckner and Hugo Wolf.'[3]

The early protagonists of Bruckner's (and Wagner's) music saw themselves as an avantgarde which, however, could not cut away the ground from under the feet of the strongly entrenched Brahmsian traditionalists. For Vienna, as Richard Strauss once ruefully observed, was unfortunately still governed by 'the same old laws of beauty, arcane secrets we should be glad to have a sight of had they not to this day remained locked in the bosoms of Messrs Hanslick & Co'.[4]

Moving patterns of sound

Eduard Hanslick was regarded by many as the supreme and infallible head of a church of musical aesthetics. His book *Vom Musikalisch-Schönen* ('Of the Beautiful in Music'), a declaration of faith in musical traditionalism, first appeared in 1854 and, by 1891, was already in its eighth edition. Here he sets the seal of approval on a concept peculiar, or at any rate not antecedent, to Viennese classicism. That concept, which defined music as 'moving patterns of sound', looked upon the formal development of musical ideas and, notably, the

254 Ferry Bératon: *Anton Bruckner.* 1889, oil on canvas, 86 x 75.5 cm. Historisches Museum der Stadt Wien.
Anton Bruckner is rightly regarded as an innovator. His happy relations with the Viennese musical establishment and notably with Eduard Hanslick soon became clouded when he openly professed his admiration for the works of Richard Wagner. Owing to Hanslick's opposition, he met with little success and it was not until his work had been enthusiastically acclaimed in Germany that it began to find acceptance in Vienna.

Dr Eduard Hanslick.

realization of those ideas, as the loftiest of goals. This axiom, inherited from the Viennese tradition, subsequently recurs in the musical thinking of Arnold Schoenberg who, despite – and, indeed, perhaps because of – the musical revolution he was to initiate, acknowledged his indebtedness to Brahms's instrumental music. Even Johann Strauss betrays the extent to which he was in thrall to 'moving sound patterns', as is discernible not only in the pretentious symphonic mannerism of the preludes to his innumerable waltzes, but also in his vocal compositions in which word stress is so often sacrificed to the musical beat.

Opera was less affected by the tension between traditionalists and progressives. From 1881 to 1897 the Court Opera was under the directorship of Wilhelm Jahn, a conductor who, at least to some extent, looked upon that establishment as a purveyor of pleasing artistic spectacles. Not that this prevented his including in the repertoire works by Mascagni, Leoncavallo, Cornelius and Humperdinck or,

for that matter, a musical play, *Der Evangelimann* ('The Preacher') by the Austrian Wilhelm Kienzl. Jahn, however, entrusted the pioneering moderns – then chiefly represented by Richard Wagner – to Hans Richter, the capellmeister and Wagner *aficionado* who, both in the opera house and as conductor (until 1898) of the Philharmonic Concerts, set his unmistakable stamp on the musical life of the city.

The capital of music, 1892

In 1892 Vienna, as a multinational capital, gave proof of its musical standing with a mammoth spectacle, the International Music and Theatre Exhibition, staged in the Prater's trade fairground.[5] The show's catalogue, nearly 600 pages in length, listed 7,149 exhibitors. No less impressive were the festival concerts put on in conjunction with the exhibition, the first of which was given on 7 May in the newly opened Musikhalle by the Philharmonic Orchestra con-

255 Peter Halm: *Eduard Hanslick.* Etching, 16.8 x 25 cm. Historisches Museum der Stadt Wien.
Eduard Hanslick, a critic who was subsequently appointed professor at Vienna University, wrote the celebrated work *Vom Musikalisch-Schönen* ('Of the Beautiful in Music') in which he set forth his views. To him music was essentially 'moving sound patterns' rather than the expression of feelings, a concept which automatically placed him in the anti-Wagner camp.

256 Otto Böhler: *Johannes Brahms, Johann Strauss und Hans Richter beim Kartenspiel* ('Johannes Brahms, Johann Strauss and Hans Richter at the Card-Table'). Silhouette on postcard, 9.2 x 14.2 cm. Historisches Museum der Stadt Wien.
Brahms and Strauss were on friendly terms and greatly appreciated each other's work. The latter's waltzes were particularly admired by Brahms.

212

257 Franz von Lenbach: *Johann Strauss.* 1895, oil on canvas, 98 x 73.5 cm. Museen der Stadt Wien (Johann Strauss's house).
This famous and much fêted composer was the undisputed 'King of the Waltz'. He was also a handsome man, a fact that contributed not a little to his fame.

ducted by Hans Richter. In addition, the Exhibition Orchestra gave no fewer than thirty 'popular symphony concerts' for the benefit of an audience seated at tables laden with food and drink. According to eyewitness accounts, so entranced did they become while listening to Anton Bruckner's Third Symphony (conducted by Ferdinand Löwe on 9 July) that they forgot the delicacies placed before them and devoted all their attention to the music. The festival, which went on until the autumn, is accorded barely a passing mention in the more recent musical historiography of Vienna. Yet its importance to the musical life of the city, if not to that of other countries, can hardly be overrated. This applies more particularly to the performances, all of them given by visiting companies, which took place in the specially built Exhibition Theatre. *Halka*, written by Stanislaw Moniuszko for the Polish National Opera and performed by the Lwów (Lemberg) City Theatre, did not win quite as much acclaim as that accorded to the works of Mascagni and Leoncavallo, staged by the 'veristic' company of Sanzogno, the Italian music publisher. The highlight of the series, however, was provided by the performances of the Czech National Opera, notably Smetana's *Bartered Bride*. This was the work which earned the most applause and which now, more than a quarter of a century after its première in Prague, was about to win international acclaim. Barely two years later *The Bartered Bride* was accepted by Gustav Mahler, principal conductor of the Hamburg Opera House. Mahler took a keen interest in musical developments in Vienna, for he had long dreamt of being summoned back to the capital and thus returning to the city where he had received his musical and intellectual training. Vienna, he would often say, was his ultimate goal; nowhere else could he feel so much at home.

Gustav Mahler

Gustav Mahler was not the kind of artist who would sit back quietly and wait for a summons to 'the god of the southern zones'

258 Ernst Klimt: Poster for the International Music and Theatre Exhibition in Vienna, 1892. Bildarchiv der Österreichischen Nationalbibliothek, Vienna. About 1900 the poster began to assume an ever more important place in the field of advertising. At first, however, it was mainly used to announce cultural events.

259 International Music and Theatre Exhibition, Tonhalle. Photograph, Bildarchiv der Österreichischen Nationalbibliothek, Vienna.

260 Emil Orlik: *Gustav Mahler.*
1916, etching, 47.3 x 31.5 cm.
Historisches Museum der Stadt
Wien.
Both as composer and conductor,
Gustav Mahler was an innovator.
From 1897 to 1907 he was conductor and director at the Court
Opera. He was an uncompromising perfectionist whose works
reflect to an unusual degree the
period in which they were composed.

(as he himself put it). It was only by dint of a great deal of manœuvring that he contrived to get himself appointed conductor of the Court Opera in May 1897 and director five months later. Indeed, recent research bears unequivocal testimony to the tactical skill shown by one who was, in other respects, so guileless and unworldly.

When Mahler took up his appointment in Vienna, the musical climate of the city had been changed, first by the death of Bruckner the previous year, then by that of Brahms on 3 April 1897. The same day saw the found-ing, under Gustav Klimt, of the Association of Austrian Artists, known as the Secession. When, on 11 May 1897, Mahler made his debut as a conductor at the Court Opera in a performance of *Lohengrin,* new aesthetic maxims were already in vogue. While he took note of these innovations, Mahler did not subscribe to them uncritically. Hans-lick, it is true, was soon to claim that he detected the influence of the Secession in Mahler's compositions. Yet no single stylistic trend could possibly have encom-passed all that the composer was attempting to achieve. His musical language incor-porates both lyrical folk music and har-monic and formal innovations; his mode of writing tends to aural transparency no less than to contrapuntal density; his instru-mentation permits a smooth transition from simplicity to exalted expression – and all this in accents which at every turn betray Mahler's unmistakable idiom. Mahler be-longed to neither of the musical factions. His championship of Bruckner's music was in no way incompatible with his deep respect for Brahms whom he would often visit in his holiday retreat at Ischl.

Mahler was director of the Vienna Court Opera from 1897 to 1907. However, the works he composed during this period – Symphonies Nos 4–8, the *Rückert-Lieder* and the *Kindertotenlieder* –were not written in the capital. For he considered his unremitting labours on behalf of the Opera to be incompatible with the exertions demanded by composition. He engaged in that activity only during his vacations when, far from the city, in the peace of his *'Häuschen'* – a cabin specially designed for the purpose – he drafted the scores he would subsequently elaborate elsewhere. Hence we cannot, as in the case of Mozart, Beethoven and Schubert, identify any par-ticular house in Vienna as a place in which he sought inspiration from his muse. His rela-tionship with the city was of a different kind, and derived from his work at the Opera. He served the latter, not only as a musician, but also – and this is the measure of his artistic stature – as a dedicated pro-ducer, in those days a very rare bird indeed, according to Bruno Walter.[6] Qualities essen-tial to the task were a total empathy with the work to be produced and the ability to iden-tify with an opera, irrespective of style or tendency. In 1900 a critic, commenting on Mahler as producer, wrote: 'Even greater, perhaps, than his energy are the suppleness and flexibility of mind that enable him so to transform himself from one work to the next and from one artist to the next as to reproduce, in his interpretation of that work or that artist, the finest distinctions of style and period.'[7]

261 Gustav Mahler, *Sixth Symphony*. Score annotated by the composer. Gustav Mahler-Gesellschaft, Vienna.
Mahler composed his *Sixth Symphony* during his summer vacations in 1903 and 1904. He incurred considerable ridicule by introducing such unusual instruments as cow-bells and a xylophone into the percussion section.

262 Play-bill for the new production of *Tristan and Isolde* on 21 February 1903 at the Vienna Court Opera. Bildarchiv der Österreichischen Nationalbibliothek, Vienna.
The performance of Wagner's *Tristan and Isolde* was one of Mahler's greatest triumphs during his term of office at the Court Opera. The scenery, designed by the Secessionist artist Alfred Roller, contributed to its success.

263 Alfred Roller: Design for set for *Tristan and Isolde* at the Vienna Court Opera, 1903.

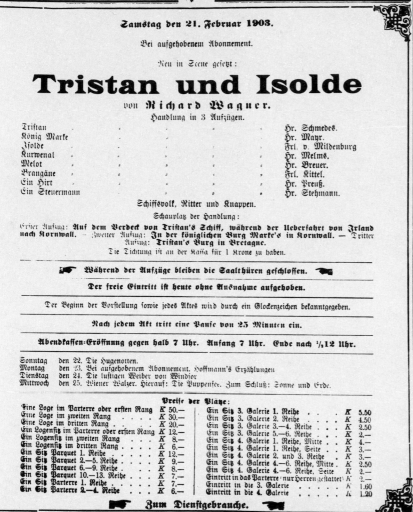

Samstag den 21. Februar 1903.

Bei aufgehobenem Abonnement.

Neu in Scene gesetzt:

Tristan und Isolde

von Richard Wagner.

Handlung in 3 Aufzügen.

Tristan	Hr. Schmedes.
König Marke	Hr. Mayr.
Isolde	Frl. v. Mildenburg
Kurwenal	Hr. Melms.
Melot	Hr. Breuer.
Brangäne	Frl. Kittel.
Ein Hirt	Hr. Preuß.
Ein Steuermann	Hr. Stehmann.

Schiffsvolk, Ritter und Knappen.

Schauplatz der Handlung:

Erster Aufzug: Auf dem Verdeck von Tristan's Schiff, während der Ueberfahrt von Irland nach Kornwall. — Zweiter Aufzug: In der königlichen Burg Marke's in Kornwall. — Dritter Aufzug: Tristan's Burg in Bretagne.

Die Dichtung ist an der Kassa für 1 Krone zu haben.

☞ Während der Aufzüge bleiben die Saalthüren geschlossen. ☜

Der freie Eintritt ist heute ohne Ausnahme aufgehoben.

Der Beginn der Vorstellung sowie jedes Aktes wird durch ein Glockenzeichen bekanntgegeben.

Nach jedem Akt tritt eine Pause von 25 Minuten ein.

Abendkassen-Eröffnung gegen halb 7 Uhr. Anfang 7 Uhr. Ende nach ¼ 12 Uhr.

Sonntag	den 22.	Die Hugenotten.
Montag	den 23.	Bei aufgehobenem Abonnement. Hoffmann's Erzählungen
Dienstag	den 24.	Die lustigen Weiber von Windsor
Mittwoch	den 25.	Wiener Walzer. Hierauf: Die Puppenfee. Zum Schluß: Sonne und Erde.

Preise der Plätze:

Eine Loge im Parterre oder ersten Rang	K 50.—	Ein Sitz 3. Galerie 1. Reihe	K 5.50
Eine Loge im zweiten Rang	K 30.—	Ein Sitz 3. Galerie 2. Reihe	K 4.50
Eine Loge im dritten Rang	K 20.—	Ein Sitz 3. Galerie 3.—4. Reihe	K 2.50
Ein Logensitz im Parterre oder ersten Rang	K 12.—	Ein Sitz 3. Galerie 5.—6. Reihe	K 2.—
Ein Logensitz im zweiten Rang	K 8.—	Ein Sitz 4. Galerie 1. Reihe, Mitte	K 4.—
Ein Logensitz im dritten Rang	K 6.—	Ein Sitz 4. Galerie 1. Reihe, Seite	K 3.—
Ein Sitz Parquet 1. Reihe	K 12.—	Ein Sitz 4. Galerie 2. und 3. Reihe	K 3.—
Ein Sitz Parquet 2.—5. Reihe	K 9.—	Ein Sitz 4. Galerie 4.—6. Reihe, Mitte	K 2.50
Ein Sitz Parquet 6.—9. Reihe	K 8.—	Ein Sitz 4. Galerie 4.—6. Reihe, Seite	K 2.—
Ein Sitz Parquet 10.—13. Reihe	K 7.—	Eintritt in das Parterre (nur Herren gestattet)	K 2.—
Ein Sitz Parterre 1. Reihe	K 7.—	Eintritt in die 3. Galerie	K 1.60
Ein Sitz Parterre 2.—4. Reihe	K 6.—	Eintritt in die 4. Galerie	K 1.20

☞ Zum Dienstgebrauche.

IX., Berggasse 7.

Such an approach was calculated, not only to bring about a departure from conventional routine, but also to turn into an event anything that was aesthetically out of the ordinary. Mahler transformed the opera house into a shrine: Wagner's works were no longer abridged in the traditional manner, but performed in their entirety; the search for the exact quality of sound demanded by each individual work led to flexibility in the composition and placing of the orchestra; 'star' singers whose sense of theatre proved inadequate were liable to be replaced by those with acting ability. A crucial role in the realization of Mahler's view of opera as theatre was played by one of the Secession artists, Alfred Roller, who, in 1903, was put in charge of sets and costume design. The production of *Tristan and Isolde* in that year and of *Fidelio* in 1904 bears eloquent testimony to their collaboration, the historical importance of which transpires, if only indirectly, from the enthusiastic notices written at the time.

The impact made by Mahler as a conductor of orchestral music was to prove less enduring. For his appointment as permanent conductor of the Philharmonic concerts in 1898 – a post previously held by Hans Richter for twenty-three years – continued only until the beginning of 1901. He did not enjoy a particularly happy relationship with the players, all of whom belonged to the Court Opera orchestra and who, when fulfilling outside engagements, went by the name of Vienna Philharmonic. Mahler's term of office coincided with a period in which they had begun to behave as though they were a law unto themselves. Thus, in 1901, they awarded the conductorship to one of their own number, Josef Hellmesberger, who held the post until 1902. In 1909 the players finally reverted to the idea of a permanent conductor when they placed themselves in the hands of Felix von Weingartner, their artistic mentor until 1927.

Expansion of orchestras

The Vienna Philharmonic Orchestra, founded in 1842, owed its high musical stan-

217

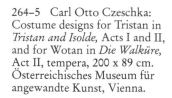

264–5 Carl Otto Czeschka: Costume designs for Tristan in *Tristan and Isolde*, Acts I and II, and for Wotan in *Die Walküre*, Act II, tempera, 200 x 89 cm. Österreichisches Museum für angewandte Kunst, Vienna.

266 Heinrich Lefler: Costume design for Richard Wagner's *Parsifal*, 1913.

267 The Musikverein Building. Photograph, Bildarchiv der Österreichischen Nationalbibliothek, Vienna.
The Musikverein building, opened by Theophil Hansen on 6 January 1870, has remained to this day one of the most important centres of the city's musical life. Numerous works were performed for the first time in the 'Golden Hall', the acoustics of which have always been renowned.

268 Max Oppenheimer: *Streichquartett* ('String Quartet'). Oil tempera on canvas, 71 x 80 cm. Österreichische Galerie, Vienna.
Max Oppenheimer, who called himself 'Mopp', was one of the most interesting Viennese artists of the post-war years. While he was known primarily as a portraitist, he also painted a large number of pictures based on musical themes.

dards largely to the contractual ties which bound each of its members to the Opera. These not only spelt greater financial security for the individual player, but also lent the orchestra as a whole both continuity and homogeneity in matters of technique. However, their duties at the Opera were such that concerts could only be given on Saturday afternoons and Sunday mornings. Thus, in the absence of new and permanent orchestras, there could be no expansion of the capital's musical life. Paradoxical though it may seem, Vienna, the city of the symphony *par excellence,* did not possess such a body until the turn of the century, for the New Philharmonic, formed in 1899, was soon disbanded owing to lack of funds. Not long afterwards a committee of music-lovers was set up with the object of promoting concerts on a properly organized basis. The result was the founding in 1900 of the Vienna Concert Society which, with the collaboration of the musicians, undertook a novel mission, namely to attract to the concert hall those elements who had hitherto shunned it.[8] Ferdinand Löwe was appointed conductor of the Concert Society Orchestra which, many decades later and after numerous legal and administrative vicissitudes, was to become the Vienna Symphony Orchestra, a company of musicians which has survived to this day and still bears the main burden of the symphony concerts performed in the city.

The Concert Society Orchestra was also instrumental in drawing attention to a young man, then a cellist in the Court Opera. This was Franz Schmidt who has, so far as form is concerned, rightly been described as the last genuine symphonist. Though his later operatic works have failed to stand the test of time, both his chamber music and his four symphonies have made a significant contribution to the Viennese repertoire of absolute music. The label 'neo-Romantic', so often attached to his style, seems to us misplaced and applicable rather to the works of Josef Marx. However, the demarcation line between neo-Romanticism as thus understood and the avant-garde of the early twentieth century cannot be defined with any precision. As examples we

might cite Franz Schreker, whose work is once more attracting notice, and Alexander Zemlinsky, in his own day a successful operatic composer and of interest to us mainly because of his instrumental music and its affinity to that of his pupil Schoenberg. In 1904 Zemlinsky was appointed director of the Vienna Volksoper, a theatre built in 1898 on the occasion of the imperial jubilee, and now about to become the capital's second operatic centre.

Zemlinsky's activities as a conductor helped to pave the way for a scheme then unprecedented in Vienna, namely the series of Working Men's Symphony Concerts inaugurated in 1905. The stimulus was provided on the centenary of Schiller's death in May of that year by the 'Schiller Memorial

269 Franz Schmidt. Photograph. Historisches Museum der Stadt Wien.
Though Franz Schmidt's compositions have a certain affinity to those of the neo-romantics, the form assumed by his instrumental works places him in the Viennese tradition of absolute music.

270 Alexander von Zemlinsky. Photograph. Historisches Museum der Stadt Wien.
The operas, symphonies and chamber music composed by Alexander von Zemlinsky long remained almost forgotten. He was, besides, a busy conductor and teacher, one of his pupils being Arnold Schoenberg who later married his sister.

271 Oskar Kokoschka: *David Josef Bach.* 1920, chalk drawing, 48.2 x 31.5 cm. Historisches Museum der Stadt Wien.
David Josef Bach, critic and musicologist, was the instigator of the Viennese Working Men's Symphony Concerts for which Anton von Webern subsequently assumed responsibility.

Festival of Viennese Labour', during which Zemlinsky conducted the Vienna Volksoper orchestra in a performance of Beethoven's Third Symphony. The keen interest shown by what was predominantly a working-class audience came as a surprise to many people and, indeed, proved so encouraging that the decision was made to organize the concerts, the first of which took place on 29 December in the Grosser Musikvereinssaal.

The concerts were initiated by David Josef Bach, an early friend of Arnold Schoenberg's. The latter was subsequently to speak of the considerable influence Bach had exerted on the development of his character. At that time music critic on the *Arbeiter-Zeitung,* Bach nevertheless entertained some doubts about his trade. 'The working man', he wrote, 'will be attracted to music, not by the expression of opinion, but by the actuality of art. The monopoly in art must cease – starting, perhaps, with the monopoly in music.'[9]

That popular concerts should have come into being at this particular time was certainly due in part to the new political situation. The demands of the so-called Fourth Estate were becoming ever more vociferous, while 1905 was the year that marked the beginning of the struggle for universal and equal suffrage. The idea that art should be made available to the people was also advocated by composers such as Schoenberg, Zemlinsky and Webern whose motives, however, were not so much political as practical and

221

educational. Schoenberg, for instance, conducted a metal-workers' choir from 1895 to 1896 and, later, also served as choir-master to the Mödling working men's choral society. His friendship with David Bach, to whose circle of friends Webern also belonged, was no doubt a contributory factor in his decision to undertake these educational tasks.

The expansion of the city's musical activities after the turn of the century provided fresh opportunities for aspiring talent. Those opportunities were further increased by the appearance of new orchestras – notably the Musicians' Orchestra founded in 1907 under Oskar Nedbal – all of which needed to expand their repertoires. Again, this period saw the founding of societies for the promotion of contemporary works, amongst them the Ansorge Society (1903), the Society of Creative Musicians (1904) under the honorary chairmanship of Gustav Mahler, and the Academic Society of Literature and Music (1908). Such an enrichment of Vienna's musical life could hardly fail to exert an influence on the creative potential of the new generation of composers.

Arnold Schoenberg

Arnold Schoenberg was one of their number. Initially self-taught, he was twenty-one by the time he applied himself, with Zemlinsky's encouragement, to the systematic study of music. Nor was it long before he himself became the teacher of a host of other composers. Profoundly influenced by Wagner though he had been, Schoenberg nevertheless continued to adhere to the compositional notions of Brahms, as is indeed evident from his String Quartet in D Major (no opus number) composed in 1897 and performed in Vienna that same year. Around the turn of the century Schoenberg embarked on the composition of his monumental choral work, the *Gurrelieder* ('Songs of the Dove'), based on poems by Jens Peter Jacobsen. He was not to succeed in completing the score until 1911, for first of all he was forced to earn his living,

partly as a conductor in the Berlin *Überbrett*, or cabaret, and partly by orchestrating other people's light music and operettas. On returning to Vienna in 1903 he was given the opportunity of directing courses in musical composition at the Schwarzwald School. Among his pupils he was soon to number Alban Berg, Anton von Webern and Egon Wellesz, to name only a few, some of whom were to enrich the repertoire of the new century with works of a highly idiosyncratic kind. Around Schoenberg there now grew up a circle of musicians who, while fully conscious of tradition, were uncompromising in their search for new means of expression. Any suggestion that the older Viennese School had left the field wide open to the innovators would be a gross oversimplification, for at this early stage the new movement was of a purely peripheral nature, despite the moral support afforded by Mahler and Richard Strauss. Even when, as in his chamber music, Schoenberg abandoned the use of vast orchestral and choral ensembles, he failed to elicit the immediate and positive response which, with hindsight, we might expect of a metropolis of absolute music dedicated to the 'obbligato accompaniment'. Neither the performance of his String Quartets Op. 7 and Op. 10 (1905 and 1909) nor that of his Chamber Symphony Op. 9 succeeded in earning the composer the approval of more than a very small circle. Indeed, in 1906, the Chamber Symphony, scored for fifteen solo instruments, caused an uproar in the concert hall. What militated against a favourable reception of the work was the fact that it was tonal only in as much as written in the key of E major, while the opalescent ambiguity of the chords and the multiplicity of leading notes left the long-familiar tonal relations far behind. That Schoenberg had nevertheless adhered to traditional formal principles necessarily eluded an audience repelled by the sounds they heard.

With his cycle of fifteen songs and piano accompaniment, based on Stefan George's *Buch der hängenden Gärten* ('Book of the Hanging Gardens'), Schoenberg entered hitherto unknown musical territory. In 1910, on its first performance in the Ehrbar-

272   Richard Gerstl: *Arnold Schönberg. C.* 1907–8, oil on canvas, 121 x 181 cm. Historisches Museum der Stadt Wien. Schoenberg was at the very centre of the modern movement in music known as the Viennese School. His friendship with Richard Gerstl, a rebellious young painter, had tragic consequences.

Saal in Vienna, the composer admitted that he had 'broken through all the barriers of past aesthetics'.[10] With this step forward came freedom of form, as in the Piano Pieces Op. 11 and the Five Pieces for Orchestra Op. 16, of which the third – with an invariant chord almost continually changing in colour – assumes the status of an experimental work, thus impressively anticipating the 'tone-colour melody' as expounded by Schoenberg in his *Harmonielehre* ('Theory of Harmony') published in 1911.

The book was dedicated to the memory of Gustav Mahler who died in Vienna on 18 May and was buried in Grinzing Cemetery, an event which is believed to have inspired the last of Schoenberg's Piano Pieces Op. 19. Mahler's death seems to have loosened the ties which bound the younger man to Vienna. Moreover, Schoenberg had departed too far from the aesthetic norms still considered *de rigueur* in the capital. His mono-drama *Erwartung* ('Expectation'), with an opera text by Marie Pappenheim, had been completed in September 1909 but, because of its idiosyncratic expressionist scoring designed to conform to musical prose, it was destined to languish for fifteen years before its first performance under Zemlinsky in Prague. Similarly, an attempt to find him an appropriate post as teacher of composition proved fruitless, despite Mahler's recommendation that he be offered a readership at the Vienna Academy of Music. In 1911, therefore, Schoenberg again betook himself to Berlin. The following year an amateur of the new music wrote: 'Art that looks to the future is out of favour. True, once someone has died (e.g. Mahler), much is forgiven him… But as for the living! Schoenberg's banishment was an evil omen. There was, of course, that lectureship – but no emoluments, no rewards, no means of sustenance. Elsewhere room is made for genius. Here the path is smoothed for its departure…'[11]

Anton von Webern

From all this we might be led to suppose that Vienna's musical culture was then divided into two opposing camps – on the one hand, the complacent traditionalists to whom anything new was anathema, on the other, the innovators, whose genius was as yet unrecognized. Yet it would be an oversimplification were we to portray the Schoenberg circle as a united band of disciples, following in the footsteps of their *guru*, Gustav Mahler. Close as were the aesthetic ties between the two parties – a fact recently confirmed beyond all doubt by Ernst Krenek[12] – their mutual relations were not, at least to begin with, entirely unclouded. As Schoenberg once remarked of his own attitude to Mahler, his conversion from Saul to Paul was by no means instantaneous. And in 1901 an eighteen-year-old music-lover, after studying one of Mahler's scores, wrote: '…the impression it makes is almost childish, despite the extravagance of the orchestration.'[13] The writer's name? Anton von Webern.

Later Webern was to become an ardent champion of Mahler's music. Yet the words cited above betray a tendency which was later to re-emerge in Webern's musical thinking, a tendency, that is, towards the elimination of unnecessary verbiage, drastic economy of means and formal compression.

Webern's intention was to become a conductor and, since the practice of that profession necessarily entailed a knowledge of theory, he entered Vienna University where he studied under Guido Adler, the founder of Austrian musicology and lifelong friend of Mahler. Probably of greater moment to Webern's artistic development were Schoenberg's courses on harmony and counterpoint, which he began attending in the autumn of 1904. On becoming acquainted with Schoenberg's Chamber Symphony Op. 9, he told himself: 'That's just the sort of thing you ought to do,'[14] and at once proceeded to attempt it, with results that were more than mere plagiarism. For it was not his teacher's wont to impose his own compositional methods on his pupils, but rather to act in accordance with the lofty educational principle of liberating their potential. In Webern's case this released a spate of compositions which far exceeded

273 Marie Arnsburg: *Eingang zum Bösendorfersaal* ('Entrance to the Bösendorfersaal'). Watercolour, 37 x 28.5 cm. Historisches Museum der Stadt Wien.
Here, in the old Bösendorfersaal, Gustav Mahler heard the first performance of a Schoenberg quartet. In the ensuing uproar he enthusiastically espoused his fellow composer's cause.

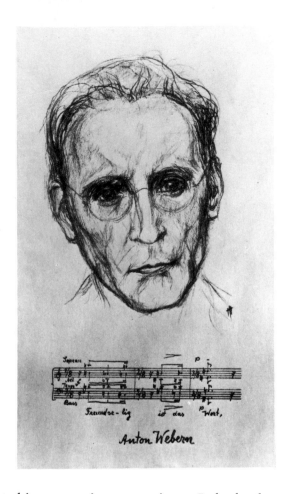

go by before 'this masterwork of extreme authenticity', as Adorno has described it, was made available in print.

The Songs Op. 3, set to texts by Stefan George, mark Webern's abandonment of the tonal centre, since there is no longer any indication of the initial key signature. Thus there was an inevitable disintegration of the formal structure that had resulted from the harmonic-tonal design. The lack of form was made good by denser motivic work. Many years later Webern was to give a pithy account of the exciting dilemma created by the renunciation of the formative power of tonality: 'As we gradually abandoned tonality', he wrote, 'it began to occur to us that nothing should be repeated, that what came next should always be something new. Needless to say, that won't work since it does away with comprehensibility.'[15]

That dilemma was undoubtedly less ineluctable in music set to a text than in purely instrumental works. For if, in absolute music, repetition is abandoned as a principle of composition and, with it, recognition as a means of reception, this will call for a closely-knit, concentrated score and, by extension, a greater degree of attentiveness on the part of the audience. Such concentration necessarily involves a reduction in playing-time, along with radical compression such as was effected by Webern in the Six Pieces for Orchestra Op. 6 (1909) and Six Bagatelles for String Quartet Op. 9 (1913).

When the latter work was published in 1924, it contained a characteristic foreword by Schoenberg: 'Just think', he writes, 'what strength of mind it takes to attain such concision. Every glance could be expanded into a poem, every sigh into a novel. But to convey a novel in a single gesture, or happiness by a catch of the breath – concision of that order postulates a corresponding lack of self-compunction.' The same comments hold good for Webern's Pieces for Orchestra Op. 10, which were written between 1911 and 1913. The longest lasts 105 seconds, the shortest fourteen seconds. Aphoristic density is the hallmark of Webern's music. Such is its economy and concision that all his numbered works (Opp. 1–31) may be accommodated on no more

his mentor's expectations. Indeed, the young composer produced a piano piece which astonished Schoenberg and, as Webern himself was later to remark, led to 'suspended tonality' and prevented the key note from coming through, although still perceptible as a point of reference. That few people were able to grasp the nature of Webern's conception is evident from the reaction to one of his piano quintets which was performed along with works by seven other pupils of Schoenberg at a concert given in 1907. According to the critic of the *Neue Zeitschrift für Musik*, only two of the young composers, Webern and Berg, were worthy of note, yet even they betrayed, he thought, the 'pernicious influence of Schoenberg's compositions'. Webern's orchestral Passacaglia Op. 1, which had its first public performance in Vienna in November 1908, was accorded a more discriminating appraisal, although fourteen years were to

than four long-playing records. To listen to them all at one sitting would be to flout the composer's intentions, since each work, indeed each section, conveys – to use the language of cybernetics – a maximum of original communication from which the banal and the redundant have been deliberately eliminated. It is that asceticism, with its refusal to pander to the desire for repetition, imitation, variation, stretta and coda, which gives rise to the problems Webern's music poses to the listener. For it calls for his unconditional assent, total surrender, unswerving attention and heightened awareness.

Alban Berg

In 1904 Alban Berg entered Schoenberg's magic circle. His early compositional attempts were confined to Lieder, the accompaniment being treated as little more than an individual 'voice'. From Schoenberg the young composer acquired a command of form and of motivic work, as may be seen from the Piano Sonata Op. 1 and the String Quartet Op. 3, which were performed for the first time in May 1911 in the Ehrbar-Saal. The latter work astonished even Schoenberg by, as he put it, 'the extent and fluency of its musical idiom, the vigour and assurance of the presentation, the painstaking attention to detail and the high degree of originality.'[16] A stage seemed now to have been reached in which the innovative elements in Viennese music could look for a greater measure of appreciation, Gustav Mahler's untimely death having, perhaps, opened people's minds to the unfamiliar. For during the Vienna music festival in June 1912 Mahler's Ninth Symphony was given its first performance under Bruno Walter.

At this time Alban Berg was engaged in making a piano transcription of Schoenberg's *Songs of the Dove*, a monumental work which was performed in Vienna in February 1913 under Franz Schreker in the presence of the composer. Since this event seemed to indicate that the Schoenberg school had at last got one foot inside the door of Vienna's musical establishment, the

Academic Society of Literature and Music decided to put on a concert whose programme would include, not only Schoenberg's Chamber Symphony, but also works by Zemlinsky, Webern and Berg. Conducted by Schoenberg, the concert took place on 31 March 1913 in the Grosser Musikvereinssaal with not altogether encouraging results, for at one stage a brawl broke out among members of the audience. The hour of the avant-garde had not yet come. While the sheer size of the orchestral complement required for the *Songs of the Dove* might, perhaps, succeed in evoking some response, the substitution of truth for beauty was too audacious to appeal to the public at large. Putting his own interpretation on the signs of the times, Richard Strauss paid tribute to Vienna's persistent conservatism with a Solemn Prelude, composed for the ceremonial opening on 19 October 1913 of the newly-built Konzerthaus. Here, too, during the first season, the public was treated to a surfeit of traditional works.

International conflict was already casting its shadow over the Viennese musical scene,[17] yet the sense of doom, so often postulated by historians after the event, was by no means omnipresent. For even the most sensitive artists were unable for the most part to register the initial tremors that heralded the devastating earthquake to come. What stirred them most deeply was not their immediate experience of social reality, but rather its reflection in literature. Only indirectly, through the medium of writers such as Ibsen, Dostoievsky and Strindberg, did the majority of artists become aware of the problems posed by the world situation. Alban Berg, for example, was moved to the depths of his being by the work of Georg Büchner, a dramatist whom most people, having omitted to read his biography, assumed to be a 'modern'. Berg had attended a performance of Büchner's play *Woyzeck* on 5 May 1914 at the Residenzbühne (later Kammerspiele), and had promptly decided 'as a matter of course' to turn the piece into an opera. He was to be engaged upon this work, with some intermissions, for more than half a decade. For the composition (unorchestrated) was not

279 László: Music Festival, Vienna, 1912. Poster, Graphische Sammlung, Albertina, Vienna.

completed until October 1921; in other words, it was written at a time that covered the war years, the collapse of the Habsburg Monarchy and the miseries of the early post-war period. Berg's experience of those days was incorporated into *Wozzeck*, the opera of 'social compassion'.

Wozzeck and the war

The success of *Wozzeck* cannot, of course, be attributed primarily to the adverse circumstances prevailing at the time. Rather, the importance of those circumstances lay in their having strengthened Berg's sense of social commitment, thus lending depth to his composition and furthering his inner aesthetic development. That particular quality, namely Berg's affinity for opera, must have been known to Schoenberg at an early date, for in 1912 the latter was already urging him 'to write something for the theatre'[18] in the belief that his pupil would be successful in this field.

Berg's spell in the army, though personally disastrous, greatly benefited his work by giving him first-hand experience of the fate suffered by Wozzeck, a fate to which he was then able to give musical form. Despite his poor state of health, he had volunteered for military service on the outbreak of war, being determined to do what he deemed to be his duty at whatever cost to himself. His correspondence at this time reveals that he soon came to regard army life as a 'moral inferno'.[19] In 1915, when strenuous guard duties had induced a physical collapse, he was admitted to a military hospital. From letters he wrote to his pupil Gottfried Kassowitz we learn that the musical picture he paints in Scene 5, Act 2 of his opera was inspired by the gloomy barrack atmosphere and the snoring of his room-mates. His military service even brought him into contact with the living counterpart of the doctor in Büchner's play – a medical officer who, instead of helping his patients, threatens them with reprimands. Some of the alterations made by Berg to Büchner's text would seem to indicate that the figure of Wozzeck depicted in his opera is to some extent autobiographical. As Berg's war-time letters show, his idealistic concept of duty was beginning to give way to a critical interest in political matters. Indeed, he once wrote to Kassowitz reproaching him for his failure to mention the war, the subject which was of greatest interest to Berg.

From his war-time experiences he gained the empathy which predestined him to give musical form to Büchner's tragedy. What he eventually achieved was, as Schoenberg put it, 'genuine theatre music'.[20] To the historian it can only be a matter for surprise that, after *Fidelio*, there should have been an interval of more than a century before the emergence of a work capable of securing and

retaining a place in the musical repertoire. Thus conditions in Vienna, a metropolis of absolute music, had evidently long been unfavourable to the genesis of operatic works whose aesthetic merit might enable them to rank alongside the symphonies and chamber music of local composers. In his own idiosyncratic way Berg, as a musical dramatist, also subscribed to the aesthetic principle of 'moving patterns of sound', for while fulfilling every dramatic requirement, he 'drew upon old and new musical forms, including those otherwise found only in absolute music'[21] to ensure that each scene and entr'acte was endowed with a musical significance all its own.

It is this specific quality that has assured the aesthetic standing of *Wozzeck*. It has also enabled us to gauge the extent to which the composer – even in those parts of the work which are primarily of a dramatic nature – continued to adhere to the Viennese tradition of tonal thinking. Both the historical significance of *Wozzeck* and much of the impact made by that work stem from the fact that it lends itself to interpretation as the artistic expression of war-time experiences, as an ethical statement not inferior to that made by Karl Kraus in *Die letzten Tage der Menschheit* ('The Last Days of Mankind') and, maybe, even surpassing the latter, unless we are much deceived, in its social and aesthetic implications.

Operetta

'I only hope this won't turn me into a composer of operettas!' Alban Berg is said to have remarked a few days before his death, when being given a transfusion of blood from an anonymous donor.[22] This esoteric joke, reflecting as it does the fear lest the 'popular muse' should 'infect' serious music, was inspired by a view which had established itself towards the end of the nineteenth century. It had been engendered by the detachment of compositional thought from musical practice and by specialization in the various musical fields. Another consequence – and this applies in particular to aesthetic theory – was the growing antagonism between musical sensuousness on the one hand and artistic truth on the other. Thus the mechanisms, which had for centuries ensured cross-fertilization between popular and aesthetically autonomous music, gradually began to decay. Never before had pioneering innovation in the art of music diverged so far from accepted practice.

Yet, paradoxical though it may seem, neither Schoenberg nor his pupils withdrew into an ivory tower, as is clear from the music the former composed for the Berlin cabaret and from the '6,000 pages of opera scores he was compelled to orchestrate'.[23] As further examples we might cite his characteristic activities both as a practical and as a politically motivated musician. Though, no doubt, he regarded his scoring of other composers' light music as tedious hack-work, it nevertheless testifies to the supreme ease with which Schoenberg was able to move in this field.

K. k. pr. Theater an der Wien.
Direktion: Wilhelm Karczag und Karl Wallner.

Samstag den 30. Dezember 1905.
4. Premieren-Abonnement.
Unter persönlicher Leitung des Komponisten.
Novität!   Zum 1. Male: Novität!

Die lustige Witwe.

Operette in 3 Akten (teilweise nach einer fremden Grundidee) von Viktor Léon und Leo Stein.
Musik von **Franz Lehár.**

Baron Mirko Zeta, pontevedrinischer Gesandter in Paris . Siegmund Natzler.
Valencienne, seine Frau . Annie Wünsch.
Graf Danilo Danilowitsch, Gesandtschaftssekretär, Leut. d. Kav. i. R. . Louis Treumann.
Hanna Glawari . . Mizzi Günther.
Camille Rosillon . . Karl Meister.
Vicomte Cascada . . Leo v. Keller.
Raoul de Saint-Brioche . Carlo Böhm.
Bogdanowitsch, pontevedrinischer Konsul . . Fritz Albin.
Sylviane, seine Frau . Bertha Ziegler.
Kromov, pontevedrinischer Gesandtschaftsrat . Heinrich Pirk.

Olga, seine Frau . . Minna Schütz.
Pritschitsch, pontevedrinischer Oberst in Pension . . Julius Bramer.
Praskowia, seine Frau . Lili Wiska.
Njegus, Kanzlist bei der pontevedrinischen Gesandtschaft . . Oskar Sachs.
Lolo . . . Mizzi Swoboda.
Dodo . . . Mizzi Dotzauer.
Jou-Jou . . . Annie Kienberger.
Frou-Frou . . . Lina Bauer.
Clo-Clo . . . Herma Cursa.
Margot . . . Helene Neumayer.
Ein Diener . . . Karl Beller.
Pariser und pontevedrinische Gesellschaft, Guslaren, Musikanten, Dienerschaft.

Spielt in Paris heutzutage, und zwar: der 1. Akt im Salon des pontevedrinischen Gesandtschaftspalais, der 2. und 3. Akt im Schlosse der Frau Hanna Glawari.
Die neuen Dekorationen sind aus den Malerateliers Burghart & Frank und Theatermaler Zabransky.
Die neuen Kostüme teils von Maison Hoffmann, teils von Frau Streischofsky und Obergarderobier Staran.
Die Tänze hat Herr Professor van Hamme einstudiert.
Die Beleuchtungsgegenstände des 2. Aktes wurden von der Bronzewarenfabrik Erdmann & Kleemann geliefert.

Nach dem 2. Akt ist eine größere Pause.

Operngläser sind bei den Billeteuren und in den Garderoben gegen eine Leihgebühr von 20 Hellern zu haben.

Kassa-Eröffnung ½ 7 Uhr.   Anfang 7 Uhr.   Ende 10 Uhr.

Sonntag den 31. Nachmittags halb 3 Uhr bei ermäß. Preisen (ohne Vormerkgebühr): **Der Zigeunerbaron.** Abends 7 Uhr: **Die lustige Witwe.**
Montag den 1. Jänner 1906. Nachmittags halb 3 Uhr bei ermäßigten Preisen (ohne Vormerkgebühr): **Vergeltsgott.** Abends halb 8 Uhr: **Die lustige Witwe.**
Dienstag den 2. **Die lustige Witwe.**

Die Tageskassen: I. Rothenthurmstraße 16 (Bazar) und VI. Millöckergasse (Theatergebäude) sind täglich von 9 Uhr früh bis 5 Uhr nachmittags geöffnet und werden Karten zu jeder im Repertoire angekündigten Vorstellung abgegeben.

K. k. Hoftheater-Druckerei, IX., Berggasse 7.

Webern also must have given proof of considerable ability to hold his own in the practical world of music for, as theatre conductor at Teplitz (now Teplice), Danzig (now Gdańsk) and Stettin (now Szczecin) between 1910 and 1912, he was required to conduct not only the operettas *Zigeunerbaron* ('Gypsy Baron') and *Fledermaus* ('The Bat') by Johann Strauss, but also Lehár's *Lustige Witwe* ('Merry Widow'), Oscar Straus's *Walzertraum* ('Waltz Dream') and Leo Fall's *Dollar Prinzessin*

281 Play-bill for the first performance of the operetta *The Merry Widow* by Franz Lehár on 30 December 1905. Bildarchiv der Österreichischen Nationalbibliothek, Vienna.
Of all the works written during the 'Silver Age' of light opera, Lehár's *Merry Widow* was the most widely acclaimed. The operetta owed its spectacular success to the frivolous view of life implicit in the libretto and to the lilting, catchy tunes.

('Dollar Princess') works, that is to say, which may be described as representative not of the 'golden' but rather of the subsequent 'silver' age of Viennese light opera, in other words, an age of decline. Contemporaries, however, saw it, not as a decline, but as an impressive rise in the nation's musical output. True, the classic exponents had departed, Franz von Suppé having died in 1895, and Johann Strauss and Karl Millöcker in 1899, yet the number of establishments purveying light opera was on the increase. Between 1900 and 1910 the population of the capital of the Habsburg empire rose from 1,650,000 to some two millions (i. e. more than Vienna possesses today). Other theatres, besides those traditionally associated with light opera (the Theater an der Wien and the Carltheater), now turned to that genre, among them the Volksoper, the Raimundtheater and, in 1910, also the Bürgertheater. Another such house was the Bundestheater, later the Metropol, built in the Prater during the First World War, a period which in its turn was to see a proliferation of establishments ranging from the small to the minute.

284 Volksoper. Xylograph, Bildarchiv der Österreichischen
Nationalbibliothek, Vienna.
The Kaiserjubiläumsstadttheater,
subsequently renamed Volksoper,
which took only eight months to
build, was opened in 1898. Initially a playhouse, it later went over
to operettas and opera. The latter
proved particulary successful during Rainer Simons's directorship.

285–6 Bürgertheater: Auditori-
um and Stage. 1906, photographs.
Historisches Museum der Stadt
Wien.
The Bürgertheater, situated near
the Stadtpark, was initially used
for plays. These were soon replaced by operettas in response to
the growing demand for such fare.

287 Hans Schliessmann: *Scham-
mel Orchestra.* Postcard,
10 x 15 cm. Historisches Museum
der Stadt Wien.
Schrammel quartets played at
Heurigers, the taverns where the
new-vintage wine was drunk. The
combination of two violins, guitar
and clarinet (later replaced by an
accordion) was originated some
hundred years ago by the Scham-
mel brothers, Johann and Josef.

288 G. Richter: Ladies' Orchestra in the Prohaska
Restaurant in the Prater, Vienna.
C. 1890, photograph. Bildarchiv
der Österreichischen Na-
tionalbibliothek, Vienna.
Restaurants in the Prater often
had their own orchestras, some of
which attained a high artistic standard. Ladies' orchestras were a
special feature.

Vienna became the hub of the light opera industry, for the works written and performed there served as prototypes for innumerable others, produced in response to popular demand not only throughout the Monarchy, but far beyond its frontiers. Among the most prominent composers of such operettas were Franz Lehár, Leo Fall, Oscar Straus, Edmund Eysler and Emmerich Kálmán. None, however, was fortunate enough to have his works accepted by the Court Opera, an accolade that was bestowed on Johann Strauss alone. His *Ritter Pazman* ('Ritter Pazman') was performed there in 1892, while in 1894 the *Fledermaus* was similarly honoured – an occasion of which the anniversary was celebrated twenty-five years later with a gala performance under Gustav Mahler. However, the twentieth century saw a widening of the rift between the solemn and the light-hearted. Slowly and almost im-perceptibly opera degenerated (if degeneration is the word) into a repository of lofty aestheticism.

Court Opera – State Opera

Felix von Weingartner, Mahler's successor at the Opera, made way in 1911 for Hans Gregor, who had the task of steering that institution through the vicissitudes of war. His term of office began with the first performance in Vienna of Richard Strauss's *Rosenkavalier* and culminated in October 1918 with the production of that same composer's *Salome,* a work persistently rejected by the censor in Mahler's day. By now, however, the old guard had long since lost its grip, and the Habsburg empire was rapidly crumbling. On 4 December 1918, following the birth of the Republic of German Austria, the Court Opera was renamed

Theater und Vergnügungen.

Theater und Vergnügungen.

Wiener Volksoper.

Zum erstenmal:

Ernani.

Oper in vier Aufzügen von Giuseppe Verdi. Dich trug nach Victor Hugos Drama "Hernani" von Francesco Maria Piave. Deutsch von Josef Ritter v. Seyfried.

Ernani, der Bandit	Hr. Schütz
Don Carlos, König von Spanien	Hr. Schützendorf
Do Ruy Gomez de Silva, Grand von Spanien	Hr. Zec
Elvira, seine Nichte und Verlobte	Frl. Wenger
Giovanna, i. Gesellschafterin	Fr. v. Kellersberg
Don Riccardo, Wissenträger des Königs	Hr. Strack
Jago, Waffenträger des Don Ruy	Hr. Markowsky

Anfang 7 Uhr.

Ende 10 Uhr.

Samstag den 12.: "Quo vadis?"
Sonntag den 13., nachmittags 2 Uhr: "Carmen." Abends halb 8 Uhr: "Quo vadis?"
Montag den 14.: "Carmen."
Dienstag den 15., nachmittags halb 3 Uhr: "Die lustigen Weiber von Windsor." Abends halb 8 Uhr: "Quo vadis?"
Mittwoch den 16.: "Quo vadis?"
Donnerstag den 17.: "Ernani."

Theater in der Josefstadt.

Hohe Politik.

Schwank in 3 Akten von Richard Sournonnet.

Ottomar v. Plunkmann	Hr. Höbling / Hr. Huber
Adalein	Frl. Schadler
Dr Buing	Hr. Biedle
Marie, s. Frau	Frl. Siedelberg
Wert	Hr. Zettl
Jonas	Hr. Jarno
Schöpfke	Hr. Erker
Rosa	Frl. Krüger
Ein Lakai	Hr. Vollner

Anfang 8 Uhr.

Ende vor 10 Uhr.

Samstag den 12.: Hohe Politik.
Sonntag den 13.: nachmittags 3 Uhr: Freie Volksbühne. Abends 8 Uhr: "Ein Doppelleben."

Hölle.

Anfang 10 Uhr.

Durchschlagender Erfolg!

Wiener Schattenspiele

von Leo Zasche und Alfred Deutsch-German.

Ihr Tugendwächter.

Ein Schelmen der von Raim Kohl.

Studentenhochzeit

Operette von A. Reinmann.

Soli-Vorträge: Fritz Grünbaum, Wilda Breiten, Trude Voigt, Arthur Hoffmann, John Frei.

Sonn- und Feiertag, 3 Uhr: Nachmittagsvorstellung bei kleinen Preisen.

Graben-Kino-Theater

I., Graben 17.

La Morte civile.

Drama von Giacometti.
(Hauptrolle: Ermete Novelli.)

Die offizielle Nunce . . . Ethn. Will'erstahl
Das Bär a. d. Lackier-Original-Aufn.
Im Marchenlande . . . Haust v Belle
Les Martignes . . . Reise-Sportspiel.
Das in geflossene Lissabon . . . Aktualität.
Der Haselstolz . . . Komödie v. Herter
Versailles . . . Varietät.
S molosko . . . Hr. roik. Studie
Winterbad im Westen . . . Naturstudie.
Altmutterliebetreue . . . V datumfnahme.
Aufgeschossen . . . Schnurre.

Vorstellungen an Wochentagen 5 Uhr nachm., 1/2 8 Uhr abends; an Sonn- und Feiertagen 2 Uhr vorm., 2 bis 5 Uhr nachm. u. 1/2 8 Uhr abends.

Johann Strauss-Theater.

Telephon 50x1 and 16814.

Das erste Weib.

Operette in drei Akten von Victor Léon. Musik von Bruno Hartl.

Prinz Palmero	Hr. Höste
Alfons Gray	Hr. Treumann
Dullenau auf Dulleuhofen	Hr. Carlo
Franz Graf Wihren	Hr. Sachs
Johann Graf Bärenburg	Hr. Jung
Alex Graf Dengenbach	Hr. Bastars
Kornel Graf Bilähy	Hr. Neumann
Reinschreiber von Sturmhauf	Hr. Grödl
Moritz Baron v. Feldberg	Hr. Gibl
Euselline, i. Frau	Fr. Günther
Netitta, i. Tochter	Fr. Haren
Ernt, sein Sohn	Fr. v. Henrici
Fürstin Tyr	Frl. Bernay
Prinzessin Clementine	
Prinzessin Poilomena	Frl. Suchy
Miß Dyson	Fr. Sintus
Dr Rohrer	Hr. Moser

Anfang 1/2 8 Uhr.

Ende nach 10 Uhr.

Samstag den 12.: "Das erste Weib."
Sonntag den 13. nachmittags halb 3 Uhr: "Der Bettelstudent." Abends halb 8 Uhr: "Das erste Weib."
Montag den 14.: "Das erste Weib."
Dienstag den 15., nachmittags halb 3 Uhr: "Die Fledermaus." Abends halb 8 Uhr: "Das erste Weib."

Lustspiel-Theater.

Zum erstenmal:

Die Jammerpepi.

Komödie in 3 Akten von Alexander Engel.

Karl Boller	Hr. Moran
Frau Therese Boller	Frl. Josephy
Iva	Frl. Oma
Steffi	Frl. Bod.
Josefine Boller	Fr. Klein
Dr Boletino	Hr. Kulinszer
Smirewinski	Hr. Viert
Eduard Kranjl	Frl. Werbezirk
Lotti	Frl. Fenster
ie Friseurin	Frl. Erben
Eusel	Hr. hl.
Hans	Hr. Butschel
Fritz	Hr. hl.
Wikki	Hr. Berger

Anfang 7 Uhr.

Ende vor 1/4 10 Uhr.

Samstag den 12.: "Die Jammerpepi."
Sonntag den 13., nachmittags 3 Uhr: Freie Volksbühne. Abends halb 8 Uhr: "Die Jammerpepi."

Theater und Kabarett "Fledermaus"

Telephon 5459. Beginn 10 Uhr.

Der fromme Selvanus. Eine Waldidylle von Veda. Musik von Leo Kleis. Der Mentor, Kabarettlein in einem von Bu .. heitheimer.

Carl Nagelmüller, Lucie Berber, Richard Godal, Georg Kundert, Wenja Horace, Ferd. Stein, Heinz Juß a. G., Mia Eberg a. G.

Nach der Vorstellung bei freiem Entrée: Bunter Teil.

Max und Moritz!

I., Annagasse 3. Telephon 9629.

Heute und täglich: Das sensationelle November-Programm.

Neu! Neu!

Der Gemeindenarr!

Tragikomödie in 1 Akt von Anton u. Donat Herrnfeld.

Neu! Neu!

Frau Elkans Friseur!

Schwank in 1 Akt von Anton und Donat Herrnfeld.

Neuer bunter Teil!

Anfang 8 Uhr. Ende nach 11 Uhr.

Warme Küche.

Die Tageskassen sind täglich in der Annagasse 3 ab 10 Uhr vormittags geöffnet.

Jeden Sonn- und Feiertag 3 Uhr: Nachmittagsvorstellung.

Carl-Theater.

Telephon 1649. (1288.)

Das Puppenmädel.

Vaudeville in drei Akten (mit Benützung eines Lustspieles von Flers und Caillavet) von Leo Stein und Dr A. M. Willner. Musik von Leo Fall.

Madame Prunier	Fr. Keplinger
Yvette, d. Tochter	Frl. Weiße
Marquis de la Tourette	Hr. Waldemar
Tiborius, s. Neffe	Hr. Bartscha
Puffou	Hr. Blaiel
Rosalitta	Fr. Zwerenz
Romuald Talmi	Hr. König
Der Pfarrer	Hr. Göttler
Maremoiselle Poche	Frl. Wilke
Madame Merlin	Frl. Halme
Babe v. Schon	Frl. Delorm
Monsieu Kandalogne	Hr. Patti
Pierre, Diener	Hr. Teichler

Anfang 1/2 8 Uhr.

Ende nach 1/4 11 Uhr.

Samstag den 12.: "Das Puppenmädel."
Sonntag den 13., nachmittags halb 3 Uhr: "Die geschiedene Frau." Abends halb 8 Uhr: "Das Puppenmädel."

Residenzbühne

I., Rotenturmstrasse 20.

Der Liebestrank.

Schwank in 3 Akten von Frank Wedekind.

Anfang 8 Uhr.

Ende vor 10 Uhr.

Intimes Theater

(II., Praterstrasse Nr. 34, gegenüber dem Carltheater).

Paris und Menelaus.

Lustspiel in einem Akt von Pierre Chaine und José de Bérys.

Wer andern eine Grube gräbt . . .

Schwank in einem Akt von Adolf Glaß.

Schlafe patent.

Schwank in einem Akt von J. und Bramarer und Alfred Grünwald.

Die nackte Dame.

Schwank in einem Akt von Julius Horst.

Anfang 8 Uhr.

Ende vor 10 Uhr.

Wiener Urania (I., Aspernplatz).

Telephon 3702

4/6 Uhr, großer Vortragssaal:

Kinematogramme
mit beleuchendem Vortrag.

Orchesterleitung: Kapelle Karl Komzal.

1/2 8 Uhr, großer Vortragssaal:

Kaif. Rat Ernst Kraul:

Der Harz.

1/2 8 Uhr, kleiner Vortragssaal:

Kurs: Dozent Dr. Franz Strunz:

Die Philosophie des Lebens.

Stadttheater in St. Pölten.

Ein Herbstmanöver.

Stadttheater in Brünn.

Madame Butterfly.

K. k. Hofburgtheater.

Ansk- u. Bestell-Bureau: Tel. 8598

Ein idealer Gatte.

Ein Spiel in vier Akten von Oskar Wilde.

Der Earl v. Cowersham	Hr. Hartmann
Lord Arthur Goring	Hr. Korff
sein Sohn	
Sir Robert Chiltern	Hr. Devrient
Unterstaatssekretär	
Lady Gertrud, seine Frau	Frl. Hönigswald
Miß Mabel Chiltern, seine Schwester	Fr. Albach-Retty
Vicomte de Nonjac, Attaché d. franz.	
Botschaft	Hr. Balch
Mr Montford	Hr. Büßler
Lady Marthy	Fr. Lewinsky
Lady Olivia v. Basildon	Frl. Wilke
Mrs. Margaret Marchmont	Fr. Bleibenberg
Mrs. Chevelen	Fr. Devrient-Reinhold
Mason, Kammerdiener bei Sir Robert Chiltern	Hr. Ruß
James, Diener bei Sir Robert Chiltern	Hr. Eimhorst
Harold, Diener bei Lord Goring	Hr. Gehre
Phipps, Kammerdiener bei Lord Goring	Hr. Sommer

Regie: Herr Hartmann.

Anfang 7 Uhr.

Ende 1/2 10 Uhr.

Samstag den 12.: "Rosenmontag." (Anfang 7 Uhr.)
Sonntag den 13.: "Monna Vanna." (Anfang 7 Uhr.)
Montag den 14.: "Die Welt, in der man sich langweilt." (Anfang 7 Uhr.)
Dienstag den 15. (der Aushilfskasse des k. u. k. Militärinvalidenvereines in Wien ist ein Teil des Ertrages gewidmet): "Egmont." (Anfang 7 Uhr.)

Wiener Bürgertheater.

Telephon 3476, 19161.

Der unsterbliche Lump.

Altwiener Stück in drei Akten von Felix Dörmann. Musik von Edmund Eysler.

Florian	Hr. Bauer
Der Bürgermeister, sein Vater	Hr. Marson
Sepp	Hr. Ludwig
Loisl	Hr. Berger
Hans Ritter	Hr. Storm a. G.
Baumgartner	Hr. Jules
Ein alter Harfenist	Hr. Letten
Die Enkelin des Harfenistenkisel Freita	Frl. Marlowa G.
Anna Reisleitner	Frl. Marion a. G.
D. alte Reisleitner	Hr. Weidinger
D alte Reisleitnerin	Hr. Baue
Rosa Raafl	Fr. Pohl-Meiser
Herr Numi elmaher	Hr. Strakmeyer
Herr Trampler	Hr. Schöntag
Frau Trampler	Frl. Stopal

Anfang 1/2 8 Uhr.

Ende 10 Uhr.

Samstag den 12., nachmittags halb 3 Uhr: "Der dicke Klaus und der lange Hans." Abends halb 8 Uhr: "Der unsterbliche Lump."
Sonntag den 13., nachmittags halb 3 Uhr: "Der Hüttenbesitzer." Abends halb 8 Uhr: "Der unsterbliche Lump."
Montag den 14.: "Der unsterbliche Lump."
Dienstag den 15., nachmittags halb 3 Uhr: "Kean." Abends halb 8 Uhr: "Der unsterbliche Lump."

K. k. Hofoperntheater.

Ansk- u. Bestell-Bur.: Tel 476, 475 und 262.

Der Ring des Nibelungen.

Ein Bühnenfestspiel für drei Tage und einen Vorabend von Richard Wagner.

Erster Tag:

Die Walküre.

In drei Aufzügen.

Siegmund	Hr. Schmedes
Hunding	Hr. Mayr
Wotan	Hr. Weidemann
Sieglinde	Fr. Förster-Lauterer
Brünhilde	Fr. Bahr-Mildenburg
Fricka	Fr. Hilgermann
Gerhilde	Fr. Kurina
Ortlinde	Fr. Pohlner
Waltraute	Fr. Bardo
Schwertleite	Frl. Kittel
Helmwige	Fr. Elizza
Siegrune	Fr. Morawetz
Roßweiße	Frl. Leschka
Grimmgerde	Frl. Saalen

Anfang 7 Uhr.

Ende 11 Uhr.

Samstag den 12.: "Die Bohème." (Anfang halb 8 Uhr.)
Sonntag den 13.: "Die verkaufte Braut." (Anfang 7 Uhr.)
Montag den 14.: "Siegfried." (Anfang 7 Uhr.)
Dienstag den 15., nachmittags 2 Uhr (bei aufgehobenem Abonnement und Saisonabonnement und zu ermäßigten Preisen): "Excelsior."

Theater an der Wien.

Teleph. Tageskassen 13180, 5245. Abendkasse 86.

Der Graf von Luxemburg.

Operette in drei Akten von A. M. Willner und R. Bodansky. Musik von Franz Lehár.

Rene Graf von Luxemburg	Hr. v. d. Bruch
Fürst Basil Basilowitsch	Hr. Langer
Gräfin Stoja	Frl. Schütz
Armand Brissard	Hr. Bötel
Angèle Didier	Frl. Mahrbach
Juliette Bermont	Frl. Percotti
Sergei Menschikoff	Hr. Saüß
Pawel Pawlowitsch	Hr. Paul
Pelegrin	Hr. Hansen
Anatole Saville	Hr. Albin

Anfang 1/2 8 Uhr.

Ende nach 10 Uhr.

Samstag den 12., nachmittags 3 Uhr: "Gänsefüßel." Abends halb 8 Uhr: "Der Graf von Luxemburg."
Sonntag den 13., nachmittags halb 3 Uhr: "Die Dollarprinzessin." Abends 8 Uhr: "Der Graf von Luxemburg."
Montag den 14.: "Der Graf von Luxemburg."
Dienstag den 15., nachmittags halb 3 Uhr: "Ein Herbstmanöver." Abends halb 8 Uhr: "Die Dollarprinzessin."

Kleine Bühne

I., Wollzeile 34. Tel. 3368.
Anfang 9 Uhr. Ende 11 Uhr.

Man steigt nach.

Die kleine Passion
v. Dörmann.

Mitzi Freller a. G.
Mella Mars
Dr. Egon Friedell a. G.
Rudolf Meinhardt a. G.

Die Dame im Kamin.

Groteske in einem Akt von A. Freksa.

Künstl. Leitung v Bela Laszky.

Jeden Sonn- u. Feiertag Nachmittagsvorstellung 1/4 4 Uhr bei ermäßigten Preisen.

Deutsches Volkstheater.

Telephon 3005.

Das kleine Schokoladenmädchen.

Lustspiel in 4 Aufzügen von Paul Gavault, deutsch von G. v. Schönthan.

Luststalle	Hr. Schreiber
Benjamine s. Tochter	Frl. Müller
Hector de Pavejac	Hr. Fürth
Ringaison	Hr. Kirchner
Eortie s. Tochter	Frl. Kueber
Heluence Bebaride	Hr. Kramer
Rosette, ein Modellgirl	Hr. Kellar
Paul Normand	Hr. Crofser
Loupet	Hr. Leopoldi
Beiuly	Hr. Huber
Julie	Frl. Menari
Pingiel, Chauffeur	Hr. Tradiy
Casimir	Hr. Gottler
Ein Kellner	Hr. Gottler
Ein Diener	Hr. Frinde

Anfang 1/2 8 Uhr.

Ende vor 10 Uhr.

Samstag den 12.: "Hasemanns Töchter."
Sonntag den 13.: nachmittags halb 3 Uhr: "Das vierte Gebot." Abends halb 8 Uhr: "Das kleine Schokoladenmädchen."
Montag den 14. (bei ermäßigten Preisen): "Der lustige Krieg."
Dienstag den 15., nachmittags halb 3 Uhr: "Ihr Korporal." Abends halb 8 Uhr: "Das kleine Schokoladenmädchen."
Mittwoch den 16., nachmittags halb 3 Uhr: "Minna von Barnhelm." Abends halb 8 Uhr: "Das Konzert."
Donnerstag den 17.: "Liebelei." "Komtesse Mizzi."

Raimund-Theater.

Gastspiel Alexander Girardi.

Das Glücksmädel.

Operette in 3 Akten von Robert Bodansky und F. Thelen. Musik von Robert Stolz.

Baron Fritz v. Waldhofen	Hr. Rohr
Erich Heulein	Hr. Flemming
Andrae Rothuber	Hr. Girardi
Anna, s. Tochter	Frl. Ruska
Franz Mitterer	Hr. Glawatsch
Resy Ramm	Frl. Waide
Rudi v. Feldbach	Hr. Werner
Mati	Hr. Even a. G.
Sch.i	Hr. Gerhardt
Willy	Hr. Ernst
Mizzi	Frl. Hallada
Hedi	Frl. Lirich
Pauline	Frl. Leisner
Aristides Bernek	Frl. ...

Anfang 1/2 8 Uhr.

Ende 10 Uhr.

Samstag den 12.: Das Glücksmädel.
Sonntag den 13., nachmittags halb 3 Uhr: "Die sieben Schwaben." Abends halb 8 Uhr: "Das Glücksmädel."
Montag den 14.: "Das Glücksmädel."
Dienstag den 15., nachmittags halb 3 Uhr: "Wiener Blut." Abends halb 8 Uhr: "Das Glücksmädel."

Neue Wiener Bühne

(ehem. Danzers Orpheum). Tel. 14101.

Der Herr Verteidiger.

Groteske in drei Akten von Franz Molnar und Alfred Halm.

Anfang 1/2 8 Uhr.

Ende nach 1/2 10 Uhr.

237

State Opera, its fortunes being entrusted to the joint care of Richard Strauss and Franz Schalk.

To many republicans, lavish expenditure on an opera house previously supported by the privy purse was now unacceptable, if not actually indefensible, in a small country beset by economic difficulties. There were some who suggested in all seriousness that, if the Imperial Court had lost its legitimacy, so too had the court theatres. However, the preservationists won the day, for in the Federal Constitution of 1920 these establishments were placed under the administrative and financial control of the state. In 1919 this change of rank was recorded in verse by Max Kalbeck.[24]

Once temple of the Muses, you have passed
From the sublime to the ridiculous,
First shrine, then palace, ending up at last
A mediocre middle-class town house.

Schoenberg Society

The end of the war and the proclamation of the Republic were generally regarded as a new beginning, as the right moment, that is, to draw up a new policy for the arts – a policy which, in the event, was not without its utopian aspects. Reform became the order of the day, a case in point being the *Richtlinien für ein Kunstamt* ('Directions for a Ministry of the Arts'), a symposium edited by the architect and theoretician Adolf Loos,[25] of which the musical section was contributed by Schoenberg.[26] Here he defends the thesis that musical performances should be free from the yoke of commerce; to achieve this, creative artists must band together in a co-operative association which, unaided by state subsidies, should look to the public for support.

These ideas found realization in the Society for Private Musical Performances set up by Schoenberg and like-minded friends on 6 December 1918. In the three years of its existence, the society gave 117 concerts at which 154 contemporary works were performed. In addition to Schoenberg himself,

292 Adolf Loos: Directives for a Ministry of the Arts, 1913.
The architect, Adolf Loos, also made a name for himself as a controversial writer on aesthetic matters, including such subjects as the encouragement of art and its acceptance by the public.
Directives for a Ministry of the Arts. Edited by Adolf Loos. Beethoven's Defective Ears.
At the turn of the eighteenth century there lived in Vienna a musician whose name was Beethoven. People mocked him, for he was small, crotchety and comical of countenance. People objected to his compositions. What a shame, they would say, that his ears should be defective. His brain keeps hatching out horrible dissonances, but since he proclaims them to be glorious harmonies, his ears must surely be defective, for our own ears are demonstrably sound. What a shame!
The nobility, however, who, by virtue of the privileges which the world had conferred upon them, were also conscious of their obligations to that world, provided him with the funds that would enable his works to be performed.
Moreover, the nobility, being persons of influence, arranged that one of his operas should be performed at the Imperial Opera House. But the citizens who packed the theatre gave the work such a savage reception that no one dared put on a second performance.
Since then one hundred years have gone by. The citizens listen spell-bound to the works of the deranged musician with defective hearing. Have they acquired patents of nobility, like the aristocracy of 1819, and now stand in awe of the will of the genius? No, they have all acquired a defect. They all have Beethoven's defective ears. Throughout the past century their ears have been maltreated by the dissonances of St Ludwig. That is more than their ears can stand. Every part of that organ's anatomy, ossicles, canals, drum and tube, has assumed a defective shape, just as Beethoven's ears did. To these people the funny face, once mocked by pursuing street urchins, has become the spiritual countenance of the world. The spirit is the architect of the body.

238

293 Carry Hauser: *Josef Matthias Hauer.* 1892, litograph, 47.6 x 31.5 cm. Historisches Museum der Stadt Wien.
In 1920 Hauser, the painter and graphic artist, and Josef Matthias Hauer, the composer, regularly foregathered for friendly discussions. Hauer evolved a twelve-tone system quite independently of Schoenberg.

it counted among its leading lights men such as Berg, Webern, Max Deutsch, Eduard Steuermann, Erwin Ratz and Erwin Stein. Schoenberg and Webern were the directors of studies. The purpose of the society was to impart an intimate knowledge of modern music and to do so, as Alban Berg put it in the prospectus of 16 February 1919, by means, first of 'lucid, thoroughly prepared performances; second, constant repetition; third, performances uncorrupted by the influence of publicity, i. e., purged of the competitive spirit, and independent of applause or the expression of disapproval'.[27] The demand for 'well-prepared performances' implied exceptionally intensive rehearsing. For example the performance of Mahler's Seventh Symphony in an arrangement for piano and four hands was preceded by no less than twelve rehearsals, each lasting several hours. The avoidance of publicity alluded to in the prospectus meant in practice that members only were admitted, and that any critic given permission to attend was required to submit a written undertaking not to mention the performance in his paper. However, there was nothing sectarian about the programmes presented by this dedicated community; not one of Schoenberg's own compositions was performed during the early days. Indeed, so wide was the stylistic range that it embraced the works of Scriabin and Reger, Mahler and Debussy, Busoni and Bartók, Schreker and Richard Strauss.

A new method of composition

Among those whose works were given their first hearing at the concerts was a composer named Josef Matthias Hauer, one of the most curious figures of the new Viennese school. His philosophical adumbrations, which had led to the establishment of a twelve-note system, were clearly contemporaneous with Schoenberg's own line of thought. In July 1921 the latter wrote to Josef Rufer, then acting as secretary to the society, informing him that he had 'discovered something that would ensure

the supremacy of German music for the next hundred years'.[28] He was referring to the method of composition with twelve notes, related only to each other, which he had employed for the first time in his Five Piano Pieces Op. 23, begun in 1920.

That method was the fruit of a lengthy search for a framework rendered essential by the abandonment of the formative energies of tonal harmony. What this mode of composition yielded in aesthetic terms falls outside the province of this essay, since it would take us beyond the period under discussion. Having evolved the above method and become aware of its convergence with Hauer's twelve-tone system, Schoenberg wrote to him in the following proud terms: 'Let us show the world that, without the Austrians, music at least would have got no further. We, on the other hand, know what it is to progress.'[29]

NOTES

1 S. Rubinstein in the Viennese literary journal, *Neue Revue*, Vol. 5, no. 5, 17 January 1894; cited from *Jugend in Wien*, Catalogue no. 24, of the Special Exhibition at the Schiller National Museum, Munich, 1974, p. 232.

2 Prospectus of the Association of Austrian Artists in *Ver Sacrum*, 1898, 1; cited from *Ver Sacrum: Die Zeitschrift der Wiener Secession 1898–1903*, Catalogue of the 77th Special Exhibition at the Historisches Museum der Stadt Wien, 1982, p. 44.

3 Hugo Wolf, letter to Hermann Bahr, 21 May 1890; cited from Rudolf Flotzinger and Gernot Gruber (eds.), *Musikgeschichte Österreichs*, Vol. II, Graz, 1979, p. 374.

4 Richard Strauss, letter to the *Grazer Tagespost;* cited from Eduard Hanslick, *Aus neuer und neuester Zeit*, 2nd ed., Berlin, 1900, p. 49.

5 Cf. Oskar Fleischer, *Die Bedeutung der Internationalen Musik- und Theaterausstellung in Wien für Kunst und Wissenschaft der Musik*, Leipzig, 1894.

6 Bruno Walter, *Thema und Variationen*, Frankfurt am Main, 1960, pp. 86 f.

7 Max Graf, *Wagner-Probleme und andere Studien*, Vienna, n. d. [1900], p. 124.

8 *Jahresbericht des Wiener Concert-Vereins 1900–01*, Vienna, 1901, p. 6.

9 David Josef Bach, letter to Victor Adler; cited from Henriette Kotlan-Werner, *Kunst und Volk: David Josef Bach 1874–1947*, Vienna, 1977, pp. 23 f.

10 Arnold Schoenberg, in the foreword to the programme of the concert held on 14 January 1910 in the Ehrbar-Saal; cited from Ernst Hilmar (ed.), *Arnold Schönberg Gedenkausstellung 1974* [Catalogue], Vienna, 1974.

11 Paul Stefan, 'Frühling', in *Der Ruf, Ein Flugblatt an Junge Menschen*, Vienna–Leipzig, no. 2, March 1912; cited from Hilmar (ed.), op. cit., p. 26.

12 The account is drawn from a biographical essay included in the first American edition of Bruno Walter, *Gustav Mahler*. Walter objected to this unauthorized but interesting contribution (cf. Bruno Walter, *Briefe 1894–1962*, p. 262), with the result that it has been omitted from later editions.

13 Anton von Webern, letter to Diez, 20 February 1902; cited from Walter Kolneder, *Anton von Webern*, Rodenkirchen, 1961, p. 13.

14 Webern said this to himself twenty-five years later. See Hans and Rosaleen Moldenhauer, *Anton von Webern*, Zurich, 1980, p. 76.

15 Cited from Walter Kolneder, op. cit., p. 50.

16 Schoenberg on Alban Berg (1936), cited from Willi Reich, *Alban Berg*, Zurich, 1963, p. 28.

17 Cf. *Jahresbericht des Wiener Concert-Vereins über das dreizehnte Vereinsjahr 1912–13*, Vienna, 1913, p. 9.

18 Letter from Schoenberg to Berg, 3 October 1912; cited from Ernst Hilmar, *Wozzeck von Alban Berg*, Vienna, 1975, p. 10.

19 On this subject cf. Kurt Blaukopf, 'Autobiographische Elemente in Alban Bergs Wozzeck' in *Österreichische Musikzeitschrift*, Vol. 9 (1954), no. 5, pp. 155 f., and Kurt Blaukopf, 'New Lights on "Wozzeck"' in *Saturday Review*, New York, 26 September 1953.

20 Letter from Schoenberg to Emil Hertzka, 24 October 1921; cited from Ernst Hilmar, op. cit., p. 26.

21 Alban Berg, 'Das Opernproblem' in *Neue Musik-Zeitung*, Vol. 49, no. 9, Stuttgart 1928; cited from Willi Reich, *Alban Berg*, Zurich, 1963, p. 61.

22 Willi Reich, op. cit., p. 96.

23 Paul Stefan, *Neue Musik und Wien*, Vienna, 1921, p. 56.

24 Max Kalbeck, facsimile of handwritten inscription in Alois Przistaupinsky, *50 Jahre Wiener Operntheater*, Vienna, 1919, p. 7.

25 Adolf Loos, 'Richtlinien für ein Kunstamt' in *Der Friede, Wochenzeitschrift für Politik, Volkswirtschaft und Literatur*, Vienna, Vol. 3, no. 62 (March 1919), pp. 232–40.

26 Ibid., pp. 239 ff.

27 Walter Szmolyan, 'Schönbergs Wiener Verein für musikalische Privataufführungen' in Ernst Hilmar, *Arnold Schönberg Gedenkausstellung 1974*, Vienna, 1974, p. 75.

28 Josef Rufer, *Das Werk Arnold Schönbergs*, Kassel, 1959, p. 26.

29 Letter from Schoenberg to J. M. Hauer, 1 December 1923, cited from Walter Szmolyan, *Josef Matthias Hauer*, Vienna, 1965, p. 45.

VIII LITERATURE AND THEATRE

Wendelin Schmidt-Dengler

Young Vienna

'Vienna's gay apocalypse of the 1880s': such was Hermann Broch's description, in his essay *Hofmannsthal und seine Zeit* ('Hofmannsthal and his Time'), of a period which to the writers of the turn of the century spelt childhood and youth. For Peter Altenburg, Arthur Schnitzler, Hermann Bahr, Richard Beer-Hofmann, Hugo von Hofmannsthal, Karl Kraus and Leopold von Andrian it was a time of gestation; but on their literature Broch pronounces a damning verdict: 'Of literary production, save for the attractive feuilleton, there was virtually none... Poetry was an affair of gilt-edged volumes on the drawing-room table.' Harsh though that verdict may seem, it is nevertheless wholly appropriate; it also explains why those authors who were embarking on their career in about 1890, found themselves deprived, not only of a supportive vernacular tradition, but also of an opposition upon which to cut their teeth. These same authors had grown up in what Broch describes as a 'value vacuum', the inevitable result of that ornamentality which had superseded art. 'Obsoleteness', a portent of things to come and symbol of Austrian decay, had consequently established itself as a surrogate for artistic creativity.

Even though the 'city of decorum' proferred no tradition of any note to the writers who set their stamp on the Viennese modern school of the turn of the century, the experience of childhood and adolescence was nevertheless incorporated into their works. The title of Broch's essay is not intended to convey the impression that Hofmannsthal was the dominant literary figure of the period between 1890 and 1920, but rather to make us aware of a paradox: for Hofmannsthal was at pains to keep aloof from social and political problems and to avoid alluding directly to such matters, yet his writings – deliberately confined, it seems, to the aesthetic if not the esoteric – give access to every sphere of human experience. It behoves us, however, to consider his work in its social context and, particularly where that context is repudiated, to ask ourselves why this should be.

Although many people refused to admit the fact, the 1880s were overshadowed by an economic crisis. The collapse of the stock market in 1873 spelt ruin for many who had thought themselves financially secure. When Hofmannsthal's parents returned from their honeymoon, they found that they had lost nearly all their money. True, the family fortunes recovered in course of time, but his mother never really got over the shock.

The mob, you say, is on the rampage?
What matter, my friend, just let them be.
Sordid their love and mean their rage,
beneath the contempt of you and me.
Until they oust us from the stage, let us
dedicate our lives to beauty,
While cold tremors of fear we can assuage
with the solace of wine's heart-warming
poetry.
What though the mob be on the rampage,
inflamed by lies and invidious oratory?
All will vanish and leave the page clean for
the truth in its pristine purity.

While it would be unjust to interpret Hofmannsthal's whole œuvre in the light of the suspiciously naïve verses he wrote as a sixteen-year-old, on 1 May 1890, we are fully justified in regarding them as symptomatic of the younger generation in the Vienna of that period. Any reader of Schnitzler's autobiography, *Jugend in Wien* ('Youth in Vienna', posthumously published in 1968) can hardly fail to see that, for all his psychological perspicuity, the author is incapable of identifying what it is that motivates the masses. And in 1895, in a letter to his friend Edgar Karg von Bebenburg, Hofmannsthal wrote:

> One hears a lot about what are commonly called social questions, superficial stuff, some not so bad, but always so remote and lifeless, like looking through a telescope at a herd of chamois grazing far away; it doesn't seem real at all... With an individual, I can get somewhere, maybe even help an individual understand an individual and, to my mind, that's all that really counts. At all events here at home, or however you describe an Austria that's so impossibly difficult to understand. In the West something else may make more sense, for there the masses are, I should say, more equal. But I'm glad it shouldn't be so here.

To him, the only valid solution is the one which helps the individual, not one that is aimed at an abstract generality. It was a position to which Hofmannsthal was to adhere until the end of his life.

Despite the crisis, exclusivity was still maintained although this was not due to wealth and social standing alone. For although the spectre of pauperization had led to a tightening of belts within the class to which authors such as Hofmannsthal belonged, there were nevertheless a number of privileges, other than purely material ones, which were still regarded as obligatory.

First among these was a good education. Hofmannsthal, Beer-Hofmann, Schnitzler Andrian, and Karl Kraus, to name only a few, were all products of the *Gymnasium*, or grammar school, the first three having attended the Akademisches Gymnasium, the most famous of them all. Most were to recall that education with condescension, or else, like Stefan Zweig in his *Welt von Gestern* ('World of Yesterday') (1942), dismiss it as unimportant. Not only did their schooling lay the foundations of a sound classical education; it also erected an effective barrier between the grammar school scholars and those who, for one reason or another, had been unable to gain admission to such establishments. An intense preoccupation with classical literature – read for the most

294   Hugo von Hofmannsthal. 1895, photograph. Theatersammlung, Österreichische Nationalbibliothek, Vienna.
Hugo von Hofmannsthal might almost rate as a child prodigy. He made his entry into the literary world under the pen-name of 'Loris' with poems and playlets which created a considerable stir. Despite his predilection for the aesthetic, his work is not divorced from real life.

part in the original text – would not have been possible had not undue emphasis been placed on the learning of Greek and Latin. Here we might mention that even Sigmund Freud, when he took his final examination in 1873, had to translate a passage from Sophocles' *Oedipus Tyrannos*.

Not only were the discourses engendered by that education unrelated to the more urgent questions of the day; they also tended to turn topical problems into general propositions. Without the salons in which representatives of different generations were able to meet, *fin-de-siècle* Viennese literature would have beeen inconceivable. One notable example was Joséphine von Wertheimstein's salon in Döbling where, as a young man, Hofmannsthal had the opportunity of consorting with Eduard von Bauernfeld and Ferdinand von Saar. The guests at these gatherings included, not only writers, but also painters, musicians, actors, industrialists, engineers, doctors and academics such as Theodor Gomperz, the famous classical scholar. Here, too, the authors of the Viennese modern school

were able to have frequent recourse to the dramatist and philosopher Alfred von Berger, whose works on aesthetics were held in high regard and whose lectures were attended by, amongst others, Hugo von Hofmannsthal.

The writers who frequented the salons bear eloquent testimony to the benefits that they gained in the form, not only of weak tea and other people's insights, but also, quite often, of lively sympathy and material assistance.

It was a world, however, in which they were among their own kind. The closed circle of the salon was, in a positive as well as a negative sense, a prerequisite for writing, just as the café was later to become. The cult of the coffee-house as a meeting-place for intellectuals has been perpetuated by its customers until the present day. Yet it could never be a real substitute for the salon, if only because of its fluctuating clientele and the mixed nature of the groups that met there. Peter Altenberg, for instance, for whom the café was a second home, would undoubtedly have cut a strange figure in the distinguished ambience of the salon. The coffee-house further differed from other forms of organization through the irregularity with which the various groups met and the failure of their members to conform to an accepted code. Indeed, this anarchic state of affairs gave rise to that very spontaneity upon which the cult of the café largely rests.

Chief among the literary coffee-houses was the Café Griensteidl (now replaced by a bank) in the Michaelerplatz. Founded in 1847, it was renamed the National-Café in a burst of nationalist fervour after the 1848 revolution, at a time when it was already a meeting-place for leading politicians, artists and writers. In the 1890s, it numbered amongst its customers men such as Andrian, Bahr, Beer-Hofmann, Felix Dörmann, Hofmannsthal, Karl Kraus, Schnitzler and Felix Salten. Such establishments were not always extolled by the critics of the day. 'The Viennese coffee-house has devoured our intelligence and our culture,' declared Edmund Wengraf in 1891, when attacking the sophisticated aesthetes who held their discussions there; not inaptly, the Grien-

295 Ferdinand von Saar. Photograph. Historisches Museum der Stadt Wien. Saar's novellas may be seen as forerunners to those of Schnitzler. Both here and in his poems he gives a brillant portrayal of the Viennese mentality and of the society of his day.

steidl was renamed by some the Café Megalomania. While the coffee-house as such was important to the writer as a place of intercourse, the very fact of his being restricted to that sphere was not without its disadvantages. As Wengraf put it: 'Here reposes the hidden seed, or rather, the visible source of the evil. Out of the brown, seemingly innocuous brew, there arise vapours which cloud our vision, which blind and stultify, thereby depriving us of one of the most unadulterated and noblest pleasures experienced by man.' It would, however, be unjust were we to overlook the positive aspects of this withdrawal to the decorative salons of the *haut monde* and to the free-and-easy haunts, for it was conducive, not only to concentration on literature as such and to the production and acceptance of literature in highly specialized form, but also to experimentation with new techniques.

The importance attached to literature in the 1890s may be judged from the profusion of literary periodicals which provided ample scope for debate. First and foremost we would cite *Moderne Dichtung*, founded on 1 January 1890 and renamed *Moderne Rundschau* a year later, in which the groups of authors known collectively as Young Vienna were able to present as well as comment upon each other's work. Other such periodicals were the *Wiener Literatur-Zeitung*, the *Wiener Rundschau, Die Zeit* and, in the field of social criticism, the *Wage*. It was a development that culminated in the appearance of the short-lived and exquisitely produced Secessionist organ, *Ver Sacrum*, in which picture and text, both of outstanding quality, are fully synthesized.

Truth and impression

The first of January, 1890, notable for the appearance of *Moderne Dichtung,* also marked a breaking point in the history of Austrian literature which increasingly came to see itself as an autonomous development and to affirm itself as such. Hermann Bahr assumed responsibility for the theoretical side of this work of identification. So prompt was he in publishing his comments

on each emerging trend that it seemed as though he was not so much keeping up with events as anticipating them. As documents, however, the essays and feuilletons are invaluable in that they render explicit at least part of what was implicit in the lyric, epic and dramatic literature of that day. Bahr reduced to a formula that to which others had given more complex expression. Though he has rightly been reproached with over-simplification, his sometimes emphatic pronouncements drew attention, both at home and abroad, to Austria's nascent literature. *Die Moderne* ('The Modern School'), one of the articles in the first issue of *Moderne Dichtung,* gave its name to the literature of the ensuing period. 'We have no grand phrases, nor can we work miracles', Bahr writes:

> We cannot promise the kingdom of heaven. All we wish is that falsehood should cease, falsehood propounded daily from podium, pulpit and throne, for such things are ugly and evil. We have but one law, and that is the truth as perceived by each of us. To that we are beholden. It is not our fault if the truth is harsh and brutal and often cruel and scornful. We are obedient to its demands alone.'

Gotthart Wunberg describes this passage as marking 'the watershed between naturalism and *fin-de-siècle*' – on the one hand, unvarnished truth, on the other, the subjective impression conveyed by that truth as seen by the artist. This is expressed even more succinctly by Bahr in *Die Überwindung des Naturalismus* ('Overcoming Naturalism') (1891), a polemic in which he dismisses the latter as 'idealist reflections on lost media'. The antidote he prescribes is the liberation of the artist, who 'objected to naturalism because he had to serve it; now, however, he is taking the tablets away from the Real and inscribing upon them his own laws'. Liberation in the guise of the nebulous, liberation in the guise of sensuality, self-abandonment to the moment 'when the unfettered nerves dream'. Thus Bahr provided a device for the works written at the turn of the century – a device to which many writers were able to

296 Reinhold Völkel: *Im Café Griensteidl* ('The Interior of the Café Griensteidl'). 1896, watercolour, 23 x 34.3 cm. Historisches Museum der Stadt Wien.
Ever since the revolution of 1848 the Café Griensteidl had been known as a meeting-place for men of note. Fifty years later it became the hub of Vienna's literary life, eventually acquiring the sobriquet 'Café Megalomania'.

297 Hermann Bahr. 1891, photograph. Historisches Museum der Stadt Wien.
Today the importance of Hermann Bahr, an exceptionally versatile writer, lies chiefly in his essays in which he submitted the world of his time to a critical scrutiny. He was often the first to draw attention to modern tendencies in Austrian literature.

respond, whether consciously or otherwise. Symptomatic of the deliberate stand taken against naturalism was the reluctance to accept Hauptmann's works, with the exception, perhaps, of his play *Die Weber* ('The Weavers') which had been enthusiastically reviewed by Karl Kraus in 1892.

No less ambivalent than the view taken of naturalism was the attitude adopted towards Nietzsche, a thinker difficult to classify and one who was to exert a lasting influence on the literature of the German-speaking world, an influence which no one could escape. Of the 'Nietzsche fuss', as Heinrich Gomperz called it, Hofmannsthal wrote in a letter to Salten: 'Three pages of Nietzsche tell us more about life than all our own experiences put together.' Increasingly decried as a false prophet in the late 1890s, Nietzsche, as an artist, was nevertheless beginning to elicit admiration. 'What then remains of Nietzsche?' Michael Fels asked in 1894, and then goes on: 'No matter where and how long we search, we find nothing but style.' Six years later, on the other hand, Alfred von Berger was to declare in a somewhat disparaging obituary that, as an artist, Nietzsche had 'come to grief mentally, and was doomed to failure'. Again, Heinrich Gomperz, son of the famous classical scholar, had founded a peculiarly esoteric society whose members subscribed to a neo-Socratic doctrine and sought to attain peace of mind by basing their lives on Socratic irony. Nietzsche, however, had dismissed the Greek philosopher as one who had used the intellect to despoil the culture of antiquity and as a 'clown who pretends to take himself seriously'. Such sentiments understandably contributed to his rejection, for they must have given deep offence to those 'decadents' who had thrown in their lot with Socrates.

Nietzsche and naturalism should in any case be regarded as necessary antecedents, since both were assimilated into the literature of the *fin-de siècle*. Of greater influence, however, was a poet described by Nietzsche as a decadent *par excellence,* namely Charles Baudelaire, whom he consigned to the same *galère* as the French Symbolists. In 1891 a translation by Felix Dörmann of Baudelaire's poem, 'Le Balcon', had appeared in the *Wiener Rundschau* at much the same time as excerpts from *Les Fleurs du mal,* translated by Stefan George. Comparisons are often drawn between Dörmann and Baudelaire. What *'spleen'* and *'ennui'* were to the latter, Alfred Gold remarked in 1895, 'madness' and 'vapidity' are to the former. That Baudelaire's aesthetic of the ugly was still strongly at work in the Young Vienna group is evident from Dörmann's poem in *Sensations,* entitled 'What I Love' (1892). The deliberately provocative tone is still able to disconcert us today:

I love what no one before
Has loved, or would even pick,
My being's own innermost core
And all that is strange and sick.

Nor was Baudelaire the only poet whose work was so intensively quarried: Joris-Karl Huysmans and Maurice Maeterlinck were

Like Hugo von Hofmannsthal, with whom he went to school, Leopold von Andrian zu Werburg *was one of a circle of younger writers. His œuvre consists of short stories and poems. For a brief period he served as* Generalintendant *(general manager) of the court theatres.*

also frequently called to the witness-box to defend this or that writer's literary principles.

Hofmannsthal, Schnitzler and Altenberg

The particular character of a period cannot, of course, be defined solely in terms of its antecedents, even were it possible to discuss every one of these in detail. We shall therefore examine certain texts which may be regarded as representative of their time. 'What is modern is antique furniture and youthful neuroses' – thus Hofmannsthal in 1893. In the same year he wrote *Der Tor und der Tod* ('The Fool and Death'), a play in which that self-critical aphorism is most strikingly exemplified. Claudio, the self-absorbed hero of the lyrical tragedy, is concerned almost exclusively with, to use Dörmann's phrase, 'his being's own innermost core'. He lives in a small, well-appointed Empire-style château, crammed with antique furniture and providing an impeccably historical ambience in which he can abandon himself to his youthful neuroses. We are reminded of the motto 'Ego Narcissus' given by Hofmannsthal's friend, Leopold von Andrian, to his novella, *Der Garten der Erkenntnis* ('The Garden of Knowledge') (1895). For the phrase implies not merely introspection, but also self-criticism. Claudio is compelled to recognize the falsity of taking refuge in his own artistic reality: 'When others took, when others gave, / I stood aside, from my birth an inner mute.' Death, in the guise of an affable god of antiquity, brings home to him the folly of such an existence. He confronts the visionary hero with three people for whom both Claudio and life itself has held some meaning – his mother, a girl and a friend, all of them capable of genuine commitment. The friend, who died in pursuit of a goal, curses Claudio, despite his own wretched end: 'Thrice blessed was I, compared with you, / Who meant nothing to others, nor they to him.' Claudio dies, and Death, in a dramatic climax to the piece, declaims a

cryptic elegy in which he expresses his astonishment at human behaviour:

Strange are these creatures, strange indeed
Who what's unfathomable, fathom,
What never yet was written read,
Knit and command the tangled mystery
And in the eternal dark yet find a way...

The above lines, we might recall, were written by a poet not yet in his twenties. But young though these writers might be, no concept was more familiar to them than death – premature death, death which precludes any immediate relationship to life. 'So the prince died, knowing nothing.' With these words, Andrian concludes *The Garden of Knowledge. Der Tod Georgs* ('The Death of Georg') (1897/1900) by Richard Beer-Hofmann has for its theme the death of a woman who, in a dream, appears to the hero Paul in the familiar guise of a wife. At the same time, another tie is broken when Paul's friend, Georg, a newly appointed

247

professor, comes to an untimely end. The text depends for its quality on the interweaving of *leitmotivs*, the integration of dreams, and the critical examination of the illusory, aesthetic existence of which Paul is made aware by the very fact of Georg's death.

Schnitzler's dubious character, Anatol, the eponymous hero of a loosely-knit sequence of episodes (1892), is likewise of the same ilk as Claudio. He is incapable of committing himself and he, too, has to fall back on traditional convention. Similarly, he reveals 'the destructive tendencies of idealism in a vacuous and aggressive sense of his own value', as Hartmut Scheible puts it. Like Claudio, he plays with women, only to be regarded by them as a plaything. He is a Narcissus, and yet he recoils from the truth. Anatol does not die but marries which, in his case, spells the end, not of a life, but of a form of life. That his marriage was questionable, to say the least, is evident from the provisional conclusion to the cycle, namely *Anatols Hochzeitsmorgen* ('Anatol's Wedding Morning'). The short scenes, whose general purpose is to put to the test either the anti-hero or his female partner of the moment, clearly betray the intervention of Schnitzler the physician who, as it were, sets up experimental situations that will enable him to portray the psychological motives behind a character's action or inaction. That this was a manifestation of Freud's influence on Schnitzler is a myth which, perpetuated in various text-books, is taking an unconscionable time to die.

The dramatic form of *Anatol* is, physically speaking, typical of the lack of magnitude which characterizes the literature of the day. No novel worthy of the name was written in the 1890s, no major or extensive play. What we have here is the novella which, however, was not, like its realistic counterpart, subject to rigorous architectonics, but rather assumed the form of short prose sketches and of one-act plays. The structure of *Anatol* anticipates that of Schnitzler's – in the event scandal-provoking – play *Der Reigen* ('La Ronde') (1900–3). Its charm lies neither in the construction of contexts nor in the continuous development of the subplots, but rather in the episodic, in the use of

299 Richard Beer-Hofmann. 1937, photograph. Historisches Museum der Stadt Wien.
A writer of novellas and plays, Beer-Hofmann was a member of Hermann Bahr's circle. His literary language is notable for its cultivated tone and exceptional musicality.

300 Arthur Schnitzler. C. 1910, photograph by J. Löwy. Historisches Museum der Stadt Wien.
The influence of Schnitzler's work has probably been more enduring than that of any of the young Austrian writers to whose circle he belonged. His play *Anatol*, a series of dramatic episodes, made him the talk of the town; not the least of his merits was his ability to cast light on the mentality of the *fin-de-siècle*.

301 Moritz Coschell: *'Weihnachtseinkäufe': Anatol verabschiedet sich von Gabriele* ('Episode from "Christmas Shopping": Anatol takes leave of Gabriele). C. 1900, design, pencil, 37.2 x 46.2 cm. Historisches Museum der Stadt Wien.

302 Moritz Coschell: *Cora in Hypnose (Die Frage an das Schicksal)* ('Cora under Hypnosis ('The Question Posed to Fate')'). C. 1900, pencil, 29.4 x 40.1 cm. Historisches Museum der Stadt Wien.

303 Manuscript page from *Liebelei* ('Playing with Love') by Arthur Schnitzler. Handschriftensammlung, Österreichische Nationalbibliothek, Vienna. Schnitzler's play *Playing with Love* was one of his greatest successes. The principal character is a *süsses Wiener Mädel* (sweet Viennese girl), or *grisette,* who comes to a tragic end.

discontinuity, in the atmospheric detail. His play *Playing with Love* (1896) reveals that a life thus negligently lived, and which turns love into mere dalliance, is constantly under threat of death, that hypocrisy and flippancy only serve to paint over the tragic background of existence.

Peter Altenberg, on the other hand, demonstrates in his prose sketches that life can be lived with intensity. Although he, too, was committed to the Viennese modern school of the 1890s, he nevertheless clung to a reality that was perceptible to the senses. 'Use your eyes', he demanded. 'To man, they are as wealth to the Rothschilds!' So as to overcome the 'depersonalization syndrome' (to use Wunberg's expression) that was proving so painful to Andrian, Schnitzler, Beer-Hofmann and Hofmannsthal, he devised a formula whereby art could remain separate from, while at the same time being united with, life. 'Art is art', he maintained, 'and life is life, but the art of living is to live artistically.' Whether Altenberg is describing a picture, expatiating on his collection of postcards, discussing a gramophone record of Schubert's Trout Quintet, whether he is enthusing over some girl or indulging in flights of fantasy about shells or butterflies, his reading of the phenomenal world is still pointillist, a reading in which a part does duty for the whole. Here, the contradictions inherent in Young Vienna assume more radical form as, for instance, in Altenberg's yearning for nature, pure and unalloyed, as opposed to a way of life that is indissolubly wedded to civilization. Yet there is every indication that nature in its pristine form was available to him only through the medium, at one remove, of postcards and, at two removes, of Schubert's Trout Quintet on gramophone records. Discernible in Altenberg's *Wie ich es sehe* ('How I See It') (1896), if nowhere else, is the rejection of naturalism, which is not to say that the baby is thrown out with the bath water.

Literature 'Demolished'

The criticism levelled by Hofmannsthal at Young Vienna, not only in *The Fool and Death,* but also in many of his early playlets, was so veiled, so hesitant, as to be barely perceptible. For a critical analysis of this literature – born, as soon became apparent, of the coffee-house – could only be made by

one who was intimately acquainted with its antecedents. Such a man was Karl Kraus, whose earlier friendship with Schnitzler, Hofmannsthal and Salten in no way deterred him from castigating them, along with Andrian, Bahr and others, in his pamphlet *Die demolirte Litteratur* ('Literature Demolished') (1897). The occasion for his onslaught was the proposed conversion of the Café Griensteidl and the fears voiced by some that this would lead to a loss of atmosphere, if not actually of decorum. Here Kraus put his finger on the very root of the evil: café conversation had become a surrogate for literature, the journalistic aphorism for the poetic stanza. Hermann Bahr was apostrophized as 'the gentleman from Linz', who 'behaved as though Weimar was a suburb of Linz, instead of Urfahr'. Of Hofmannsthal he says: 'He set about writing a fragment and was impelled by altruism to prepare his manuscripts for posthumous publication.' Schnitzler, in his turn, faces the charge of innocuousness, for since 'his *bonhomie* prevents him from coming to grips with a problem, he has concocted a world of *grisettes* and men-about-town, a world above whose platitudes he seldom rises, and then only to the height of bogus

tragedy.' And 'even if, say, a death should occur, pray do not take fright – the pistols are loaded with insipidity.' Again, Andrian's *Garden of Knowledge* is transmogrified into a Garden of Ignorance. It is perfectly possible to appreciate, at one and the same time, both the pungency of Kraus's satire and the merits of the works he so violently attacks. Indeed, he may be said to owe his verve, if indirectly, to the achievements of his victims.

The year 1899, in which his periodical *Die Fackel* first appeared, marked the end of yet another era. From the outset Kraus inveighed against the language employed by journalists – or *journaille,* as he called them. *Die Fackel,* which he edited until he died in 1936, and which offered complex commentaries on the happenings of the day, bears comparison with nothing else in the world of literature. It was run by a man whose allegiance to language was so absolute and uncompromising that even the contradictions to which that allegiance gave rise must compel our admiration. The press responded to his repeated attacks by completely ignoring him. And yet, to many Austrian intellectuals, what he was saying was precisely what they felt to be incumbent

upon them. Today, it is not easy to subscribe unreservedly to the views he put forward. Yet his critique of language sharpens our perceptions. His treatment of the decadents, the group known as Young Vienna, was far from gentle, Peter Altenberg alone being spared. Kraus praises Wedekind and Strindberg, honours Nestroy and execrates Heine, thus testifying to a commitment to life, the primal source – a commitment that was hostile to a literature characterized by excessive artificiality.

Re-orientation

The emergence of Karl Kraus as satirist undoubtedly marks a breaking point in the development of Viennese literature. Nor did the signs of the times go unnoticed by Hermann Bahr. It was a re-orientation that may be summed up in two phrases, 'the irredeemable self' and 'the discovery of the provinces'. Bahr believed that in Mach's *Beiträge zur Analyse der Empfindungen* ('Contributions to the Analysis of the Feelings') (1886), he had discovered what had been tormenting him over the past three years: '"The self is irredeemable"', he wrote in 1904. 'It is but a name. It is but an allusion. A device which we need for practical purposes to help us sort out our ideas.' Such is the background we should bear in mind when reading, say, Schnitzler's novella, *Leutnant Gustl* ('Lieutenant Gustl') (1900). The action takes the form of an interior monologue which reveals the many contradictory elements which go to make up

306 Karl Kraus: *Die demolirte Litteratur* ('Literature Demolished'), 5th ed., Verlag A. Bauer, Vienna, 1899. Cover designed by Hans Schliessmann.
Karl Kraus's satire was inspired by the closure of the Café Griensteidl. His shafts were directed primarily at Hermann Bahr, 'the gentleman from Linz' and later also at Hugo von Hofmannsthal.

307 Karl Kraus: *Die Fackel*, No. 1, 1899.
From 1899 Karl Kraus was first editor of, and then sole contributor to, this satirical journal. He used it to combat the corruption of language by journalists and certain other literary coteries.

the character of an otherwise unremarkable officer who, having become embroiled in an affair of honour, believes suicide to be the only way out. The reader is presented with Gustl's stream of consciousness immediately before this desperate solution, the necessity for which, however, is obviated by his opponent's sudden death. So a meaningless existence continues as hitherto... The novella depends for its effect primarily upon artistic innovation. Schnitzler's use of soliloquy enabled him to achieve the highest measure of authenticity, an authenticity so provocative that he was subsequently stripped of his officer's rank by a court of honour.

Although at first glance the theme of Hofmannsthal's famous piece, *Ein Brief* ('A Letter') (1902), appears to be very dissimilar, it nevertheless belongs in the same context. The fictitious letter is written by twenty-six-year-old Lord Chandos to Francis Bacon, describing a predicament very similar to that in which Hofmannsthal found himself at the turn of the century. That it is primarily a crisis of identity is evident from Chandos's words: 'I scarcely can tell whether I am the same man to whom your amusing letter is addressed.' Personal inconsistency manifests itself in a linguistic crisis which begins with the young man's inability to broach an abstract subject, since words such as 'mind', 'soul' and 'body' arouse in him an 'inexplicable unease'. Such abstractions 'crumble in the mouth like rotten mushrooms'. Nor is he in better case when it comes to the language of everyday life. By calling language itself in question, *A Letter* introduced a theme which was to loom large in Austrian literature – as, indeed, it still continues to do. What we have here is not a problem thought up by a self-indulgent poet to reflect the premises of his calling, but rather one of immediate import to all forms of communication. Utterly different in kind, but still having the same constant, are Fritz Mauthner's *Beiträge zu einer Kritik der Sprache* ('Contributions to a Critique of Language') (1901–), and Ludwig Wittgenstein's *Tractatus logico-philosophicus* (1921). Ingeborg Bachmann and Peter Handke also wrote important works which bear the stamp of linguistic scepticism, as opposed to the unqualified faith in language demonstrated, more notably, by Karl Kraus.

From Chandos's letter it is apparent that Young Vienna itself harboured doubts about its own literature. Since those who had celebrated death in their writings still lived on, they found themselves compelled to seek a new idiom. Recourse to the past and a diversity of styles – rendered suspect by Hofmannsthal with his apt term 'craze for stylistic distortion' – invariably proved disastrous. It is significant that Hofmannsthal should have evaded the issue and turned to the writing of highly successful librettos for Richard Strauss, namely *Elektra* (1904), *Der Rosenkavalier* (1910), *Ariadne auf Naxos* (1912), *Die Frau ohne Schatten* (1916), *Die ägyptische Helena* (1928) and *Arabella* (1933).

Ernst Mach also prepared the way for Robert Musil's (1880–1942) first novel *Die Verwirrungen des Zöglings Törless* ('Young Törless') (1906), in which the 'depersonalization syndrome' of the youthful cadet is credibly attributed to a pubertal crisis. The latter is followed by an epistemological crisis when Törless turns to mathematics for the answer to a fundamental and unanswerable question. Musil who, as a mathematician and engineer, possessed a different educational background from that of the Young Vienna writers, sought in his works to comprehend what was feasible in literature, now that such strides had been made in the exact sciences. He provides a partial answer to the above question in the motto, borrowed from Maeterlinck, to his novel: 'No sooner do we express something than we strangely devalue it.' Not only is the quotation a reminder of one of the key figures of the turn of the century; it also brings the novel within the scope of linguistic scepticism. At the turn of the century few important works appeared of which the themes or, for that matter, the influence extended beyond the cultural sphere of the bourgeoisie. Notable exceptions are a novel by the Nobel Peace Prize winner, Bertha von Suttner, *Die Waffen nieder!* ('Lay Down Your Arms') (1889), Philipp Langmann's successful working-class play, *Bertl*

Turaser (1897) and, in particular, the narrative works of Jakob Julius David, whose pithy, realistic idiom is utterly different from anything to be found in the writings of the decadents. His Viennese novels, *Am Wege sterben* ('Dying by the Wayside') (1897–9) and *The Transition* (1902) should be considered in conjunction with the prints current at the time, in which Vienna is depicted in all its glory. Again, his tales of the countryside have nothing in common with the neo-Romantic cult of rusticity which had then come into vogue in the capital.

Anti-Semitism and the provinces

Hermann Bahr's essay 'The Discovery of the Provinces' (1899) is an expression of the disquiet caused by Vienna's preponderance. As Peter Rosegger, perhaps the most popular writer of the day, remarked: 'The provinces are being ignored', thereby prompt-

ing Bahr, despite his earlier support of the 'decadents', to ask:

> Is it not a matter for surprise that the authors of Young Vienna should turn their backs on everything that must surely be of the greatest consequence? Has Austria really nothing more to offer than that *süsses Mädel** of Schnitzler's, for ever the same save, perhaps, for an occasional change of dress, and that charming, pernicious world of the theatre from which I cannot tear myself away, and the few, strange tones of the extreme, indeed, sublime, yet by now scarcely comprehensible refinement peculiar to Hofmannsthal? Is that the whole of our Austria? If so, it means that everything is already worn out and exhausted and that no path remains untrodden.

---

* The Viennese version of the *grisette.*

255

Once again, Bahr pointed the way out of the dilemma, a way that led to the provinces, no longer regarded as in any way contemptible. 'If our dream of a new Austrian art is to come true', he said, 'we must look to the people.' In the provinces, success was assured, as the example of Rosegger's periodical *Heimgarten* showed; Vienna, on the other hand, had now become a target for the barbs of those writers who drew exclusively on the provinces for their themes.

Whereas urban art connoted sickness and over-refinement, the art of the countryside would, according to Bahr, proffer health and naturalness. His pronouncements were accompanied by the rapid growth of the vernacular art movement. Inspired by naturalist modes, literature became the handmaiden of rusticity. In the city's theatres, folk plays came into their own, the great majority being set in the countryside. The trend is most clearly marked in the highly successful works of the Tyrolean Karl Schönherr, notably *Erde* ('Earth') (1908), a comedy in which the principal character, old Grutz, recovers from a serious injury and, in the spring, returns to take charge of the farm, in defiance of his frail son. Of some significance was the fear expressed at the time that people might see in the old peasant an allusion to the Emperor Francis Joseph, now in the sixtieth year of his reign. This was a time in which fathers had the upper hand over their sons.

Schönherr was conscious both of the extent to which his work was dependent on the city, and of the paradoxical nature of such a situation. For his plays, which owed their success to an exact representation of the rural scene, were all conceived in the capital, 'for the most part at small marble-topped tables, amidst the clatter and chatter of big coffee-houses, or else during solitary walks through the hurly-burly of the busiest streets'.

What chiefly distinguished provincial art from decadence was the stand adopted, not only against modernism and internationalism, but also against capitalism, thereby entering the socio-critical arena. Nor (if we except Schönherr and Rosegger) was anti-Semitism absent from their attacks on the

311 Otto Weininger. Photograph. Bildarchiv der Österreichischen Nationalbibliothek, Vienna.
Otto Weininger was the author of the much-acclaimed book *Geschlecht und Charakter* ('Sex and Character') in which he analyzed the psychology and metaphysics of the sexes.

Viennese writers and critics, the great majority of whom happened to be of Jewish origin. Indeed, it was not until the emergence of anti-Semitism (around the turn of the century) that the question of origin, hitherto almost ignored, began to be treated as a literary theme, even by assimilated Jews. In 1898 Kraus, himself of Jewish stock, wrote a pamphlet entitled *Eine Krone für Zion* ('A Crown for Zion'), in which he vehemently denounced Zionism. Arthur Schnitzler, who had himself been savagely attacked by the anti-Semites, also criticized Zionism, if more subtly, by including in his book, *Der Weg ins Freie* ('The Way into the Open') (1908), a character whose traits irresistibly recall those of Theodor Herzl.

The extent to which sentiment had become inflamed between the two by now irreconcilable camps is exemplified by the fate of Schnitzler's play, *Professor Bernhardi*

(1912), which revolves round a clash between a liberal Jewish scholar and the Church. Permission for its performance was refused by the authorities on the grounds that the theme might unleash a similar clash between factions in the audience.

Anti-Semitism, however, should not be regarded solely as a manifestation of the provincial, anti-Vienna tendency, for amongst the middle classes of the capital it had become tantamount to a dogma. Otto Weininger's *Geschlecht und Charakter* ('Sex and Character') (1903), in which women and Jews are denied a soul, was believed to have provided a genuine basis for discussion. That the man who enriched the anti-Semites' arsenal with this dangerous essay in pseudo-science should himself have been a Jew lends poignancy to the paradoxical confusion of camps that prevailed in the years prior to the First World War.

Actors

The uproar created by Schnitzler's plays, *La Ronde* and *Professor Bernhardi*, demonstrates the importance of the theatre to an understanding of those times. Literature would appear to have been almost wholly geared to the theatre. 'This is how we act our parts out,/Acting plays of our own making,/Early-ripe and sad and tender,/ the commedia of our spirit...' Thus Hofmannsthal, in his celebrated prologue to Schnitzler's *Anatol*. The theatrical metaphor was by no means a superficial one, so far as that generation was concerned, for an actor was regarded as an object of veneration. And in 1888 a suitable place of worship was created with the ceremonial opening of the new Hofburgtheater in the Ring. The poems written by Hofmannsthal in memory of Friedrich Mitterwurzer and Josef Kainz take on an almost elegiac quality and extol in particular the actor's capacity for metamorphosis, for becoming wholly and completely another. It was that gift, above all others, which gave expression to the problem that perplexed and troubled the writer, namely, his inability to see himself as a consistent personality rather than as the

performer of a role. The extent to which the theatre had become a cult is evident from an article on Eleonora Duse, written by Hofmannsthal in 1892 on the occasion of a guest performance in Vienna. She enacted, he wrote, 'not just the actual reality, but also the philosophy of her role'.

The veneration felt for actors was not idolatry pure and simple; rather it corresponded to the prevailing mood of the time. The most outstanding actress of the day was Charlotte Wolter, whose dynamic performances marked a break with the time-honoured declamatory ritual of the Burgtheater. Many of the actors, however, had not been schooled in that tradition and, indeed, the director himself, Adolf von Wilbrandt, was of north German provenance. Himself a playwright, he was succeeded by Max Burckhard. The latter not only brought with him the actor, Mitterwurzer, but frequently put on plays by Ibsen, and was also responsible for introducing Gerhart Hauptmann to the Viennese stage. Again it was he who, in defiance of the powers-that-be, turned Schnitzler into a Burgtheater author by accepting his work *Playing with Love.*

A more controversial figure was Burckhard's successor, Paul Schlenther from Berlin, a consistent advocate of naturalism, whose mainstay in the company was the actor, Josef Kainz. Karl Kraus repeatedly inveighed against the way in which Schlenther ran the theatre. In his view it was a betrayal of the great art of acting as exemplified by performers such as Wolter. He referred to Kainz as an 'unfledged actor' and contrasted him with others more suited to his taste, among them Alexander Girardi, whom he described as 'one of the most unusual and charming personalities ever to have employed the drama as a vehicle for creative performance'. According to Kraus, Girardi was a man of genuine talent who, by careful attention to emphasis, was able to bring out the point of even the most feeble joke. He appeared, not at the Burgtheater, but in houses where folk plays were the rule – at the Theater an der Wien and, later, at the Raimundtheater and the Deutsches Volkstheater. His Valentin in Raimund's *Spend-*

312 Friedrich Mitterwurzer as
Mephistopheles. 1894,
photograph. Historisches Museum
der Stadt Wien.
Mitterwurzer appeared at the
Burgtheater and other playhouses
in Vienna, where he specialized
mainly in character parts.

313 Eleonore Duse. Photograph.
Historisches Museum der Stadt
Wien.
Duse, the Italian actress who appeared in many countries besides
her own, scored her chief
triumphs as an interpreter of
modern roles. She was therefore
greatly adulated by the authors of
the time who regarded her as the
very essence of a modern
tragédienne.

314 Adolf von Sonnenthal as
Rudolf von Habsburg in Grill-
parzer's *König Ottokars Glück und
Ende* ('King Ottokar's
Fortunes and Death'). Photo-
graph. Historisches Museum der
Stadt Wien.
Adolf von Sonnenthal, who was
much respected as an actor,
worked for many decades as the
Burgtheater's producer and also,
for a time, as its interim director.

315 Charlotte Wolter.
Photograph. Historisches
Museum der Stadt Wien.
Charlotte Wolter was a member
of the Burgtheater company from
1862 until her death in 1897. So
highly regarded was she that
several plays were specially commissioned to suit her particular
talents. She was renowned for the
musicality of her delivery and for
what became known as 'La
Wolter's cry', this last being
quintessential to her emphatic
style.

316 Josef Kainz. Photograph. Theatersammlung, Österreichische Nationalbibliothek, Vienna.
Kainz, one of the most famous actors of his day, ranked high as an elocutionist and interpreter of character. In his roles he combined spiritual intensity with a high degree of physical expressiveness.

317 Anna Bahr-Mildenburg as Brünnhilde. Photograph. Historisches Museum der Stadt Wien.
Anna Bahr-Mildenburg was for many years a member of the Vienna Opera where she made her name chiefly as an interpreter of Wagnerian roles. She was married to the writer Hermann Bahr.

318 Alexander Girardi. Photograph. Historisches Museum der Stadt Wien.
Girardi appeared in a number of Viennese theatres. The manner in which he interpreted his roles, notably in Raimund's plays, inevitably led to his being described as a 'folk actor'.

319 Alexander Moissi as Everyman. 1926, photograph. Historisches Museum der Stadt Wien.
Alexander Moissi came to Vienna in 1898 where he was discovered by Josef Kainz, and became a popular actor who performed frequently both in Vienna and in Salzburg.

259

thrift was hailed by Kraus as 'the most momentous event in the Viennese folk theatre'.

'The Grouser'

In 1881 there occurred a disaster which was regarded as an evil omen, not only in the world of the theatre, but also in that of politics – the destruction by fire of the Ringtheater. So catastrophic did this seem as almost to portend the end of the world. Yet the outbreak of war in 1914 appeared to dispel that sense of impending doom, and to present, for most writers, a mean of escape from the ivory tower of 'art for art's sake', a tower in which they had been immured by a literature that was both highly specialized and over-sensitive. They welcomed the fact that they would now be able to use their talents in furtherance of the war effort. A triumphalist spirit – all too premature, as subsequent disasters were to show – characterizes the poems, produced by the dozen, sometimes even by writers of high repute. A case in point is Anton Wildgans, a poet with a social conscience whose work is undoubtedly worthy of respect. Yet in 1914 he demeaned himself so far as to write '*Vae victis!* A solemn hymn to the Allied Armies'.

> Woe to the conquered! Inexorable decree
> Coldly executed upon craven necks,
> With a slaughterer's phlegm, ne'er a curse nor contumely,
> Crushed, the *canaille* and all its effects.
> No mercy will the conqueror show,
> When upon the bowed backs of the cringing foe
> He tramples, as though upon loathly insects.

That such stuff should be written, let alone read and republished in the form of flysheets, should give pause for thought, even today. Wildgans's bloodthirsty rhetoric was not an isolated phenomenon; even Hofmannsthal, if in far more cautious vein, dutifully flexed his patriotic muscles. Yet voices were also raised in opposition. Schnitzler openly deplored such warlike sentiments, Alfred Polgar, an astute critic, remained profoundly sceptical, Franz Werfel was, from the outset, an opponent of war, and Stefan Zweig, after several disquieting lapses, wrote a highly important play, *Jeremias* (1917), instinct with the spirit of pacifism. Having paused briefly for reflection after the outbreak of war, Kraus was not slow in making his opinions known. In a speech 'At this momentous hour' (November 1914), he hit out at all those who believed that the conflict would lend political relevance to their work. 'To the writer', he said, 'voluntary war service connotes his entry into journalism. Here, right in the front line, we have one Hauptmann, not to mention Messrs Dehmel and Hofmannsthal, all agog for a decoration while, battling behind them, we see dilettantism let loose.' Particularly worthy of note is Kraus's *Die letzten Tage der Menschheit* ('The Last Days of Mankind') (1918–22), a gigantic tragedy in five acts, one for each year of the war, whose events they depict with uncompromising realism. So vast was its compass that, according to Kraus, it could only be performed on a parade ground. With a satirist's sharp perception, he demonstrates the destructive power of journalistic catchwords and the dangers inherent in the abuse of language, themes which still remain disturbingly topical today. Just as a fly is preserved in amber, so Kraus, in his quotations, encapsulates for posterity the monstrous statements that were published at that time. His play, he tells us, is an attack on the unholy alliance of 'ink, death and technology'.

Although every region of the Danubian Monarchy is included in Kraus's picture, Vienna is the anonymous centre whence 'the Grouser' (easily recognizable as Kraus himself) broadcasts his opinion of those who have hounded the soldiers into war. These five acts also bear witness to the capital's decline. Kraus unmasks not only the hollowness of language, but also the worthlessness of the florid ornamentation in which reality had been shrouded during the *Gründerzeit*.

320 Rudolf Hirschenhauser: *Anton Wildgans.* Etching. Historisches Museum der Stadt Wien.
In his writings the poet and dramatist Anton Wildgans reveals a particular love for his native city. This attitude emerges clearly from his reminiscence *Musik der Kindheit* ('Music of Childhood'). He served two separate terms as director of the Burgtheater.

More plainly than anywhere else, the collapse of the Danubian Monarchy left its mark on the capital. Soon to be denounced by the forces of conservatism as 'red Vienna', it became a place of change and, concomitantly, a symbol of sheer wretchedness. The sudden and irreversible impoverishment of the middle classes nurtured their animosity towards the forces which had been conjured up by the general cataclysm. It is, therefore, of some significance that many writers should have elevated exclusiveness and nostalgia into principles of their art. In his brilliantly conceived comedies, *Der Schwierige* ('The Difficult Man') (1922) and *Der Unbestechliche* ('The Unbribable Man') (1923), Hofmannsthal depicts, in stark contrast to the surrounding poverty and inflation, the mores of a society that has vanished for ever. In 1920 a prolific novelist, Karl Hans Strobl, produced a utopian tale entitled *Gespenster im Sumpf* ('Phantoms in the Swamp'), the swamp being Vienna and the phantoms the new authorities. Though little more than a pot-boiler, it nevertheless gives an idea of the distorted view of reality taken by the majority of writers after 1918.

For all its expressionist pathos and, to us, somewhat incongruous stylistic solecisms, Albert Ehrenstein's poem, *Vienna* (1920), succeeds in conveying the mental confusion that prevailed at the time.

Vienna, in ruins, is weeping.
Vienna, you old, cold-hearted whore, you,
I cowered against your graveyard wall,
When you still lured,
A scrofulous pander to this world,
And hastened to whore with chauvinist demons,
All through the war with triumphalist drones.

Now famished, you whimper,
So heavy does your wickedness weigh:
An empire frittered away.

A belated renunciation of decorum and the 'value vacuum'. For many writers, such as Schnitzler, Hofmannsthal, Musil and Joseph Roth, the submerged world provided a rich source of material. Yet during that same period Vienna was to witness new initiatives in the fields of philosophy and social theory – initiatives whose importance is only now becoming apparent. But these are developments which belong to another, if no less exciting, chapter of Austria's intellectual history.

SELECT BIBLIOGRAPHY

Bettelheim, Anton, *Karl Schönherr. Leben und Schaffen,* Leipzig, 1928.

Broch, Hermann, 'Hofmannsthal und seine Zeit', in H. B., *Kommentierte Werkausgabe,* ed. P. M. Lützeler, Vol. 9/1, Frankfurt am Main, 1975, pp. 111–284.

Fischer, Jens Malte, Fin de Siècle. *Kommentar einer Epoche,* Munich, 1978.

Von Hofmannsthal, Hugo, *Poems and Verse Plays,* ed. Michael Hamburger, Pantheon Books, New York, 1961, pp. 60, 63, 98–9, 133, 137.

Johnston, William M., *The Austrian Mind,* Berkeley, 1972.
'Jugend in Wien. Literatur um 1900'. *Eine Ausstellung des Deutschen Literaturarchivs im Schiller Nationalmuseum,* Marbach, 1974.

Nielsen, Erika (ed.), *Focus on Vienna 1900. Change and Continuity in Literature, Music, Art and Intellectual History,* Munich, 1982.

Österreichische Avant-garde 1900–1938. Ein unbekannter Aspekt. Visual arts by Oswald Oberhuber, Literature and Science by Peter Weibel. Vienna, 1975.

Scheible, Hartmut, *Arthur Schnitzler in Selbstzeugnissen und Bilddokumenten.* Reinbeck near Hamburg, 1976.

Schorske, Carl E., Fin-de-siècle *Vienna. Politics and Culture,* London, 1979, New York, 1980.

Weigel, Hans, Lukan, Walter, and Peyfuss, Max D., *Jeder Schuss ein Russ. Jeder Stoss ein Franzos. Literarische und graphische Kriegspropaganda in Deutschland und Österreich 1914–1918,* Vienna, 1983.

Wunberg, Gotthart (ed.), *Das Junge Wien. Österreichische Literatur- und Kunstkritik 1887–1902,* 2 vols., Tübingen, 1976.
– (ed.), *Die Wiener Moderne. Literatur, Kunst und Musik zwischen 1890 und 1910,* Stuttgart, 1981.

GUIDE TO PERSONS MENTIONED IN THE BOOK

ADLER, FRIEDRICH (Vienna) 1879–1960 (Zurich): socialist politician, leader of the Left in the Austrian Parliament.

ADLER, GUIDO (Eibenschitz) 1895–1941 (Vienna): founder of the 'Viennese School' of musicology.

ADLER, VIKTOR (Prague) 1852–1918 (Vienna): politician, doctor of medicine and Social Democratic leader, impassioned advocate of universal suffrage.

ALT, FRANZ, (Vienna) 1824–1914 (Vienna): water-colourist.

ALT, RUDOLF VON (Vienna) 1812–1905 (Vienna): water-colourist, honorary president of the Secession.

ALTENBERG, PETER (Vienna) 1859–1919 (Vienna): feuilletonist, aphorist.

ANDRI, FERDINAND (Waidhofen/Ybbs) 1871–1956 (Vienna): painter and graphic artist, taught at the Academy of Fine Arts, 1905–6 president of the Secession.

ANDRIAN-WERBURG, LEOPOLD VON (Vienna) 1875–1951 (Fribourg): author, diplomat, literary historian.

AUCHENTALLER, JOSEF MARIA (Grado) 1865–1949 (Grado): painter, 1898–1905 member of the Secession.

BACH, DAVID JOSEF (Vienna) 1874–1947 (London): musicologist and critic, founder of the Viennese Working Men's Symphony Concerts.

BACHER, RUDOLF (Vienna) 1862–1943 (Vienna): painter and sculptor, professor at the Academy of Fine Arts, member of the Secession.

BADENI, COUNT KASIMIR (Surochów) 1846–1909 (Krasne): Minister President and Minister of the Interior 1895–7.

BAHR, HERMANN (Linz) 1863–1934 (Munich): novelist, essayist, critic, prolific playwright.

BARTH, OTTO (Vienna) 1876–1916 (Waidenhofen/Ybbs): painter, lithographer and illustrator.

BAUER, LEOPOLD (Jägerndorf) 1872–1938 (Vienna): architect, pupil of Carl von Hasenauer and Otto Wagner, professor at the Academy of Fine Arts.

BAUER, OTTO (Vienna) 1881–1938 (Paris): Social Democratic politician, exponent of Austro-Marxism.

BAUERNFELD, EDUARD VON (Vienna) 1802–1890 (Vienna): writer of comedies, resident playwright at the Burgtheater.

BAUMANN, LUDWIG (Seibersdorf, Silesia) 1853–1936 (Vienna): architect.

BEER-HOFMANN, RICHARD (Vienna) 1866–1945 (New York): author and dramatist.

BENEDIKT, MORIZ (Kwassitz) 1849–1920 (Vienna): liberal publicist, editor-in-chief of the *Neue Freie Presse*.

BERG, ALBAN (Vienna) 1885–1935 (Vienna): composer and a member of Schoenberg's circle.

BERGER, ALFRED FREIHERR VON (Vienna) 1853–1912 (Vienna): author and dramatist, director of the Burgtheater.

BERNATZIK, WILHELM (Mistelbach) 1853–1906 (Hinterbrühl): painter and draughtsman, founder member of the Secession.

BLAU-LANG, TINA (Vienna) 1845–1916 (Vienna): landscape painter.

BOEHM, ADOLF (Vienna) 1861–1927 (Klosterneuburg): painter and designer, founder member of the Secession.

BRAHMS, JOHANNES (Hamburg) 1833–97 (Vienna): composer.

BREITNER, HUGO (Vienna) 1873–1946 (Clairemont): Social Democrat, prominent in local politics and in the creation of 'Red Vienna'.

BROCH, HERMANN (Vienna) 1886–1951 (New Haven): novelist and social philosopher.

BRUCKNER, ANTON (Ansfelden) 1824–96 (Vienna): composer, one of Austria's most important symphonists.

BURCKHARD, MAX (Korneuburg) 1854–1912 (Vienna): author, jurist, director of the Burgtheater.

CANON, HANS (Vienna) 1829–85 (Vienna): painter.

CHARLES I, last emperor of Austria and, as Charles IV, king of Hungary (Persenburg) 1887–1922 (Funchal).

CZESCHKA, CARL OTTO (Vienna) 1878–1960 (Hamburg): designer and book illustrator, taught in Vienna and later in Hamburg.

DARNAUT, HUGO (Dessau) 1851–1937 (Vienna): painter.

DAVID, JAKOB JULIUS (Mährisch-Weisskirchen, now Hranice) 1859–1906 (Vienna): author and journalist.

DÖRMANN, FELIX [Biedermann] (Vienna) 1870–1928 (Vienna): author, dramatist and theatrical producer.

EDERER, CARL (Vienna) 1875–d.?: painter, etcher and lithographer.

EHRENSTEIN, ALBERT (Vienna) 1886–1950 (New York): novelist, pioneer of Expressionism.

ENGELHART, JOSEF (Vienna) 1864–1941 (Vienna): painter and sculptor, founder member of the Secession, subsequently an opponent of the Klimt group.

EYSLER, EDMUND (Vienna) 1874–1949 (Vienna): composer of operettas.

FABIANI, MAX (Kobdil) 1865–1962 (Görz, now Gorizia): architect.

FAHRINGER, KARL (Wiener Neustadt) 1874–1952 (Vienna): figure, animal and landscape painter.

FALL, LEO (Olmütz, now Olomouc) 1873–1925 (Vienna): composer of operettas.

FERSTEL, HEINRICH VON (Vienna) 1828–1883 (Vienna): architect, pupil of von Sicardsburg and van der Null.

FRANCIS FERDINAND, ARCHDUKE (Graz) 1863–1914 (Sarajevo): heir apparent to the throne; his assassination by Serbian nationalists sparked off the First World War.

FRANCIS JOSEPH I, emperor of Austria and king of Hungary (Vienna, Schönbrunn) 1830–1916 (Vienna, Schönbrunn): ruled from 1848 up to the time of his death.

FREUD, SIGMUND (Freiberg, now Příbor) 1856–1939 (London): neurologist, founder of psychoanalysis.

FRIEDELL, EGON (Vienna) 1878–1938 (Vienna): historian, author, feuilletonist, critic and actor.

FRIEDLÄNDER, OTTO (Vienna) 1889–1963 (Waidenhofen/Ybbs): author and pacifist.

FRIEDRICH, OTTO (Raab, now Györ) 1862–1937 (Vienna): visited Spain and North Africa, founder member of the Secession.

FUCHS, JOHANN NEPOMUK (Frauenthal) 1842–99 (Bad Vöslau): composer and conductor.

FUCHS, ROBERT (Frauenthal) 1847–1927 (Vienna): composer and court organist.

GERSTL, RICHARD (Vienna) 1883–1908 (Vienna): painter.

GEYLING, REMIGIUS (Vienna) 1878–1974 (Vienna): stage designer, painter and craftsman.

GIRARDI, ALEXANDER (Graz) 1850–1918 (Vienna): folk actor.

GOLDMARK, KARL (Keszthely) 1830–1915 (Vienna): composer, music teacher.

GOMPERZ, HEINRICH (Vienna) 1873–1942 (Los Angeles): philosopher.

GOMPERZ, THEODOR (Brünn, now Brno) 1832–1912 (Baden near Vienna): classical scholar, professor at Vienna University.

GRÄDENER, HERMANN 1844–1929: composer.

GRAF, MAX (Vienna) 1873–1958 (Vienna): musical historian, author.

GRANITSCH, SUSANNE (Vienna) 1869–1946 (Vienna): painter.

HAMPEL, SIGMUND WALTER (Vienna) 1867–1949 (Nussdorf on Lake Atter): painter.

HANAK, ANTON (Brünn, now Brno) 1875–1934 (Vienna): sculptor.

HANSEN, THEOPHIL VON (Copenhagen) 1813–1891 (Vienna): architect, one of the designers of the Ringstrasse.

HANSLICK, EDUARD (Prague) 1825–1904 (Baden near Vienna): music critic, professor at Vienna University.

HASENAUER, KARL VON (Vienna) 1833–94 (Vienna): architect, one of the designers of the Ringstrasse.

HAUER, JOSEF MATTHIAS (Wiener Neustadt) 1883–1959 (Vienna): composer, teacher, discoverer of a twelve-tone system

HELLMER, EDMUND (Vienna) 1850–1935 (Vienna): sculptor who produced a large number of sculptures and monuments for the city.

HELLMESBERGER, JOSEF (Vienna) 1855–1907 (Vienna): conductor and composer.

HERZL, THEODOR (Budapest) 1860–1904 (Edlach): dramatist, critic and journalist, founder of theoretical Zionism.

HEVESI, LUDWIG (Heves) 1842–1910 (Vienna): author and journalist.

HITLER, ADOLF (Braunau) 1889–1945 (Berlin): Leader of the National Socialist Party and Chancellor of the Third Reich.

HODLER, FERDINAND (Berne) 1853–1918 (Geneva): Swiss painter closely connected with the Secession.

HOFFMANN, JOSEF (Pirnitz) 1870–1956 (Vienna): architect and designer, professor at the School of Arts and Crafts, founder member of the Secession and Wiener Werkstätte, founder of the Austrian Werkbund.

HOFMANNSTHAL, HUGO VON (Vienna) 1874–1929 (Vienna-Rodaun): essayist, poet and dramatist.

HOPPE, EMIL (Vienna) 1876–1957 (Vienna): architect.

HÖRMANN, THEODOR VON (Imst) 1840–95 (Graz): landscape painter.

JETTEL, EUGEN (Johnsdorf) 1845–1901 (Lussingrande): landscape painter.

JETTMAR, RUDOLF (Zawodzie near Tarnów) 1869–1939 (Vienna): painter and graphic artist, teacher at the Academy, member of the Secession.

JUNGNICKEL, LUDWIG HEINRICH (Weinsiedel) 1881–1965 (Vienna): painter, draughtsman and graphic artist, known chiefly for his animal studies.

KAINRADL, LEO (Klagenfurt) 1872–1943 (Munich): painter and graphic artist, later editor of the Munich *Fliegende Blätter*.

KAINZ, JOSEF (Wieselburg) 1858–1910 (Vienna): actor.

KÁLMÁN, EMMERICH (Siófok) 1882–1953 (Paris): composer of operettas.

KIENZL, WILHELM (Waizenkirchen) 1857–1941 (Vienna): composer and conductor.

KLIMT, ERNST (Vienna) 1864–92 (Vienna): painter.

KLIMT, GUSTAV (Vienna) 1862–1918 (Vienna): painter and draughtsman, founder member and first president of the Secession and the most prominent figure in Viennese Art Nouveau.

KLINGER, MAX (Leipzig) 1857–1920 (Grossjena near Naumburg): graphic artist, painter and sculptor.

KRAUS, KARL (Gitschin, now Jičin) 1874–1936 (Vienna): satirist deeply concerned with the use of language, actor, journalist and translator.

KREMSER, EDUARD (Vienna) 1838–1914 (Vienna): composer and conductor.

KŘENEK, ERNST (Vienna) 1900: composer and novelist.

KOKOSCHKA, OSKAR (Pöchlarn) 1886–1980 (Villeneuve): painter, graphic artist and writer, associated with the Wiener Werkstätte, professor at the Dresden Academy.

KÖNIG, FRIEDRICH (Vienna) 1857–1941 (Vienna): painter, graphic artist, designer, founder member of the Secession.

KROIS, FERDINAND (Písek) 1869–1944 (Innsbruck): painter and graphic artist, member of the Secession.

KUNDMANN, CARL (Vienna) 1838–1919 (Vienna): sculptor.

KURZWEIL, MAX (Bisenz, now Bzenec) 1867–1916 (Vienna): painter and graphic artist, founder member of the Secession.

LANGMANN, PHILIPP (Brünn, now Brno) 1862–1931 (Vienna): naturalist writer concerned with social questions.

LASKE, OSKAR (Czernowitz, now Chernovtsy) 1874–1951 (Vienna): painter and graphic artist.

LAUFBERGER, FERDINAND (Mariaschein, Bohemia) 1829–1881 (Vienna): painter, etcher and lithographer.

LEFLER, HEINRICH (Vienna) 1863–1919 (Vienna): painter, graphic artist and sculptor; with his brother-in-law Urban founded the Hagenbund.

LEHÁR, FRANZ (Komárom) 1870–1948 (Bad Ischl): composer of operettas.

LENZ, MAXIMILIAN (Vienna) 1860–1948 (Vienna): painter, graphic artist, and sculptor, founder member of the Secession.

LEWINSKY, JOSEF (Vienna) 1835–1907 (Vienna): character actor.

LIEBENWEIN, MAXIMILIAN (Vienna) 1869–1926 (Munich): painter and graphic artist, member of the Secession.

LÖFFLER, BERTHOLD (Nieder-Rosenthal near Reichenberg, now Liberec) 1874–1960 (Vienna): painter, graphic artist, illustrator and designer, taught at the School of Arts and Crafts; together with Michael Powolny, founded the Vienna Pottery.

LOOS, ADOLF (Brünn, now Brno) 1870–1933 (Kalksburg): architect and writer of works on art.

LÖWE, FERDINAND (Vienna) 1865–1925 (Vienna): conductor, founder of the Vienna Symphony Orchestra.

LUEGER, KARL (Vienna) 1844–1910 (Vienna): Christian Social politician, 1897–1910 Mayor of Vienna.

LUKSCH, RICHARD (Vienna) 1872–1936 (Hamburg): sculptor and medallist.

MACH, ERNST (Turas) 1838–1916 (Haar near Munich): physicist, psychologist and philosopher.

MAHLER, GUSTAV (Kalisht, now Kaliště) 1860–1911 (Vienna): composer, notable symphonist and conductor, director of the Court Opera.

MAKART, HANS (Salzburg) 1840–84 (Vienna): historical and portrait painter, professor at the Academy of Fine Arts.

MARX, JOSEPH (Graz) 1882–1964 (Graz): composer, professor at the Academy of Music and the Visual Arts.

MATSCH, FRANZ VON (Vienna) 1861–1942 (Vienna): painter and sculptor; collaborated with the Klimt brothers.

MAYREDER, ROSA (Vienna) 1858–1938 (Vienna): writer and champion of women's rights.

MITTERWURZER, FRIEDRICH (Dresden) 1844–1897 (Vienna): actor specializing in heroic and character parts.

MOLL, CARL (Vienna) 1861–1945 (Vienna): founder member of the Secession.

MYRBACH, FELICIAN VON (Zaleszczyki, Galicia) 1853–1940 (Klagenfurt): painter, graphic artist and designer, founder member of the Wiener Werkstätte; moved to Spain in 1914.

NEUMAYER, JOSEF (Vienna) 1844–1923 (Vienna): Mayor of Vienna.

NÜLL, EDUARD, VAN DER (Vienna) 1812–68 (Vienna): architect.

OHMANN, FRIEDRICH (Lemberg, now L'vov) 1858–1927 (Vienna): architect.

OLBRICH, JOSEPH MARIA (Troppau, now Opava) 1867–1908 (Düsseldorf): architect, founder member of the Secession whose building he designed.

ORLIK, EMIL (Prague) 1870–1932 (Berlin): painter, graphic artist and designer, member of the Secession.

PAJER-GARTEGEN, ROBERT (Vienna) 1886–1944: painter and graphic artist, member of the Hagenbund.

PECHE, DAGOBERT (St Michael) 1887–1923 (Mödling): architect, painter and designer; worked for and, later, managed the Wiener Werkstätte.

PETZOLD, ALFONS (Vienna) 1882–1923 (Kitzbühel): writer of working-class novels.

PLEČNIK, JOSEF (Ljubljana) 1872–1957 (Ljubljana): architect and designer, pupil of Otto Wagner at the Academy of Fine Arts.

POLGAR, ALFRED (Vienna) 1873–1955 (Zurich): author, satirist and theatre critic.

POPP, ADELHEID (Vienna) 1869–1939 (Vienna): Social Democratic women's leader.

POWOLNY, MICHAEL (Judenburg) 1871–1954 (Vienna): sculptor and potter; together with Berthold Löffler founded the Vienna Pottery under the aegis of the Wiener Werkstätte.

RENNER, KARL (Untertannowitz) 1870–1950 (Vienna): statesman, Social Democratic politician, Chancellor, President.

RICHTER, HANS (Raab, now Rába) 1843–1916 (Bayreuth): conductor, principally in Vienna and Bayreuth.

ROESSLER, ARTHUR (Vienna) 1877–1955 (Vienna): writer on art, essayist and publicist.

ROLLER, ALFRED (Brünn, now Brno) 1864–1935 (Vienna): painter, graphic artist, stage designer at the State Opera House under Gustav Mahler, member of the Secession.

ROSEGGER, PETER (Alpl near Krieglach) 1843–1918 (Krieglach): writer of folk literature.

ROTH, JOSEF (Schwatendorf near Brody) 1894–1939 (Paris): author and feuilletonist.

RUDOLF, CROWN PRINCE OF AUSTRIA (Laxenburg) 1858–89 (Mayerling): was known for his liberal outlook, committed suicide.

SAAR, FERDINAND VON (Vienna) 1833–1906 (Vienna): writer and poet.

SALTEN, FELIX [SATZMANN] (Budapest) 1869–1945 (Zurich): author.

SCHACHNER, FRIEDRICH 1841–1907: architect.

SCHALK, FRANZ (Vienna) 1863–1931 (Edlach): conductor and, with Richard Strauss, co-director of the State Opera.

SCHIELE, EGON (Tulln) 1890–1918 (Vienna): painter, draughtsman and graphic artist, co-founder of the 'Neukunstgruppe'.

SCHIMKOWITZ, OTHMAR (Tárts, Hungary) 1864–1947 (Kroisbach): sculptor.

SCHINDLER, EMIL JAKOB (Vienna) 1842–92 (Westerland on island of Sylt): painter.

SCHLENTHER, PAUL (Insterburg) 1845–1916 (Berlin): director of the Burgtheater.

SCHLÖGL, FRIEDRICH (Vienna) 1821–92 (Vienna): writer of humorous folk tales, feuilletonist.

SCHMIDT, FRANZ (Pressburg, now Bratislava) 1874–1939 (Perchtoldsdorf): composer and symphonist.

SCHMIDT, FRIEDRICH VON (Frickenhofen) 1825–91 (Vienna): architect, one of the designers of the Ringstrasse.

SCHNITZLER, ARTHUR (Vienna) 1862–1931 (Vienna): novelist and dramatist.

SCHOENBERG, ARNOLD (Vienna) 1874–1951 (Los Angeles): composer, leader of the 'Vienna school'.

SCHÖNERER, GEORG VON (Vienna) 1842–1921 (Rosenau): politician, landowner, leader of the German National movement in Austria.

SCHÖNHERR, KARL (Axams) 1867–1943 (Vienna): writer of folk-plays.

SCHÖNTHAL, OTTO (Vienna) 1878–1961 (Vienna): architect, pupil and colleague of Otto Wagner.

SCHREKER, FRANZ (Monaco) 1878–1934 (Berlin): composer.

SCHUCH, CARL (Vienna) 1846–1903 (Vienna): painter.

SEITZ, KARL (Vienna) 1869–1950 (Vienna): leading Social Democratic politician, Mayor of 'Red Vienna'.

SEMPER, GOTTFRIED (Hamburg) 1803–79 (Rome): architect and writer of works on art.

SICARD VON SICARDSBURG, AUGUST VON (Budapest) 1813–1868 (Weidling near Vienna): architect, first president of the Künstlerhaus.

SITTE, CAMILLO (Vienna) 1843–1903 (Vienna): architect and town-planner.

SOPHIE, ARCHDUCHESS (Munich) 1805–72 (Vienna): mother of the Emperor Francis Joseph I.

SPEIDEL, LUDWIG (Vienna): 1830–1906 (Vienna): writer and critic.

SPITZER, DANIEL (Vienna) 1835–93 (Meran, now Merano): satirist and feuilletonist.

STÖHR, EMIL (St Pölten) 1860–1917 (St Pölten): painter, graphic artist, novelist and musician, founder member of the Secession.

STRASSER, ARTHUR (Adelsberg) 1854–1927 (Vienna): sculptor.

STRAUS, OSCAR (Vienna) 1870–1954 (Bad Ischl): composer of operettas.

STRAUSS, EDUARD (Vienna) 1835–1916 (Vienna): composer and conductor.

STRAUSS, JOHANN (Vienna) 1824–99 (Vienna): composer and conductor, known as the King of the Waltz.

STRAUSS, RICHARD (Munich) 1864–1949 (Garmisch): composer and conductor.

STROBL, KARL HANS (Iglau, now Jihlava) 1877–1946 (Perchtoldsdorf): author.

SUPPÉ, FRANZ VON (Spalato, now Split) 1819–95 (Vienna): composer of operettas.

SUTTNER, BERTHA VON (Prague) 1843–1914 (Vienna): author, first woman to win the Nobel Peace Prize.

TANDLER, JULIUS (Iglau, now Jihlava) 1869–1936 (Moscow): anatomist, Social

UHL, FRIEDRICH (Teschen, now Těšín) 1825–1906 (Mondsee): author, editor-in-chief of the *Wiener Zeitung.*

URBAN, JOSEPH (Vienna) 1872–1933 (New York): book illustrator, founded the Hagenbund with his brother-in-law Heinrich Lefler.

VEITH, EDUARD (Neutitschein, now Nový Jičín) 1856–1925 (Vienna): decorative painter.

WAGNER, OTTO (Vienna) 1841–1918 (Vienna): architect; the most important architect of the period.

WEBERN, ANTON VON (Vienna) 1883–1945 (Mittersill): composer, pupil of Schoenberg, conductor.

WEINGARTNER FELIX (Zara) 1863–1942 (Winterthur): conductor, composer and director of the Court Opera in Vienna.

WEININGER, OTTO (Vienna) 1880–1903 (Vienna): philosopher.

WILBRANDT, ADOLF VON (Rostock) 1837–1911 (Rostock): author, director of the Burgtheater.

WILDGANS, ANTON (Vienna) 1881–1932 (Mödling): novelist, poet and director of the Burgtheater.

WINTER, MAX (Tarnów) 1870–1937 (Hollywood): author, editor of the *Arbeiter-Zeitung.*

WISINGER-FLORIAN, OLGA (Vienna) 1844–1926 (Vienna): painter.

WITTGENSTEIN, LUDWIG (Vienna) 1889–1951 (Cambridge): philosopher.

WITTMANN, HUGO (Ulm) 1839–1923 (Vienna): journalist.

WOLF, HUGO (Windischgraz, now Slovenjgradec) 1860–1903 (Vienna): composer.

WÖLFLING, LEOPOLD (Salzburg) 1868–1935 (Berlin): in 1902, the Archduke Leopold Franz Salvator renounced his title and assumed the name of Leopold Wölfling.

WOLTER, CHARLOTTE (Cologne) 1834–97 (Vienna): Burgtheater actress and celebrated tragedienne.

ZEMLINSKY, ALEXANDER (Vienna) 1872–1942 (New York): composer and conductor.

ZWEIG, STEPHAN (Vienna) 1881–1942 (Petrópolis): novelist and dramatist.

PHOTO CREDITS

The publishers wish to thank all the photographers who collaborated on this book, as well as the museums, archives and other institutions which supplied additional photographic material. The illustrations not listed below were kindly put at our disposal by the Historisches Museum der Stadt Wien. The numbers refer to the plates.

Basle, Kunsthalle 189 (Colour photo Hinz)
Cologne, Theatermuseum des Instituts für Theaterwissenschaft der Universität 266
Vienna, Bundesdenkmalamt 150, 212
   Graphische Sammlung, Albertina 279
   Graphische Sammlung, Albertina, Loos-Archiv 240, 241, 243
   Gustav Mahler-Gesellschaft 261 (photo Vouk), 280
   Dr.-Karl-Renner-Institut 30, 36, 38
   Österreichische Galerie 152, 181, 188, 195–7, 201, 268
   Österreichische Nationalbibliothek 33, 42, 209, 228, 258, 259, 262, 267, 281–4, 288, 289, 298, 303, 308, 309, 311

Österreichische Nationalbibliothek, Theatersammlung 52, 294, 316
Österreichisches Museum für angewandte Kunst 144, 146, 161 167, 264, 265
Sigmund Freud-Gesellschaft 117–19, 122
Gerhard Trumler 221
Wiener Stadt- und Landesbibliothek 51, 64, 65, 292, 306, 307

The city plan (p. 10) was kindly provided by the Verlag Hallwag, Berne; Pl. 216 is reproduced from *Der Architekt*, XXII, 1919; Pl. 224 from Marco Pozzetto, *Max Fabiani*, Vienna, 1983; Pls. 233, 234 and 239 from Eduard F. Sekler, *Josef Hoffmann – Das architektonische Werk*, Salzburg–Vienna, 1982 (with kind permission of the Residenz Verlag).

INDEX